# LAND, SEA & TIME

## Book Three

### EDITORS

Edward A. Jones

Shannon M. Lewis

Pat Byrne

Boyd W. Chubbs

Clyde Rose

BREAKWATER

# LAND, SEA & TIME

*Book Three*

Land, Sea & Time is a three-volume collection of a variety of Newfoundland and Labrador texts.

Text is defined as any language event, whether oral, written, or visual. In this sense, a conversation, a poem, a poster, a story, a photograph, a tribute, a music video, a television program, a radio documentary, and a multi-media production, for example, are all texts.

The series, Land, Sea & Time, Book One, Book Two, and Book Three offers a blend of previously neglected voices, new voices, and those often found in anthologies. Together, these books give readers an opportunity to explore the literary and cultural heritage of Newfoundland and Labrador.

The picture on the cover of this book was taken by photographer, Dennis Minty. The publisher gratefully acknowledges the Newfoundland Museum who kindly permitted us to photograph the Beothuk moccasins that appear in the photo.

BREAKWATER
100 Water Street
P.O. Box 2188
St. John's, NF
A1C 6E6

*Series motif by Boyd W. Chubbs, featuring* Avalon, *an original typeface by Boyd W. Chubbs.*

*Design and production: Nadine Osmond*

**National Library of Canada Cataloguing in Publication Data**

Main entry under title:

    Land, sea & time

Includes indexes.
ISBN 1-55081-160-6 (v. 1).—ISBN 1-55081-175-4 (v. 2).—
ISBN 1-55081-177-0 (v. 3)

1. Canadian literature (English) — Newfoundland.    2. Canada literature (English) — 20th century.    3. Art, Modern — 20th century — Newfoundland. I. Jones, Edward, 1939-

NX513.A3N452000        C810.8'09718        C00-950054-5

Breakwater wishes to thank the Department of Education whose cooperation on this project is much appreciated. In particular we wish to express our indebtedness to Eldred Barnes, Language Arts Consultant, (and his successor, Rex Roberts), all the pilot teachers and the school boards in Newfoundland and Labrador who worked with us on this educational venture. Best wishes to you all.

 We acknowledge the financial support of the Government of Canada through the Book Publishing Industry Development Program (BPIDP) for our publishing activities.

# Table of Contents

Excerpt from *On the Rim of the Curve* — Michael Cook — 10

Excerpt from *A History and Ethnography of the Beothuk* — Ingeborg Marshall — 10

Excerpts from *Shanawdithit's People* — Ralph Pastore — 11

Game pieces found in Beothuk graves — BBL Archives — 12

The Dig — Robert O. Norman — 12

Excerpt from *A History and Ethnography of the Beothuk* — Ingeborg Marshall — 13

*Beothuk Hunting Seabirds* — Gerald Squires — 16

Now that there are no cobblestones — Des Walsh — 17

Beothuck IV — Wallace Bursey — 17

At Red Indian Lake — Paul O'Neill — 18

Wooden comb — BBL Archives — 18

Mary March — Robert Burt — 19

Excerpt from *Liverpool Mercury*, 1829 — E. Slade — 19

Excerpt from *A History and Ethnography of the Beothuk* — Ingeborg Marshall — 22

Miniature portrait of Mary March (Demasduit), 1819 — Lady Hamilton — 23

Excerpts from *All Gone Widdun* — Annamarie Beckel — 25

Boyd's Cove, site of Beothuk encampment — BBL Archives — 26

Excerpt from the Film Script *Finding Mary March* — Ken Pittman — 27

A necklace of carved bone pieces and an animal tooth — BBL Archives — 28

Be Sure to Bring the Kids to See *Finding Mary March* — John Holmes — 29

Film Injects Beothuck Legend with Life — Beth Ryan — 30

Shaa-naan-dithit, or the Last of the Boêothics — John McGregor — 32

Staves — Shanawdithit — 32

Display of food — Shanawdithit — 33

Excerpts from a Diary — Bishop John Inglis — 34

Mamateeks — Shanawdithit — 34

A sealing harpoon and a spear — Shanawdithit — 35

Excerpt from *The Colony of Unrequited Dreams* — Wayne Johnston — 36

Shanadithit — Al Pittman — 38

Excerpt from a Journal — Gerald Squires — 41

Gerald Squires sculpting the maquette — BBL Archives — 42

Luben Boykov at Boyd's Cove site — BBL Archives — 43

Clay statue in Gerald Squires's studio — BBL Archives — 43

*Spirit of the Beothuk* — Gerald Squires & Luben Boykov — 44

Excerpts from *On the Rim of the Curve* — Michael Cook — 45

Carved bone pendants — BBL Archives — 46

Dancing woman — Shanawdithit — 47

Aich-mud-yim — Shanawdithit — 48

Extract from *The Newfoundlander*, June 11th, 1829 — Anonymous — 49

Extract from *The Public Ledger* June 12th, 1829 — Anonymous — 49

Extract from the *London Times*, September 14th, 1829 — W. E. Cormack — 50

Small birch bark dish found in a grave — BBL Archives — 50

Excerpt from *On the Rim of the Curve* — Michael Cook — 51

| | | |
|---|---|---|
| Carved bone pendant found in a grave | *BBL Archives* | 51 |
| Shanawdithit's Dream | *Robert O. Norman* | 52 |
| A bone harpoon head with an iron point | *BBL Archives* | 53 |
| In There Somewhere | *Tom Dawe* | 54 |
| Excerpt from *The Beothuk of Newfoundland* | *Ingeborg Marshall* | 55 |
| End profile of Beothuk canoe replica | *Cliff George* | 56 |
| Excerpts from *Beothuk Bark Canoes* | *Ingeborg Marshall* | 57 |
| Miniature birch bark canoe found in a grave | *BBL Archives* | 57 |
| Replica of Beothuk canoe | *BBL Archives* | 58 |
| *Sketch of a Beothuk Camp* | *John Cartwright* | 59 |
| Obligatory Beothuk Poem | *James Candow* | 60 |
| dead Indians | *Mary Dalton* | 60 |
| Excerpt from *Reports and Letters by George C. Pulling* | *Ingeborg Marshall* | 61 |
| Two moccasins from a boy's grave | *BBL Archives* | 64 |
| Mamateeks | *Dennis Minty* | 65 |
| bedoret ahune | *Randolph Paul* | 66 |
| A string of flat beads | *BBL Archives* | 66 |
| heart of the rock | *Randolph Paul* | 67 |
| A stone knife | *BBL Archives* | 67 |
| Excerpts from *Shanadithit: The Musical* | *Eleanor Cameron-Stockley* | 68 |
| Concrete slab grave marker | *BBL Archives* | 70 |
| Boyd's Cove Museum display | *Dennis Minty* | 71 |
| A Profile of Georgina Ann Stirling (1867-1935) | *Editors* | 72 |
| Georgina Stirling | *Provincial Archives* | 73 |
| To Miss Twillingate Stirling | *Isabella Whiteford Rogerson* | 74 |
| A Picture of the Past | *Addison Bown* | 75 |
| Excerpt from the *Dictionary of Newfoundland English* | *Story, Kirwin & Widdowson* | 84 |
| Goin Hout | *David Glover* | 85 |
| Dictionary Sam | *Geraldine Rubia* | 86 |
| newfoundland dialect | *DNE* | 87 |
| To Whittle an Alder Whistle | *Gary Saunders* | 88 |
| A Chant for One Voice | *Harold Horwood* | 91 |
| Second Heart | *Michael Winter* | 93 |
| The Hunt | *Larry Small* | 102 |
| Seasons | *Neil Murray* | 103 |
| mauzy | *DNE* | 104 |
| Elemental Poem | *Roberta Buchanan* | 105 |
| Excerpt from *Suspended State* | *Gene Long* | 107 |
| Newfoundland's Dream | *W. P. Williams* | 110 |
| The Announcement of the Rooster Tax | *Gregory Power* | 111 |
| Excerpts from *As Loved Our Fathers* | *Tom Cahill* | 113 |
| The Black Tie | *Grace Butt* | 122 |
| To Mark the Occasion | *Bernice Morgan* | 124 |
| Text of an Address | *Joseph R. Smallwood* | 127 |
| woods work | *DNE* | 132 |

| | | |
|---|---|---|
| The Bowl | Lillian Bouzane | 133 |
| *Stoneware Bowl* | Bonnie Leyton | 134 |
| Raku: Sod | Mary Dalton | 135 |
| *Sod, 1989* | Sharon Puddester | 136 |
| *Ash Wednesday: Portrait of Poet, Al Pittman* | Gerald Squires | 137 |
| Portrait of the Artist as a Young Mortician | Al Pittman | 138 |
| fetch | DNE | 140 |
| With Love from The Andes | Kathleen Winter | 141 |
| The Brule Men | Peter Leonard | 143 |
| Excerpt from *The Broadcast* | Jim Wellman | 145 |
| Let Me Fish Off Cape St. Mary's | Otto Kelland | 148 |
| Eighteen | Janet Fraser | 149 |
| Jeans | Peggy Smith Krachun | 150 |
| Greenhair Goes for a Smoke | Randall Maggs | 153 |
| green man | DNE | 154 |
| Adam and Eve on a Winter Afternoon | Carmelita McGrath | 155 |
| *Basket with Pears* | Helen Parsons Shepherd | 156 |
| In the Chambers of the Sea | Susan Rendell | 157 |
| A Piece of Toast | Kathleen Winter | 164 |
| The Prisoner | Irving Fogwill | 166 |
| *Winter Morning* | Reginald Shepherd | 167 |
| Preface to *The Labradorians* | Lynne Fitzhugh | 168 |
| Some Labrador Narratives by Nat Igloliorte | Phyllis Artiss | 173 |
| *Love* | Kathleen Knowling | 179 |
| Excerpts from *Woman of Labrador* | Elizabeth Goudie | 180 |
| Woman of Labrador | Andy Vine | 182 |
| Excerpts from a play: *Woman of Labrador* | Sherry Smith | 183 |
| Tragedy of CF-BND | Leonard McNeill | 184 |
| ranger | DNE | 188 |
| *Christmas Fire* | Mary Pratt | 189 |
| Miracles | Michael Crummey | 190 |
| The Home | Raymond Hillier | 197 |
| *The Trunk of Tir-na-n-og* | Eamonn Rosato | 198 |
| *Seaman's Chest* | Eamonn Rosato | 199 |
| Help Me Hepplewhite | Anne Hart | 200 |
| *Hepplewhite Chair* | Gerald Squires | 206 |
| Excerpts from *Wind in My Pocket* | E. B. Obed & S. Steffler | 207 |
| Excerpts from *Borrowed Black* | E. B. Obed & J. Mogensen | 210 |
| Excerpt from *Down by Jim Long's Stage* | A. Pittman & P. Hall | 212 |
| Excerpt from *On a Wing and a Wish* | A. Pittman & V. Tomova | 213 |
| *Polar Bear on the Labrador Coast* | Ray Fennelly | 214 |
| *Cotton Grass* | Dennis Minty | 215 |
| The White Fleet | Richard Greene | 216 |
| A Seaman of the White Fleet | Wayne Ralph | 219 |
| *The White Fleet* | Ben Hansen | 221 |

| | | |
|---|---|---|
| *The Creoula*, a Portuguese Training Ship | *BBL Archives* | 222 |
| Excerpts from *Terras de Bacalhau* | *RCA Theatre Company* | 223 |
| poor john | *DNE* | 232 |
| The Incubus | *Carmelita McGrath* | 233 |
| The Rain Hammers | *Michael Wade* | 242 |
| Empty Nets | *Jim Payne* | 243 |
| If Sonnets Were in Fashion | *Tom Dawe* | 245 |
| *City Homes* | *Paul Parsons* | 246 |
| Message | *Adrian Fowler* | 247 |
| waking from a dream | *Nick Avis* | 248 |
| springsmistory | *Nick Avis* | 249 |
| Old Flame | *Gildas Roberts* | 250 |
| *Satin Wrap* | *Barbara Pratt Wangersky* | 251 |
| To Be a Bee | *Nellie Strowbridge* | 252 |
| Purgatory's Wild Kingdom | *Lisa Moore* | 253 |
| Ballad of Captain Bob Bartlett, Arctic Explorer | *A. C. Wornell* | 261 |
| *Bartlett's World, 1995* | *Janice Udell* | 262 |
| Print: Captain Robert A. Bartlett | *Janice Udell* | 263 |
| In Memoriam: Captain Arthur Jackman | *Daniel J. Carroll* | 264 |
| Tribute to James (Jimmy) Butler, Blacksmith | *Anonymous* | 265 |
| This Is My Home | *Harry Martin* | 266 |
| A Statement | *Samuel Broomfield* | 267 |
| A Tribute to Samuel Broomfield | *Author Unknown* | 268 |
| A Tribute to Samuel Broomfield | *Mabel Manak* | 269 |
| Dr. Agnes C. O'Dea, 1911-1993 | *Anne Hart* | 270 |
| A Tribute to Michael Cook | *Clyde Rose* | 272 |
| In Memoriam: Cassie Brown—A Tribute | *Helen Fogwill Porter* | 274 |
| Noel Dinn | *Harold Paddock* | 275 |
| figgy duff | *DNE* | 276 |
| Pamela Morgan: A Voice for Newfoundland Roots | *Ken Roseman* | 277 |
| newfoundland dance | *DNE* | 281 |
| It Ain't Funny | *Pamela Morgan* | 282 |
| More Than a Monument | *Luben Boykov* | 283 |
| *The St. Lawrence Miners* | *Luben Boykov* | 286 |
| Loss of a Friend: A Personal Memoir | *Irving Fogwill* | 287 |
| Excerpt from *The Rock Observed* | *Patrick O'Flaherty* | 289 |
| The Literature of Newfoundland | *Adrian Fowler* | 292 |
| Excerpt from *The Colony of Unrequited Dreams* | *Wayne Johnston* | 302 |
| sealing crew | *DNE* | 304 |
| *Iceberg Alley* | *Diana Dabinett* | 305 |
| Excerpt from *Doctor Olds of Twillingate* | *Gary Saunders* | 306 |
| myrrh | *DNE* | 311 |
| We Will Remain | *Shane Mahoney* | 312 |
| nipper | *DNE* | 313 |
| Newfoundland | *E. J. Pratt* | 314 |

from "This is My Home"

'Cause I've seen the mountains,
I've been to the sea..
And all of that beauty
is like heaven to me.
Where the wild birds are flying
and the caribou roam
Many places I've rambled,
but this is my home

by Harry Martin

Excerpt from

# On the Rim of the Curve

Michael Cook

AUTHOR: Look! I never knew my grandfather but it would be easy to write about him. There's something of him in my father and ultimately, me, and we did, at least, share a mythology of sorts.

But how do you write of a vanished people? Out of a bone? A book? A lock of hair? A litany of lies? Or simple honest confusion. Sooner write of Atlantis…

Excerpt from

# A History and Ethnography of the Beothuk

Ingeborg Marshall

The Beothuk were the original inhabitants of Newfoundland at the time of the island's discovery by Europeans in 1497. They were hunters, gatherers, and fishers who moved seasonally in order to harvest coastal and inland resources. In spring and summer they lived on the coast, pursued marine mammals and seabirds, and caught salmon and other seafood; in fall and winter they moved to small camps or to settlements in the wooded interior, where they hunted caribou and other fur-bearing animals.

Archaeological and historical evidence suggests that, at contact, the Beothuk group would have numbered between 500 to 1,000. At that time, they ranged throughout the island. By the mid-1700s, due to encroachment into their territory from all sides, the majority of the Beothuk had retreated to secluded harbours and islands in Notre Dame Bay, and to the watershed of the Exploits River and Red Indian Lake. The continued expansion of hunting and trapping activities into this region by the English and their opening of salmon stations in river mouths led to strife and acts of violence by Beothuk and English alike. Isolated incidents developed into an increasingly vicious cycle of retaliation. In these conflicts the Beothuk were outnumbered and, without guns, were unable to defend important food resources. Starvation, harassment by Europeans and by other native groups, and diseases brought from Europe contributed to a steady population decline.

At the end of the eighteenth century several private citizens, naval officers, and governors submitted proposals to British authorities to improve the situation of the Beothuk and to put an end to hostilities by English settlers. Decades passed before such plans were considered. Eventually, in the early 1800s, naval parties were sent to make contract with the Beothuk, but to no avail. Although captives were taken to be used as mediators, plans to return them to their people with messages of goodwill never materialized. Measures taken to appease the Beothuk were either ineffective or came too late to prevent the extinction of the tribe. Stragglers may have led a sequestered existence for a few more years, but the Beothuk as a viable cultural unit had ceased to exist by the late 1820s.

The demise of the Beothuk is, at once, the most distressing aspect of their history, and the most complex, having rooted itself most deeply in public consciousness. Oral traditions of violent interaction between Beothuk and English settlers that formerly flourished in the northern bays were later replaced by stories in which the Beothuk were characterised as mild and inoffensive forest dwellers who had been cruelly extirpated by Newfoundlanders. But the facts were elusive and lack of information led to the idea that the Beothuk were a people whose origin, history, and fate were shrouded in mystery. In the last few decades the basis for these traditions has been widely questioned and a new interest in the Beothuk has emerged, inspiring scholarly investigations as well as poetry and fiction, the latter frequently centering around questions of blame and guilt.

Excerpts from

# Shanawdithit's People: The Archaeology of the Beothuks

**Ralph Pastore**

For years the Beothuks, the aboriginal inhabitants of the Island of Newfoundland, were regarded as a mysterious people who shrank from contact with Europeans and whose last member, Shanawdithit, died in 1829. In the past twenty years, discoveries made by archaeologists, historians and linguists have helped to lift much of the mystery from these people, but the tragedy of their demise remains. The extinction of an entire people is a terrible thing, and it requires us to try to understand what happened. Often, that process of understanding is a difficult one. It may be easy to accept the simple explanation that the ancestors of today's Newfoundlanders were criminals who slaughtered the Beothuks 'for fun' as one writer expressed it. But the past is seldom that simple, and it is not enough to accept the easy answer that early Newfoundland settlers were more cruel and more violent than other Europeans in other parts of Canada who did not exterminate the Native peoples whose lands they also took.

Game pieces found in Beothuk graves

While in St. John's, Shanawdithit provided Cormack (and us) with a wealth of information about Beothuk language and culture. In fact, much of what we know about the later culture and history of the Beothuks comes from Cormack's notes. Not the least of that information was in the form of a remarkable series of drawings that Shanawdithit made illustrating a number of facets of Beothuk life as well as a pictorial representation of the final events of her people.

Tragically, those drawings would be her last tangible legacy to the future—a future devoid of her own people forever. Shawnadithit, too, fell ill, almost certainly of tuberculosis. She died in June, 1829. Her death marked the end of an entire people—one of the most tragic forms of loss that humanity can experience. We owe it to Shanawdithit, her people, and the rest of the human species, to understand what happened to the Beothuks. The cheap, lurid explanations that portray the ancestors of today's Newfoundlanders who killed the Beothuks 'for fun' should no longer be sufficient. The demise of Shanawdithit's people came out of an intricate interaction of factors which included the ecology of the island and its surrounding seas, the extension of a European migratory fishery to the region, and the ultimate colonization of the island by Europeans. It was not genocide, but this, that brought about Beothuk extinction, but it was no less tragic.

12

# The Dig
Robert O. Norman

Inch by inch they dig
to uncover a truth
about a people who once
lived in this bay.
With pick and brush they
forge a cover like a book
to reveal how it was
that such a people disappeared.

For now, where there was once
rising smoke from the camp
and the sound of laughter
there remains only holes in the
ground surrounded by sticks
that look like little picket fences
and a story waiting to be told.

Excerpt from

# A History and Ethnography of the Beothuk

Ingeborg Marshall

| | |
|---|---|
| 1497 | Discovery of Newfoundland by John Cabot. |
| 1560s-1700s | Conflict between Beothuk and Inuit. |
| 1594 | The crew of the English fishing vessel *Grace* discovers a Beothuk camp at St. George's Bay and later experiences hostile acts from Beothuk at Presque, Placentia Bay. |
| 1612 | John Guy and a party of colonists explore Trinity Bay and meet Beothuk with whom they feast and trade. |
| 1613-14 | The crew of a fishing vessel are said to have shot at Beothuk in Trinity Bay. |
| 1694 | Beothuk refuse contact with French fishing crews. |
| 1719 | Salmon posts are erected by Skeffington and others in Freshwater Bay, Gander Bay, and Dog Creek; Beothuk protest by killing some of the salmon catchers; this is the first record of Englishmen being killed by Beothuk. |
| 1720s | Confrontations between Beothuk and Micmac take place in St. George's Bay; the Beothuk are defeated. |
| 1729-31 | English furriers kill Beothuk and Beothuk retaliate by killing furriers. |
| 1730s | Barter between Beothuk and settlers in Bonavista Bay terminates after a Beothuk woman is shot while selecting a trade item. |
| 1750s | Renewed confrontations between Beothuk and Micmac occur at Grand Lake; Beothuk are defeated again and lose access to Newfoundland's west and south coasts. |
| 1758 | The Beothuk boy June is captured by furriers and his mother and a child are killed. |
| 1760 | Shipmaster Scott attempts to build a station in the Bay of Exploits; in an encounter with Beothuk, Scott and five of his men are killed. |
| 1760s | Captain Hall is killed by Beothuk when he tries to settle in Hall's Bay. |
| 1768 | Governor Hugh Palliser sends Lieut. John Cartwright to explore the Exploits River and to contact the Beothuk; Cartwright, who did not meet the Beothuk, submits a detailed report about the Beothuk's way of life and two maps of the river on which he |

marked Beothuk habitations; he also reports that Beothuk are persecuted by fishermen and settlers.

1768    Furriers capture the Beothuk boy August and kill his mother.

1781    John Peyton, Sr. his partner Miller, and their headman raid a Beothuk winter camp on the Exploits River; many Beothuk are wounded or killed.

1784    George Cartwright submits a proposal to the Colonial Office suggesting that a reserve be set aside for the Beothuk; his proposal is not accepted.

1790    Eight English furriers raid a Beothuk winter camp on the Exploits River and wound occupants; they burn three of four houses and carry away caribou skins.

1791    Fishermen capture the Beothuk girl Oubee; a Beothuk man and child are killed in the encounter.

1792    Capt. G. C. Pulling questions northern fishermen and furriers about relations with the Beothuk. He submits a lengthy report and a Beothuk wordlist collected from Oubee; his report shows that Beothuk are consistently persecuted. He suggests remedial action and states that many residents are in favour of his plan; Chief Justice Reeves supports his proposal.

1797-1806    Governors William Waldegrave, Charles Morris Pole, and James Gambier submit proposals to authorities in Britain to improve relations with Beothuk. The plans call for sending a peace mission, capturing Beothuk to be used as mediators, and setting aside a Beothuk reserve. None of the proposals are approved.

1803    A Beothuk woman is captured by William Cull and returned to the Exploits River the following year.

1807-09    Governor John Holloway sends one of his officers with trade goods and a painting of trading Englishmen and Beothuk into Beothuk country; he is unable to contact Beothuk.

1811    Governor Thomas Duckworth sends Lieut. David Buchan on a peace mission into Beothuk country. Buchan, with twenty-three marines and furriers as guides, treks up the Exploits River in midwinter and finds the Beothuk's principal settlement at Red Indian Lake. He believes he has convinced the Beothuk of his friendly intentions and leaves two hostages; during his absence the Beothuk kill the marines and flee.

| 1814-15 | John Peyton, Sr. kills a Beothuk woman on the Exploits River, near Rushy Pond. |
|---------|---|
| 1818 | Settlers and fishermen kill Shanawdithit's brother, mother, sister, and a young child on their way to an island where they intended to collect bird eggs; Shanawdithit's father, a swift hunter, dies a few months later. |
| 1819 | In March of this year, the John Peytons, father and son, with eight of their men capture Demasduit (Mary March) at Red Indian Lake; her husband, Nonasabasut, and his brother are killed in the encounter. The Peytons claim to have acted in self-defence. Rev. John Leigh collects a Beothuk vocabulary from Demasduit. |
| 1820 | On 8 January 1820 Demasduit succumbs to pulmonary tuberculosis. Captain Buchan brings her coffined body to the Beothuk camp at Red Indian Lake. |
| 1822 | William E. Cormack, an explorer and entrepreneur, and the Micmac Joseph Sylvester walk across Newfoundland from Trinity Bay to St. George's Bay in search of Beothuk; they fail to meet any. |
| 1823 | Two furriers kill a Beothuk man and his daughter; taken to court they are declared to be "not guilty." |
| 1823 | Shanawdithit, her mother and sister, ill and starving, give themselves up to furriers; the mother and sister die within a few weeks. Shanawdithit is taken into the household of John Peyton, Jr. on Exploits Islands. |
| 1827 | In October William E. Cormack founds the Boeothick Institution whose aim it is to open communication with the Beothuk and promote their civilization. |
| 1827 | In November, Cormack and three native guides search Beothuk territory for the remnants of the tribe; the party finds only abandoned camps and a cemetery. |
| 1828 | The Boeothick Institution sends two Abenaki and one Montagnais to search for Beothuk inland from St. George's Bay, around Red Indian Lake, on the Exploits River, on the Northern Peninsula south of Croque Harbour, in White Bay, and on the coast of Notre Dame Bay; the men are unsuccessful in finding survivors, though they come across many signs of Beothuk habitation. |
| 1828 | In September Shanawdithit is transferred to St. John's under the auspices of the Boeothick Institution. William E. Cormack questions her extensively about the history and culture of her people. |

1829      On 6 June Shanawdithit dies of pulmonary tuberculosis. Though some of her people would still have been alive, either in the interior of Newfoundland or in Labrador, the Beothuk tribe as a cultural entity has become extinct.

*Beothuk Hunting Seabirds*, Gerald Squires, 1988

# Now that there are no cobblestones

**Des Walsh**

Now that there are no cobblestones
and few old photographs
we are free at last,
we owe nothing to anyone.
The indigenous race,
we are responsible,
it was our choice.
Now that we have kept down
the souls of garrison soldiers
and with dirt and stone
moved the Beothuk once more
we can embrace this century,
and those to come…
once more, as in 900 or there about,
looking into the hazy July morning
there will be bona vista,
no obstruction of guilt and memory.
But cry no more for the leaf
that swirls in the wake of panic,
the young man who drowned
in the harbour of North America's oldest city.
It is as it seems.

# Beothuck IV

**Wallace Bursey**

I ask no more vengeance
On the white man,
There is no need;
His fathers pity him
And the spirits of his fathers,
Even the spirits of my fathers,
For the vengeance he has exacted
On himself.

And the beauty of our land
Shall pity him,
When he has destroyed the tribes
Who could have taught him
How to live with the land
He could have shared.

# At Red Indian Lake

Paul O'Neill

O my wild and lonesome land
of snowflake and the frosted moon
look on these shores of Shanadithit
and lament the wounds that have
annihilated traces
of her tribe.

Where silence hangs
from looting of their song
sit in the hush
and weep among the dead.
Orphans of the crime
we track Beothuk blood
among the roots
of ripening
and turn in shame from
whispers of old acts indelible
where in star chill of tears
that fell among the withered leaves
they floated out of time
along a yellow stream
from strands of birch
and tamarack
in which
the footfalls of forever
fill the emptiness.

Wooden comb

# Mary March

Robert Burt

Mary March shines on
Aloof and distant as the stars
Hanging over Red Indian's spirit waters.
Your existentialist plight
Is now a thing of legends.
You knew not if you were the last;
You would not want to
Bear the fame of your genes' extinction.
Better to take the purity of your Beothuk race
Into the ochre sunset sky,
Leaving this dark Island
For its next extinction.

Excerpt from

# A Letter to the Editor of the *Liverpool Mercury*, 1829

E. Slade

Sir: Observing among the deaths in the *Mercury* of September 18th that of "Shanawdithit" supposed to be the last of the "Red Indians" or aborigines of Newfoundland, I am tempted to offer a few remarks on the subject, convinced as I am that she cannot be the last of the tribe by many hundreds. Having resided a considerable time in the north of Newfoundland which they most frequented, and being one of the party who captured Mary March in 1819, I have embodied into a narrative the events connected with her capture, which I am confident will gratify many of your readers....

In the summer of 1818 a person who had established a salmon fishery at the mouth of the Exploits River, had a number of articles stolen by the Indians; they consisted of a gold watch, left accidently in the boat, the boats, sails, some hatchets, cordage and iron implements. He therefore resolved on sending an expedition into the country, in order to recover his property.

The day before the party set off I arrived accidently, at the house, taking a survey of numerous bodies of wood cutters belonging to the establishment with which I was connected. The only time anyone can penetrate into the interior is in the winter season, the lakes and rivers being frozen over, even the Bay of Exploits, though salt water, was then (the end of January) frozen for sixty miles. Having proposed to accompany the party they immediately consented. Our equipment consisted of a musket, bayonet, and hatchet; to each of the servants, a pistol; Mr—— and myself had, in addition, another pistol and a dagger, and a double-barrel gun instead of a musket; each carried a pair of snow shoes, a supply of eight pounds of biscuits and a piece of pork, ammunition, and one quart of rum; besides we had a light sled and four dogs, who took it in turns in dragging the sled, which contained a blanket for each man, rum and other necessities. We depended on our guns for a supply of provisions, and at all times could meet with plenty of partridge and hares, though there were few days we could not kill a deer. The description of one day's journey will suffice for all, there being but little variation. The snow was all the time about eight feet deep.

On the morning of our departure we set off in good spirits up the river, and after following its course for about twelve miles, arrived at the rapids, a deer at full speed passed us; I fired, and it fell the next instant, a wolf in full pursuit made his appearance; on seeing the party he haulted for an instant, and then rushed forward as if to attack us. Mr—— however, anticipated him; for taking a steady aim and at the same time sitting cooly on an old tree, he passed a bullet through the fellows head, who was soon stretched a corpse on the snow, a few minutes after another appeared, when several firing together he also fell, roaring and howling for a long time, when one of the men went and knocked him on the head with a hatchet.

And now ye effeminate feather-bed loungers, where do you suppose we were to sleep? There was no comfortable hotel to receive us; not even a house where a board informs the benighted traveller that there is "entertainment for man and horse," not even the skeleton of a wigwam; the snow eight feet deep, the thermometer nineteen degrees below the freezing point. Everyone having disencumbered himself of his load, proceeded with his hatchet to cut down the small fir and birch trees. The thick part of the trees was cut into lengths, and heaped up in two piles between which a sort of wigwam was formed of the branches; a number of small twigs of trees, to the depth of about three feet were laid on the snow for a bed; and having lighted the pile of wood on each side, some prepared venison steaks for supper while others skinned the two wolves, in order, with the deerskin to form a covering to the wigwam; this some opposed as being a luxury we should not every day obtain. Supper being ready, we ate heartily and having melted some snow for water, we made some hot toddy, that is, rum, butter, hot water and sugar; a song was proposed and acceded to: and thus in the middle of a dreary desert far from the voice of our fellow men, we sat cheerful and contented, looking forward to the morrow without dread, anxious to renew our labors. After about an hour thus spent the watch was appointed, and each wrapped in his blanket; we vied in convincing each other, with the nasal organ, which was in the soundest sleep; mine was the last watch about an hour before daybreak. The Aurora Borealis rolled in awful splendour across the deep blue sky, but I will not tire my readers with a description. When the first glimpse of morn showed itself in the light clouds, floating in the Eastern horizon, I awoke my companions, and by the time it was sufficiently light, we had breakfasted and were ready to proceed. Cutting off enough of the deer shot the night before, we proceeded on our journey, leaving the rest to the wolves. Each day and night were a repetition of the same; the country being in some places tolerably level, in general covered with wood, but occasionally barren tracts, where sometimes for miles not a tree was to be seen. Mr—— instructed the men in which way he wished them to act, informing them that his object was to open a friendly communication with the Indians, rather than act on the principle of intimidating them by revenge; that if they avoided him, he should endeavour to take one or two prisoners and bring them with him, in order that by the civilization of one or two an intercourse might be established that would end in their permanent civilization. He strictly exhorted them not to use undue violence; everyone was strictly enjoined not to fire on any account. About three o'clock in the afternoon two men, who had led the party were about two hundred yards before the rest; three deer closely followed by a pack of wolves, issued from the woods on the left, and bounded across the lake, passing very near the men, whom they totally disregarded. The men incautiously fired at them. We were then about half a mile from the point of land that almost intersected the lake, and in a few minuted we saw it covered with Indians, who instantly retired. The alarm was given; we soon reached the point; about five hundred yards on the other side we saw the Indians' houses, and the Indians, men, women, and children rushing from them, across the lake, here about a mile broad. Hurrying on we quickly came to the houses; when within a short distance from the last house, three men and a woman carrying a child issued forth. One of the men took the infant from her, and their speed soon convinced us of the futility of pursuit; the woman, however, did not run so fast. Mr—— loosened his provision bag from his back and let it fall, threw away his gun and hatchet and set off at a speed that soon overtook the woman. One man and myself did the same, except our guns. The rest, picking up our things followed. On overtaking the woman, she instantly fell to her knees, and tearing open the cossack, (a dress composed of deer-skin bound with fur), showing her breasts to prove she was a woman, and begged for mercy. In a few moments we were by Mr—'s side. Several of the Indians, with the three who had quitted the house with the woman, now advanced, while we retreated towards the shore. At length we stopped and they did the same. After a pause three of them laid down their bows, with which they were armed, and came within two hundred yards. We then presented our guns, intimating that not more than one would be allowed to approach. They retired and fetched their arms, when one, the ill-fated husband of Mary March, our captive, advanced with a branch of a fir tree (spruce) in his hand. When about ten yards off he stopped and made a long oration. He spoke at least ten minutes; towards the last his gesture became very animated and his eye "shot fire." He concluded very mildly, and advancing, shook hands with many of the party then he attempted to take his wife from us; being opposed in this he drew from beneath his cossack, an axe, the whole of which was finely polished, and brandished it over our heads. On two or three pieces being presented, he gave it up to Mr—— who then intimated that the woman must go with us, but that he might go also if he pleased, and that in the morning both should have their liberty. At the same time two of the men began to conduct her towards the houses. On this being done he became infuriated, and rushing towards her strove to drag her from them; one of the men rushed forward and stabbed him in the back with a bayonet; turning round, at a blow he laid the fellow at his feet; the next instant he knocked down another and rushing on like a child laid him on his back, and seizing his dirk from his belt brandished over his head; the next instant it would have been buried in him had I not with both hands seized his arm; he shook me off in an instant, while I measured my length on the ice; Mr—— then drew a pistol from his girdle and fired. The poor wretch first staggered then fell on his face: while writhing in agonies, he seemed for a moment to stop; his muscles stiffened: slowly and gradually he raised himself from the ice, turned round and with a wild gaze surveyed us all in a circle around him. Never shall I forget the figure he exhibited; his hair hanging on each side of his sallow face; his bushy beard clotted with the blood that flowed from his mouth and nose; his eyes flashing fire, yet with the glass of death upon them, they fixed on the individual who first stabbed him. Slowly he raised the hand that still grasped young——'s dagger, till he raised it considerably above his head, when uttering a yell that made the woods echo, he rushed at them. The man fired as he advanced, and the noble Indian again fell on his face; a few moments struggle and he lay a stiffened corpse on the icy surface of the limpid waters. The woman for a moment seemed scarcely to notice the corpse, in a few moments however, she showed a little motion; but it was not until obliged to leave the remains of her husband that she gave way to grief, and vented her sorrow in the most heartbreaking lamentations.

Excerpt from

# A History and Ethnography of the Beothuk

**Ingeborg Marshall**

Once the Peytons had safely conveyed Demasduit from Red Indian Lake to the coast, they placed her under the care of the Reverend John Leigh in Twillingate. The women who took care of her washed the ochre from her person and clothed her in English garb. Demasduit was named Mary March after the month in which she had been captured. For some time she was ill at ease in Leigh's household and twice during the night attempted to escape to the woods. Thereafter she was carefully watched and a few weeks later seems to have been tolerably reconciled to her situation, enjoying "the comforts of civilization, particularly the clothes." Her own clothes, made of caribou skins tastefully trimmed with marten, she would neither put on nor part from. Rev. John Leigh (as recorded by Robinson) described her as being

> tall and rather stout, having small and delicate limbs, particularly her arms. Her hands and feet were very small and beautifully formed and of these she was very proud, her complexion a light copper colour became nearly as fair as an European's after a course of washing and absence from smoke, her hair was black, which she delighted to comb and oil, her eyes larger and more intelligent than those of an Esquimaux, her teeth small, white and regular, her cheek bones rather high, but her countenance had a mild and pleasing expression.

Miniature portrait of Mary March (Demasduit), painted by Lady Hamilton in 1819.
Hamilton, Lady Henrietta Martha/National Archives of Canada/C-087698.

As Demasduit spent many weeks in his household, Leigh came to know her fairly well and later recalled some of her character traits, abilities, and behaviour to Capt. Hercules Robinson, who recorded much of Leigh's account. Demasduit ate sparingly and disliked spirits but was fond of sleep. She was playful and endowed with an astute "perception of anything ridiculous" (an unmarried man seemed an object of great ridicule to her), and her general "knowledge of character showed much archness and sagacity." She had a remarkable innate sense of delicacy and propriety and a power of mimicry that quickly enabled her to speak the language she heard. Before she could express herself, she described people she could not name, such as a shoemaker, tailor, blacksmith, and a man who wore glasses, "with a most happy minuteness of imitation." Leigh also found that Demasduit could be quite obstinate. She was glad to be of help but only if she were not asked to assist. Once Demasduit understood English reasonably well, Leigh compiled a Beothuk vocabulary of about 180 words, which he sent to the Society for the Propagation of the Gospel.

Demasduit rarely spoke freely about her people but told Leigh once that they lived in separate mamateeks, her own housing sixteen. She routinely divided trinkets that were given to her into sixteen shares and once secreted some blue cloth in her room, which she converted into sixteen pairs of moccasins. Robinson recorded that she had two children (he probably erred here; Shanawdithit later said she had only one), which was "the tie that held her to her wigwam." Although she had adjusted to life in Leigh's household, she seemed to "drag a lengthened chain," and "all her hopes and acts appeared to have a reference to her return." Leigh drew a crew and a female figure representing Demasduit in a boat that was going upriver; when he portrayed the people stopping at a wigwam and then returning, Demasduit cried "No, no." Leigh then altered the sketch by leaving the woman behind at the wigwam, whereupon Demasduit responded joyfully, "Yes, yes good for Mary."

In spring, after the breakup of the ice, Leigh took Demasduit to St John's, where she remained for a short time. Governor Hamilton, in his official report, described her as a woman of about twenty-three years, "of a gentle and interesting disposition and acquiring and retaining without much difficulty any words which she was taught." Many years later, Mr. Curtis, who had seen Demasduit in Twillingate, said she was of medium height and slender and "for an Indian very good looking."

While in St John's, Lady Hamilton, the first governor's wife to reside in Newfoundland, painted a watercolour portrait of Demasduit in miniature. She portrayed her as an attractive, sensitive young woman with black eyes and short cropped black hair, clad in a skin robe that was trimmed with fur. The portrait was said to be a striking likeness and is the only fully authenticated picture of a Beothuk. The original, now in the National Archives in Ottawa, was later copied by several artists.

**Excerpts from**

# *All Gone Widdun*

## Annamarie Beckel

*[Speakers in the following excerpts are William Cormack and Shanawdithit]*

Wretched. So stands Newfoundland. A barren rock-strewn coast, a cruel devouring sea, dreadful fog loom. Belligerent winds that pummel all life into submission. A melancholy wasteland of interminable forests and bogs.

And yet, she beckons. In 1822, at the age of 26, I returned to my boyhood home to mount an expedition into the wilderness, to be the first white man to cross the island's unexplored interior. The adventure nearly cost me my life. Nonetheless, I did not regret it, for I discovered Newfoundland's desolate beauty.

Five years later I went into that wilderness again, to search for the Beothuk, the island's aborigines. How could I know that I would encounter not only Newfoundland's stark beauty, but also her enduring soul? That I would discover her soul not in the forests and bogs, nor in the restless sea, but in my own drawing room in St. John's?

Willem will never bring them back. I know that now. Yet, it does not matter so much. I have learned that it is not so easy for the Strangers to steal our souls.

Nonosabasut and Demasduit are not at peace. I am not at peace. But we are where we belong, with the Beothuk. And that pleases us. We sing with the wind, drum with the sea, dance with the stars in the sky. We howl with the raging storms, smile when the sun gives light to the day. We are there when Caribou gives birth to her calf, when Salmon fights against the rushing waters, flinging himself toward life, then death. We are there when the tender pink blossoms of laurel open to the sun, when the leaves of cup plant lure flies to their death. We are there when Gannet falls from the sky, brought down by Eagle's talons.

We are Eagle's talons. Loon's song. Whale's misty spray.

Never can we be taken from this rock, from the earth who gave us birth, who welcomes us back to life in our death.

I fell into a restless sleep, shifting between wakefulness and slumber. I dreamed that the white coffin lay in the lodge where I slept. I saw myself rise from the blankets, open the lid, and lift Mary's skull from its muslin shroud.

Someone watched from the shadows. Dark eyes, in an ancient face.

Bright red blood spurted from the skull's grinning mouth, streamed down the alabaster chin, and dripped through my fingers. I dropped the skull, raised my blood-covered hands, and screamed.

I woke, sweating and shivering. The fire had burned down to embers, and the wind shrieked at the smoke hole. Trying to calm myself, I recited psalms and Shakespearean sonnets, but could bring to mind no comforting lines. Perversely, unwillingly, I summoned Macbeth: *Here's the smell of the blood still: all the perfumes of Arabia will not sweeten this little hand….What's done cannot be undone.*

Why these lines? There was no blood on my hands. I was here in this abominable place to prevent more bloodshed. To save the Beothuk, not to kill them.

Rising from my bed, I pulled the canvas pack with the skulls to the far side of the wigwam as far away as possible then returned and wrapped myself in my blankets, willed my heartbeat to slow. I recited all the poetry I could bring to mind, then recalled Professor Jameson's lectures on botany and geology until there was no room in my head for ghosts. I imagined Katherine. Try as I might, however, I could not keep my thoughts from shifting back to the dream.

Sleep did not visit me again that night, and I decided we would leave the Beothuk camp first thing in the morning. I even considered leaving the skulls behind, then berated myself for my irrational fears.

In the morning, when I joined Louis, Stevens, and Peter John, they looked at me as if I were the very spectre they feared. They sat apart from me while we ate our breakfast of boiled oats and bitter tea. Raising the tin cup to my lips, my hands shook, but I convinced myself that my trembling, my lack of sleep came from the ache in my jaw, not my dream.

The men needed no word from me to know we were leaving. After breakfast, they quietly packed our gear while I consulted my maps. I kept the pack at my feet, under careful watch. If the Indians learned I had taken the skulls, they might abandon me in the wilderness.

Boyd's Cove: site of Beothuk encampments

Excerpt from the Film Script

# Finding Mary March

## Ken Pittman

PROLOGUE
(INTERIOR OF NEWFOUNDLAND. SUMMER, 1987)

1    EXT. HELICOPTER VIEW OF OCEAN. DAY                                1

The helicopter passes over islands that spot a long narrow bay and flies up the mouth of the Exploits River, winding its way through tree-covered mountains.

SUPERIMPOSED ON THE SCREEN: The following passage:

The Beothuck Indians once inhabited the island of Newfoundland. No one knows what caused their demise. Some say the white settlers hunted them for sport. Others say they died of natural causes. By the late 1820s they had disappeared from the face of the earth.

FADE OUT

2    FROZEN SURFACE OF THE EXPLOITS RIVER. DAY.                        2

It is a cold windy day in the winter of 1820. A small party of men drags a wooden coffin over the ice on a sled. A few of them are mere boys. They are tired, cold and fearful of their surroundings.

SUPERIMPOSED OVER THE SCREEN:

"Interior of Newfoundland, Winter of 1820."

DISSOLVE TO:

3    EXT. MARY MARCH GRAVE. DAY.                                      3

A structure of four cut tree trunks rises out of the snow. At the top of these twelve-foot posts, the wooden coffin has been lashed into place. Wolves emerge from snow-laden trees. They circle the structure, sniffing the air, their noses pointed upward at the snow-covered coffin.

DISSOLVE TO:

4    EXT. MM GRAVE. DAY                                               4

Spring. Melting snow. The coffin is still held by the posts, but the bindings have loosened and it tips at a sharp angle. Crows sit in the nearby trees, clucking and growling. They take flight in a black spray as something below disturbs the landscape.

A small group of INDIANS, Beothucks, come out of the trees. Wrapped in shabby hides and furs, showing signs of hunger and sickness, they approach the structure. Gathering beneath the coffin, the stronger ones begin to release it from its perch.

When the box has been lowered to the ground, the top boards are removed, revealing the decaying remains of a young Indian woman clothed in a white woman's dress. The people begin to stack large stones against all sides of the box. They pause in their work, to let an old, old woman advance from the periphery. Kneeling feebly beside the coffin she opens the front of her ragged tunic. Inside she wears against her weathered skin, a wide bib-like breast piece made of caribou hide, and completely covered with two-inch rectangles of bone which are attached with lacing of fine sinew. Each bone piece is intricately engraved with vertical columns of minuscule figures, some of them suggesting animal and human forms.

A necklace of carved bone pieces and an animal tooth

As the old woman's finger struggles to untie the leather thong that holds the elaborate display of bone shapes in place, the other Indians look on with eyes that tell of finality and doom. Their eyes never leave the woman's movements. She removes the breast piece and with reverent sadness, places it on the breast of the woman's body in the coffin. The ancient hands disappear into her tunic and emerge with a small hide pouch. She opens it, and turns her head in the direction of the nearest adult. It is a woman; her age is obscured by hunger and illness. She dips her fingers into the pouch and lifts out red-clay powder. She sprinkles it onto the dead woman. The red dust falls on the withered face, and on the hide and bone breast piece that now adorns the body. When she is finished sprinkling, she rubs the residue of clay on her face, slowly, deliberately, with eyes closed. When her face is covered with the stain, she backs away. Another figure moves into her place and repeats the same ritual. One by one, the remaining Indians sprinkle clay into the coffin and smear it on their faces. The Indians are women and children, not a man left among them. When they have finished, the old woman, with open arms bent upward like a priest at an altar, faces the clouds and utters faint prayers. Light rain and wind. Boards are placed back on the coffin: stones are stacked one by one.

DISSOLVE TO:

5    EXT. MM GRAVE. DAY.                                                          5

Later that same spring day in 1820. The stones form a dark mound surrounded by patches of melting snow on the bank of the still frozen river. Except for the faint whistle of the wind and the distant sound of crows, the wide landscape is still.

DISSOLVE TO:

6    EXT. EXPLOITS RIVER. PRESENT DAY.                                            6

HELICOPTER VIEW of the Exploits River winding its way through tree-covered mountains.

# Be Sure to Bring the Kids to See
# *Finding Mary March*

John Holmes

In Ken Pittman's movie we have a feature length film of which Newfoundland can be very proud in the way that has been denied up to now. It is a serious, fictional story, that develops slowly through a series of stunning inland visual images, a dozen or more first rate performances with an evocative and moving musical score by Paul Steffler and Pam Morgan. It has none of the hackneyed, stale stereotypes so frequently trotted out as being "typically Newfoundland" which usually include interminable seascapes, rubber boots and winking nitwits.

The most criticism I heard from the capacity invited audience last night at Cinema One in the Avalon Mall was that *Finding Mary March* is slow moving. Thank goodness! For a change the audience can sit back and luxuriate in Michael Jones's magnificent cinematography, and the restrained and at times moving performances from the three leading actors.

The story is simple. Nancy George (Quebec actress Andrée Pelletier) is a photographer of archeological sites who comes to central Newfoundland to take pictures of Beothuk burial sites along the Exploits River. Ted Cormack, played by Rick Boland, is recommended to her as the best possible guide. But Ted and his daughter Bernardette, played by Tara Manuel in her first movie, live away in the woods, and Ted is in deep trouble with the authorities for intimidating mineral prospectors and also for keeping his 14-year-old daughter out of school. Nancy offers Ted a large enough fee to settle his financial problems and he reluctantly agrees to take her up river.

But Ted has a quest of his own. A year ago his Micmac Indian wife took off in search of the grave of Mary March, one of the last of the Beothuks whom she believes was in some mysterious way, her ancestor. But she disappeared, her body was never recovered and Ted is determined to find some trace of her.

The story of the genocidal destruction of the native Beothuk Indians by British and Irish come-from-aways is woven into this story and some of the most stunning and heart-rending scenes in the film show the capture of Mary March, played by Jacinta Cormier, the shooting of her mate, her return to her people in a pine box and her ritual burial by her own people. These are winter scenes, so realistically shot and acted that one felt a shiver of anticipation of what is soon to come.

In these silent scenes Mary Vavasour is outstanding as the old Beothuk woman, lovingly adorning the dead Mary March with the carved necklace. These scenes are the most memorable for me and bring to mind a fine radio drama by Michael Cook called *On the Rim of the Curve* on the same subject, produced years ago on the CBC network. The tragic story of the slaughter and disappearance of a whole race of people because of advancing "progress" is an epic movie in itself.

*Finding Mary March* is a modern story too, with clear implications of what unbridled development threatens to do to virgin land, with its ubiquitous helicopters and avaricious land-grabbers.

Ken Pittman, his cast and crew and all who supported him are to be highly commended for producing a beautiful, moving film which is as professional and gripping as any of the usual trash that appear on our screens, large and small. *Finding Mary March* will be released for general distribution during the next few weeks, and it will appear on CBC television sometime later. Wherever it appears near you, be sure to see it; take your children and let them learn some of the sad but true history of their province.

# Film Injects Beothuck Legend with Life

## Beth Ryan

In the opening shot of *Finding Mary March*, the camera pans a winter wilderness scene and titles roll up on the screen to give historical information on the last Beothucks in Newfoundland. But instead of giving the audience a dry lesson in Newfoundland history, writer/director/producer Ken Pittman injects the legend of Mary March with life.

Mary March, one of the last surviving Beothucks, was captured by white settlers in a bitter struggle that left her husband dead. When she died in captivity, the white men sent her back to her people, who decorated her with a hand-carved stone necklace and gave her the traditional Beothuck burial. As scholarly and public interest in the history of the Beothucks increased in the past few decades, the search for Mary March's burial site and any other remains of the Beothuck culture has intensified, making this a timely film.

In *Finding Mary March*, a Quebec archeologist/photographer Nancy George (Andrée Pelletier) comes to the Buchans area under the guise of researching the environmental impact of mining operations. But her real aim is to find Mary March. She enlists the help of local trapper Ted Cormack (Rick Boland) as her guide and sets out to re-discover the Beothuck heritage. But Ted and his daughter Bernadette (Tara Manuel) are reluctant guides because they have recently found Mary March's grave themselves. Ted's Micmac Indian wife Monica disappeared the previous year during one of her attempts to find Mary March, whom she believed was a distant relation. So the wounds are still raw for Ted and Bernadette and they are fiercely protective of Monica's dream and the burial site of Mary March.

This fictionalised account blends history and speculation about Mary March into a credible and sensitive story that allows Pittman to explore a myriad of related themes and issues. The struggle between the Cormacks and Nancy George over the Beothuck burial sites raises important questions about our perceptions of history and heritage. While Nancy indignantly proclaims that everyone should be able to explore and understand the Beothuck culture, Ted reminds her that these are people she's talking about, not just interesting rocks or trees. When she tries to take a piece of ceremonial pendant from Mary March's grave, Ted tells her it's as if he had opened her mother's coffin and stole her wedding band, a comparison that shakes Nancy's philosophy of archeology.

The film intelligently tackles the difficult questions that social scientists, particularly archeologists and anthropologists, must ask themselves when they explore the lives of real people. When does the culture, heritage and experiences of a people become open to public scrutiny? As Ted asks Nancy, when is it all right? After a few days, or a few months or many years? In the end, Nancy chooses to leave the burial sites intact, forsaking the archeological find she's discovered. But it doesn't resolve the question for her.

Pittman carefully uses images of the Beothuck spiritual world as a link between Nancy and the Indian culture. In a particularly effective scene, the scene flashes from Bernadette huddled in her tent in the midst of a storm, to Ted and the young Micmac boy at Monica's grave in the woods, to Nancy wrapped in a blanket and standing atop a hill in the rain and wind. She has smeared her face with the red ochre (in an attempt to keep the flies away) and for a moment, the audience wonders if they've just seen the ghostly apparition of Mary March.

Throughout the film, the links between Nancy and the Cormacks grow stronger when they learn of the Indian father who left her years ago to return to his Indian roots. And the Cormacks' fierce protectiveness of the Beothuck legends becomes more understandable when Ted explains that Monica believed she was related to Mary March, through an intermarriage between a Beothuck and a Micmac.

Most of the conflict is resolved in a final climactic scene when Nancy returns the ceremonial pendant to Mary March's burial site. While the dialogue implies that Nancy is going to stay with Ted and Bernadette, Ken Pittman wisely chose not to muddy an important script with a trivialized romance between Nancy and Ted. The very genuine relationship that the three shared was a more effective way to humanize the story than a love story could have been.

The acting and dialogue of the film were carefully understated, allowing the setting and story to tell itself. Rick Boland successfully resists any temptation to over-dramatize in scenes where he discovers the graves of Mary March and later of his missing wife and he creates a credible and sympathetic character. Quebecois Andree Pelletier was well cast as Nancy George, sensitively and effectively portraying the outsider with the hidden heritage. Tara Manuel approached her film debut with maturity and gave an impressive performance in the role of the proud defender of her heritage. The main actors were supported by a talented local cast including Des Walsh, Austin Davis, Mary Lewis and Paul Rowe as Buchans townspeople and mining company employees. As well, another group of actors made up of Newfoundland Micmac Indians and white actors in Beothuck dress reenacted the chilling abduction of Mary March (Jacinta Cormier) by the white settlers and the burial ceremony performed by a Beothuck leader.

The film features the cinematography of Michael Jones and the film editing of Derek Norman as well as a beautiful musical score by Pamela Morgan and Paul Steffler.

31

# Shaa-naan-dithit, or the Last of the Boêothics

## John McGregor

She was the last of the Boêothics. Her person, in height above the middle stature, possessed classical regularity of form. Her face bore striking similarity to that of Napoleon, and the olive cast of her complexion added to the resemblance. Her hair was jet black; her finely pencilled brows her long, darting lashes her dark, vigilant, and piercing eyes, were all remarkably striking and beautiful. Her teeth were white, even, and perfectly sound. Her hands and feet, small and well formed. She never laughed. Her smile was an exertion to do so, not a feeling. She from the first exhibited a predisposition to pulmonary disease: yet her appetite was sharp, and she ate more food than most European women. Having been four years among the English settlers in the remote part of the northern coast, and being remarkably apt to learn, she could, on arriving at St. John's, make herself tolerably well understood in English. Great hopes were entertained of her becoming the instrument of establishing an intercourse with her tribe. She, however, constantly persisted in refusing to accompany any of the expeditions in search of the Boêothics; saying it was an invariable religious principle laid down by her people to sacrifice to the names of the victims slain by the whites and Mik-maks any Boêothic who had been in contact with them.

Mr. Cormack provided her with crayons, and teaching her how to use them, in a few months she was able to represent various subjects which he requested her to draw relative to the customs of her tribe. She always preferred red crayons, and with them

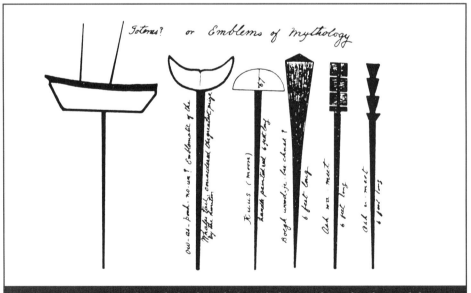

Two-metre-long staves with symbols of Beothuk mythology, as drawn by Shanawdithit. Cormack wrote the names of the staves, but failed to give a proper explanation of their significance. The first three represent a fishing boat, a whale's tail, and a half moon.

drew the profiles of various persons of her nation. That they were resemblances seems probable; for if taken from her, and if afterwards requested to draw the same persons, the likenesses exactly resembled those she previously sketched. The features of her father were uniformly the same, particularly his nose, which was consistently Roman. She also sketched groups, exhibiting the Boêothics in their camps, villages, and in their canoes; also rude sketches of their mode of hunting and snaring deer....

She said "her father and her lover and her mother were with the good spirit, and that she would go there too; but that she would not go back to Red Indian Lake, because she would be killed there, and not be buried with the things she should want for her journey."

She declared that it was impossible for any of her tribe to exist much longer. Her reasons were satisfactory. At the time when she and the other two females surrendered, the tribe had been reduced to so small a number that they were unable to keep up the deer-fences; and being driven from the shores, and from the fish and oysters, and the nests of water fowl, their means of existence were completely cut off.... Impelled by hunger, she and her mother and sister ventured to the coast, and were, as has been stated, captured. The other women died soon after. She, although her youth adapted her more readily to a new mode of living, was never after in good health; and, as she grew up, her predisposition to consumption, a disease common, it appears, to her tribe was apparently sapping her vitals. Her manners were easy and graceful—her temper generally calm; but on occasions, when some of the servants treated her, as she thought, with disrespect, her fierce Indian spirit kindled—the savage eye darted fire and vengeance; and the uniform kindness of Mr. Cormack alone would subdue the tempest which raged in the bosom of Shaa-naan-dithit.

He had occasion to return to England, and during his absence the attorney-general of the colony took her to his house. Consumption now crept rapidly through her frame; she became uneasy in her new dwelling, and was carried to the hospital, where, a few weeks afterwards, on the 6th June 1829, expired the last of the Boêothics.

(1836)

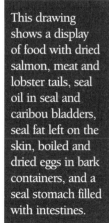

This drawing shows a display of food with dried salmon, meat and lobster tails, seal oil in seal and caribou bladders, seal fat left on the skin, boiled and dried eggs in bark containers, and a seal stomach filled with intestines.

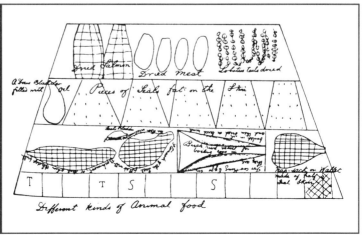

# Excerpts from a Diary

## Bishop John Inglis

### 2 July 1827. Exploits Island.

At Mr. Peyton's we saw Shanawdithit the Red Indian Girl, supposed to be the last of her race, of which, however, I have many doubts. She is like a well-looking Micmac squaw about 23 years of age, very stout, with mild and pleasing expression of countenance and a soft voice. She supposes three of her race to be still alive….

This woman with her Father, Mother and Sister were in this neighbourhood in the year 1823 in April separated from the rest of the party in search of food and when one of the inhabitants who were up the Bay for wood in their winter station, saw traces of the wild Indians (as they are generally called but sometimes Red from the quantity of ochre with which they are covered in such quantities that their tracks are sometimes distinguished by it) he collected two or three others and discovered a wigwam with an old woman nearly blind whom they brought in. When she was taken away her husband and the two girls who had been looking for food, moved to some distance through fear and as they were crossing some weak ice the old man fell in and was drowned. The old woman after being well treated for several days was returned to her own wigwam where she found the daughters or soon afterwards discovered them. They were afterwards taken to St. John's and treated with all possible kindness in hope that they might be used in calling in for protection, the wretched remnant of the tribe….

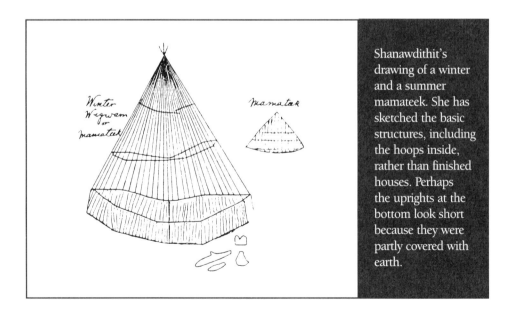

Shanawdithit's drawing of a winter and a summer mamateek. She has sketched the basic structures, including the hoops inside, rather than finished houses. Perhaps the uprights at the bottom look short because they were partly covered with earth.

## 4 July 1827.

Shanawdithit (now called Nancy) was left with Mr. Peyton, in whose service she has remained ever since. She is fond of his children who leave their mother to go to her and soon learned all that was necessary to make her useful in the family. Her progress in the English language has been slow…. She is now 23 years old, very interesting, rather graceful and of a fine disposition. Her countenance mild and her voice soft and harmonious. Sometimes a little sullenness appears and an anxiety to wander, when she will pass 24 hours in the woods and return but this seldom occurs. She is fearful that her race has died from want of food….

Shanawdithit was at church this day dressed in clothes given her by Capt. Jones [for whom she made a birchbark canoe replica] looking remarkably well and behaving with great propriety, kneeling when others kneeled. She perfectly understood that we were engaged in religious services and seemed struck with their solemnity. Her whole deportment was serious and becoming. I greatly regretted that her information was not such as to justify me in directing her to be baptised that I might confirm her.

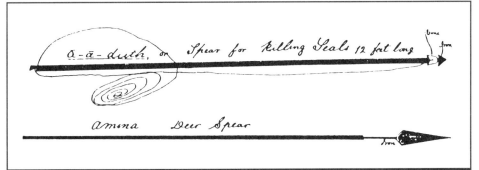

A sealing harpoon and a spear used for hunting caribou as drawn by Shanawdithit. The explanations she gave were recorded by Cormack.

# The Colony of Unrequited Dreams

## Wayne Johnston

Field Day, June 6, 1959

On this day 130 years ago a woman who was known to the people of this city as Nancy April and to herself as Shawnawdithit died in St. John's. She was the last Beothuk Indian.

When I was in my early twenties, I came down with tuberculosis and was confined for two years to the San. There was little to do but read and one of the books I read was Howley's book about the Beothuks.

Nancy was named April after the month that she was captured, as her sister was named Easter Eve after the day that she was captured and her mother Betty Decker after the boat on which she was transported from her place of capture to St. John's.

In 1823, the three of them were often seen walking the streets of St. John's together, wearing deerskin shawls over the dresses they were given by the whites with whom they lived.

When curious children gathered around them, Nancy made as if to chase them, which caused them all to scatter at the sight of which she laughed out loud. Everywhere they went, people gathered round to gape. Of the three of them, only Nancy seemed unafraid. She sometimes went so far as to mimic the looks of wonderment on the faces of the people that they passed. She was perhaps too young to understand; or perhaps she was feigning unconcern to reassure her mother and her sister, who were sick.

People reported seeing them so laden down with ironmongery, which they planned to take home with them, that they could barely move. I have often, since reading Howley, thought of those three women, not two months removed from their world, wandering around in one full of things they had no names for, laden down with bits of iron that they found discarded on the ground but that in their world, if only they could make their way back to it, could be put to precious use.

After a failed attempt to reunite them with their tribe, of whom there were by this time not more than two dozen left, they were sent to live with magistrate John Peyton and his wife in the town of Exploits, near the river of that name on which, for no one knows how long, the Beothuk depended for their livelihood, and where Nancy's mother and her sister died in the fall of 1823.

Nancy was for several years a servant in the Peyton household, where she learned very little English, but enough to tease Mrs. Peyton about how hard she worked her servants.

A society to prevent the extinction of the Beothuks was created in 1828 by William Cormack, who brought Nancy back to St. John's to live with him. Cormack suggested that she learn English and, in turn, teach him her language and way of life. She could not read, but she could draw quite well and name what she drew and some of what she saw. Cormack introduced her to people as "my interesting protegé."

She drew many sketches for Cormack, some depicting Beothuk dwellings, clothing, weapons and burial practices, and narrative maps showing where certain members of her tribe were killed or captured and the path of what is thought to have been their final expedition. When Cormack left Newfoundland, Nancy was sent to live with Attorney-General James Simms.

I think often, too, of Cormack leaving Newfoundland in the spring of 1829, when it was certain that she would soon die, unwilling to wait a few weeks more. It is not recorded why he left, though as he was single and quite well off, it seems likely that, if he had wanted to, he could have stayed.

She knew she was the last Beothuk. How, other than sad, this made her feel, she was unable to communicate. Nor can I imagine it, any more than I can a world that would seem as alien to me as ours must have seemed to her. "As for beds," Cormack said, "she did not understand their use," and instead slept on the floor beside them.

I am not much better able to imagine the point of view of the men at whose hands so many of her people died. I like to think that in their place, I would not have done what they did, but that is something I can never know.

But when I was in the San, I was drawn, morbidly drawn perhaps, to read and re-read Howley's book, and I was young enough to think that Nancy and I had a lot in common.

It was said of her that "she could not look into a mirror without grimacing at what she saw." That sentence would not be out of place in my obituary. She was described as having been "stout but shapely before she fell ill." Some people might say the same of me. We contracted tuberculosis at about the same age. I survived, for no other reason I can think of than because I understood the use of beds.

My father could not bear to watch me die. When he was told my death was certain, he stopped coming to the San to see me. I had very few other visitors. It was partly my father's abandonment of me that made me identify with Nancy. I fancied that Cormack had been in love with her and had gone away because he could not bear to watch her die. There are times when I still think it might be so.

She made a great impression on people long before they knew that she would be the last Beothuk. But it is hard not to think of her as that, "the last Beothuk," perhaps presumptuous to try in what is, after all, an address to absence, silence.

She was buried on the south side of St. John's, below the Brow, not with those whose graves she drew, not with those whose beads she wore, but with the Church of England dead, the Church of England poor, her grave unmarked. Her remains lie somewhere near the Church of St. Mary the Virgin, but where exactly no one knows.

According to one person who knew her while she stayed with Peyton, she had left behind her in the interior two children about whom she "fretted constantly." Nowhere else except in this one account are these children mentioned, so l am almost able now to persuade myself that they did not exist.

When I was in the San, I liked to think otherwise, however, because I had two lost children of my own.

I had a son and have a daughter who were conceived in St. John's and born in New York. I met my daughter and my granddaughter for the first time two years ago.

# Shanadithit

## Al Pittman

What I know of you is only
what my grade seven history book
told me.
That you were young when they caught you.
That your people lived in deerhide houses.
That you drew lovely pictures.
That they changed your name to Nancy.
That you died soon after.
That you were the last of the Beothuks.

You probably didn't know that
did you?
That you were the last of your people.
That when you went there was no one
to take your place.
I suppose you died thinking
there were uncles and cousins
with toothaches and babies
that there were hunters,
young men you'd like to be with,
coming home game-laden to campfires
on the shore of the lake
your executioners call Red Indian.

You didn't know
you'd end up in my grade seven history book
did you?

And when you died your lonely death,
when the white disease put an end to you,
you didn't know that all these years
beyond your decay I would long
to be with you, to tell you
I wouldn't forget. You didn't know
that I would have kissed you
and cried when you went.

Of course that has all to do
with my own images of you and they are
much too mixed up with technicolor movies
and my own boyish musings.

I see you as beautiful as Debra Paget
who played the role of an Indian girl
in a movie I barely remember.
I can't see you, no matter how hard
I try, mud-caked and offensive smelling.
I can't see you groaning and twisting
on the floor of your smokey mamateek
locked in any embrace with your rough
raw-boned cousins.

I see you
(and I know this is all wrong)
leaning over a blue pool. The sun
filters through the alders
and sends little shivers of light
bouncing off your golden thigh
where your beautifully embroidered dress
(like the one marked yours in the St. John's museum)
parts to let you bend.
Your reflection looks up at me
from the still water and your eyes
are two hollows deeper than any this brook
could fill. The eyes of a martyr,
of one who waits patiently for death
knowing that beyond all kindred deaths
yours will mater most.

Yet in all this there is a sadness
about you for you had not always
consented to your martyrdom. Before this,
before it had all been revealed to you
through witchcraft and religion,
you had wished rather that I would walk
buckskinned into your forest and take you
upstream to a place the shaman
and the gods had ordained for us.
And there in an eternity of summers,
we would have loved each other gently
in the brook-cooled summer sun.

That dream, of course,
(though it pleases me that you had it)
was entirely impossible. For you had
to die as you did, you had to be the last
of your race before I could love you
at all.

I admit now
(putting this poem aside)
that my love for you has nothing
to do with you. Not as you were
or might have been in those few
of your own dead end days.
For in those days surely my affection
would have been given over to some
Newfoundland lass with fair hair
and delicate English-pink skin.
There might have been times when I
would have impressed her with stories
of how I raided your village, killed
your cousin, and laughed heartily
all the way home.

The workman who destroyed your grave
to build his portion of road
did not know what he was doing, did
not know that I would have knelt
in awe at that spot loving you
and condemning your death all in one prayer.
He did not know he ruined forever
my one chance to come close to you.
and therefore what is he guilty of
but depriving me of one singular
and pitiful indulgence? One moment
in my history when I could have knelt
over your fleshless remains and said
"Shanadithit, I love you." What did he do
but save you the agony of one more lie?
Lie easy in your uneasy peace girl
and do not, do not, forgive those
who trespass against you.

# Excerpt from a Journal

## Gerald Squires

We're heading towards Exploits Island; it's a clear, bright, dancing butterfly day in early June, 1996. I'm aboard a longliner out of New World Island. Suddenly a storm comes out of nowhere, the islands in the distance turn black. I see lightening flashes over Exploits. The rain tears down in white sheets. Everyone scrambles for cover. I stay and watch the drama of the changing atmosphere. The small islands in the foreground turn a dark greenish-yellow ochre. It's hard to define the trees from the rocks; everything is one dimension. A renegade wind is churning the sea near the shore. Exploits disappears in the dark driving rain. I see a stooping figure walking along the edge of the rocks in the nearest island [Grassy Island]. It seems unconcerned about the weather. Its body-language tells me it's looking for something or someone. It also ignores the longliner and its lone witness. Standing erect now, it wraps itself in a heavy cloak and turns its face to the wind. The rain beats down. The weather and the figure become one. It disappears. The storm stops. The sun returns. We motor damply in the harbour and dock at the government wharf.

We stay on the island for eight days visiting old friends, photographing, drawing and painting. There is a heavy numbing sense of responsibility nagging at the base of my skull. The vision flashes on and off the screen of my imagination. I feel a strong urge to return to the apparition's island; to leave some sort of marking, build a stone cairn, make a sculpture out of driftwood, or maybe just sit and meditate. But none of these thoughts removed the numbing sensation I was feeling.

It was later, after returning home that I would entertain the thought that the image might have been Shanawdithit making herself known to me. I discussed it with Gail and Lois. I phoned Ingeborg. I made a small clay image of her. But art like the flashing weather and the dark rain is as fleeting as the lone figure itself.

Gerald Squires in his Holyrood studio sculpting the maquette

Clay statue in Gerald Squires's studio

Luben Boykov at Boyd's Cove site

Creating the bronze statue of Shanawdithit was a three-stage process: first a "maquette" was sculpted; secondly, a "life-size" clay model of the figure was made and thirdly, a bronze figure was cast by Bulgarian-born sculptor Luben Boykov.

*Spirit of the Beothuk*, Gerald Squires and Luben Boykov

**Excerpts from**

# *On the Rim of the Curve*

## Michael Cook

1. Nonasabasut, last Chief of the Beothuck, speaks from
   the Rim of the Curve.

> I, Nonasabasut, laboured
> to free myself of the old mortality,
> the obsession with wind and stars,
> her body, salmon silver in moonlight.
>
> I atoned for blood,
> the blood of my enemies,
> the blood of caribou and bear,
> the cold blood of fishes.
>
> I rendered up
> the gift of mysteries,
> my inheritance,
> the knowledge of water and birds,
> the conversation of trees.
>
> And now, on the Rim of the Curve,
> when all should be one,
> wife, child, self, the People,
> spirit moulded to spirit,
> daring the final journey,
> the unspeakable regions,
> I am troubled once more
> with lost voices,
> the ancient thunder of dying.
> I am tired, Father,
> of sifting that truth for meaning.
>
> I am tired of drowning in old deaths.
>
> I am tired of my external surprise…
> feeling the stab in the back,
> the shot in the back,
> the hole in the chest,
> watching the water of my body
> slip and freeze on my hands,
> the tented fabric of dreams folding.
>
> Do not keep us alive
> in the minds of men,
> or let their dreams

arrest our journey.
It was a good destiny
I have learned,
we walking in sleep
not to wake in the New World,
and those grim men…
became our saviours
and the inheritors of our suffering.
Ever we were what we were
and nothing changed us
from our coming to our going.

Let us pass on

2. Nonasabasut and his wife Demasduit reach out to Shanadithit
   from the Rim of the Curve

**SHANADITHIT:**
I, Shanadithit,
the last of my people,
laboured to free myself
of the old mortality,
the remembrance of wind and stars,
light,
and the limbs of light on the water,
light on the limbs of the water…

I, Shanadithit, was chosen
to be the book of my people,
was asked to render up
the mysteries of word and faith,
to chant, in a strange tongue,
our mythologies…

Carved bone pendants

Female figure, drawn by Shanawdithit and described as a "dancing woman," suggests that even during the last desperate days of the Beothuk it was possible to find some joy in their lives.

The Beothuk feared the "black man" or 'Red Indian devil' called Aich-mud-yim. Shanawdithit, who drew this picture, said he had a long beard, was short and very thick and dressed in beaver skin. He had been seen at Red Indian Lake.

Extract from

# The Newfoundlander

Thursday, June 11th, 1829

**Anonymous**

Died: The Red Indian woman, Shanawdithit better known by the name of Nancy who was taken some years ago by Mr. Peyton, and lived for the last twelve months in this town died of consumption of the lungs on Saturday last, aged, it is supposed about 28 years. She resided during her stay in St. John's with the Attorney-General and W. E. Cormack, Esq, who provided her the best medical attention, but the mode of life, so different from that to which she had been accustomed, appeared to have hastened her dissolution.

Extract from

# The Public Ledger and Newfoundland General Advertiser

Friday, June 12th, 1829

**Anonymous**

Died: on Saturday night, the 6th instant, at the hospital, SHANANDITHIT, the female Indian, one of the Aborigines of this Island. She died of consumption, a disease which seems to have been remarkably prevalent among her tribe, and which has unfortunately been fatal to all who have fallen into the hands of settlers.

Since the departure of Mr. Cormack from the Island, this poor woman has had an asylum afforded her in the house of James Simms, Esq. Attorney-General, where every attention has been paid to her wants and comfort; and under the able professional advice of Dr. Carson, who has most kindly and liberally attended her for many months past, it was hoped that her health might be reestablished. Lately however, her disease had become daily more formidable, and her strength had rapidly declined, and a short time since, it was deemed advisable to send her to the hospital, where her sudden decease has but too soon fulfilled the fears that were entertained for her.

With SHANANDITHIT has probably expired nearly the last of the Native Indians of the Island; indeed it is considered doubtful by some, whether even any of them now survive. It is certainly a matter of regret that those individuals who have interested themselves most to support the causes of science and humanity, by the civilization of these Indians, should have so unfortunately failed by this sudden termination to their hopes. They have, however, notwithstanding the calculating apathy with which their views have been met by some, the satisfaction of knowing, that their object has been to mitigate the sufferings of humanity and that at least they have endeavoured to pay a portion of that immense debt which is due from the European settlers of Newfoundland to these unfortunate Indians, who have been so long oppressed and persecuted, and are finally almost exterminated.

Extract from the

# London Times

*September 14th, 1829*

## W. E. Cormack

Died, at St. John's, Newfoundland, on the 6th of June last, in the 29th year of her age, Shawnawdithit, supposed to be the last of the Red Indians or Boeothicks. This interesting female lived six years a captive among the English, and when taken notice of latterly, exhibited extraordinary strong natural talents. She was niece to Mary March's husband, a chief of the tribe who was accidently killed in 1819, at the Red Indian's Lake, in the Interior, while endeavouring to rescue his wife from the party of English who took her, the view being to open a friendly intercourse with his tribe. This tribe, the Aborigines of Newfoundland, presents an anomaly in the history of man. Excepting a few families of them soon after the discovery of America, they never held intercourse with the Europeans, by whom they have been ever since surrounded, nor with the other tribes of Indians since the introduction of fire-arms among them. The Chinese have secluded themselves from the interference of all other nations, their motives being understood only to themselves, and the moral peculiarities of that people are slowly developed to others. But in Newfoundland, nearly as far apart from China as the Antipodes, there has been a primitive nation, once claiming rank as a portion of the human race, who have lived, flourished, and became extinct in their own orbit. They have been dislodged, and disappeared from the earth in their native independence in 1829, in as primitive a condition as they were before the discovery of the new world, and that too on the nearest point of America to England, in one of our oldest and most important colonies.

Small birch bark dish found in a grave

**Excerpt from**

# On the Rim of the Curve

## Michael Cook

RINGMASTER: Listen. Hang on a minute before you all rush off about whatever business sustains you. I've got something to read to you. It's from *The Times* of London. Of course. September 14th, 1829. It's about her and them. An obituary. Very big on obituaries, *The Times*. Only the best people get noticed in there, of course. Funny isn't it. All the crowd that scratched and fought and settled the place…none of them got in. Took an Indian to put Newfoundland on the map. A dead one. Here it is…"Died at St. John's, Newfoundland, on the 6th June last in the 29th year of her age, Shanadithit, supposed to be the last of the Beothuks." *(He folds the paper.)* Supposed to be. She was. We made no mistake about that, did we? Oh well…there you have it….Good night ladies and gentlemen, sweet ladies and gentlemen. God bless you all, and may you all be saved. Don't forget to tell your friends about us. Without your support, we'd never keep a show like this running….

*The lights fade…on a prolonged drum role.*

CURTAIN

Carved bone pendant found in a grave

# Shanawdithit's Dream

Robert O. Norman

As she lay in bed
weak with consumption
she dreamed of a time
when the snow was piled
high around their mamateek

and she was listening to her
mother tell the tale of
Shaw-na-yet.

Like a warm salty summer
wind blowing in from the sea
Shanawdithit could smell
Shaw-na-yet's sweet scent
of wild rose and see the
tiny embers of blazing sun
in her eyes.

Always, she loved the ending.
The part that told of how the
reuniting of Shaw-na-yet
and her mother Obo-dish
brought spring back to the world

and as she awoke Shanawdithit
felt the joy that Shaw-na-yet felt
for she too would soon be reunited
with her mother and they would dance
in the warm summer breeze.

A bone harpoon head with an iron point

# In There Somewhere

**Tom Dawe**

"What if they are not all dead?
Suppose a group of them
were wise enough to hide
somewhere deep in the island's interior?"

"Just think…
they could still be
in there somewhere!"

Somebody laughed at her
and it rattles like the chains
of beaver traps.

I could not laugh
at what the lady tourist said.
Why should I scorn
a little ignorance
(or call it what you will)
of Newfoundland geography?

Besides, I know that
deep within my island
there are austere voices
in the August birch
and slow dawns are caught
in great wooden bowls
where the meek still inherit.
And a moon is always
a moving canoe
across blue acres of the night.
And a child is always
laughing
in the splash of white water
down the long bakeapple hills.

I could not laugh
because they are
still
in there
somewhere.

Excerpt from

# The Beothuk of Newfoundland: A Vanished People

## Ingeborg Marshall

Beothuk canoes were between 3.5 and 6.5 metres long and could carry up to 8 or 10 adults. Their special features were a high-curved front and back to protect the occupants from spray, and sides that rose high in the middle so that water would not pour into the craft when it tipped sideways. While most bark canoes of other Indians had a flat or rounded bottom from which the sides rose up gently, the sides on Beothuk canoes flared straight out from the central timber or keelson; seen from the front, Beothuk canoes looked pointed at the bottom. This feature gave the canoes great depth and prevented them from being blown off course.

To build a canoe, the Beothuk stripped sheets of birch bark from large trees and sewed them together to form a single sheet. It was laid out on the ground with the smooth inner bark facing down. This smooth surface became the outside of the canoe. A piece of spruce the length of the canoe was placed in the centre of the bark sheet to serve as a keelson or frame. The bark was then folded upwards along the keelson to form the sides and was held up by stakes driven into the ground.

Now the canoe was ready to be strengthened. The upper edges of the sides were fortified with long, tapered poles of spruce, called gunwales, that were lashed to the bark. At both ends of the canoe, the bark cover was cut to its proper shape and sewn together. All lashing and sewing was done with split spruce roots. Since the women were the most skilled at sewing, they usually completed this part of the job. When all the sewing was done, the two sides of the canoe were sprung open like a purse.

The next step was to place crossbars or "thwarts" at the middle and at each end, to hold the sides apart. Inside, the birch bark was protected with wooden slats laid lengthwise. Curved sticks known as ribs were placed over them to hold the slats and keelson in place. The rib ends were tucked under the gunwales. The seams and any thin patches in the bark were waterproofed with a thick coating of heated tree gum, charcoal, and red ochre. When the coating had cooled and dried, the canoe could be launched. Because Beothuk canoes were very light and had no flat bottom to rest on, they would not stay upright in the water without ballast. Rocks, covered with moss and sods to make them more comfortable to kneel on, were often used for ballast. How tippy could a canoe with a pointed bottom be? To find out, Scott James from Grand Falls built one from plywood. He found it took time and patience to ballast it with rocks but, once this was accomplished, the canoe was very stable and easily cut through the waves.

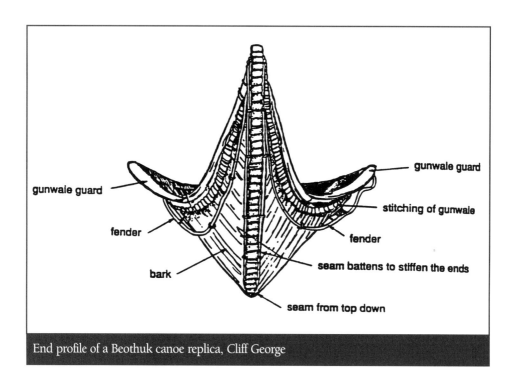

End profile of a Beothuk canoe replica, Cliff George

Excerpts from

# Beothuk Bark Canoes: An Analysis and Comparative Study

## Ingeborg Marshall

The earliest source of relatively detailed information on the Beothuk canoe is John Guy's "The Journall of the voiadge of discoverie made in a barke built in Newfoundland called the *Indeavour* begunne the 7th. of October 1612 and ended the 25th. November following." Guy, an alderman of Bristol, co-founded a settlement in Cupids, Newfoundland, in 1610 and acted as its first governor. In October 1612 he set out with 17 men on an exploration of Trinity Bay. Having met with a group of Beothuk Indians and their canoes and having found and expropriated one of their birch-bark vessels, Guy was in the position to give fairly accurate data on these craft.

> Theire canoaes are about 20 foote long, & 4 foote & a halfe broad in the middle alofte, & for their keele, & timbers they have thinne lighte peeces of dry firre rended, as yt weare lathes and in steede of boorde they vse the vtter birche barke which is thinne & hath many foldes, sowed togeather with a thread made of a small roote quartered, they will carrie fower persons well, & way not one hundred weight. They are made in forme of a new moone, stemme, & sterne alike & equallie distant from the greateste breadth. From the stemme & sterne theare riseth a yarde highe a lighte thinne staffe whyped about with small rootes, which they take hold by to bring the canoa ashoare. That serveth in steede of ropes and a harbour, for every place is to them a harboorugh, wheare they can goe ashoare them selves they take a land with them theire canoa, & will neaver put to sea but in a calme, or very fayre weather. In the middle the canoa is hygher a great deale than in the bow & quarter. They be all bearing from the keele to the porteles, not with any circular line but with a righte line.

Miniature birch bark canoe found in a grave

Captain Richard Whitbourne's long time association with Newfoundland began in 1579 when he first visited this island. In 1620 he published A Discourse and Discovery of the *Newe-founde-lande* which includes a description of Beothuk canoes. Whitbourne had been given a bark canoe by sailors from the "Tapson" (probably Topsham), a Devonshire fishing vessel. They had surprised an Indian encampment near Heart's Ease in Trinity Bay and had taken their three canoes. Following the description is a systematized summary of the text.

> Natiues of those parts haue great store of red Okar, wherewith they vse to colour their bodies, Bowes, Arrowes and Cannowes, in a painting manner; which Cannowes are their Boats, that they vse to goe to Sea in, which are built in shape like the Wherries on the Riuer of Thames, with small timbers, no thicker nor broader than hoopes; and in stead of boards, they vse the barkes of Birch trees, which they sew very artificially and close together, and then ouerlay the seames with Turpentime, as Pitch is vsed on the seames of Ships, and Boats.

Replica of Beothuk canoe

*Sketch of a Beothuk camp*, John Cartwright
Provincial Archives of Newfoundland and Labrador, Cartwright Collection, MG 100.

# Obligatory Beothuk Poem

**James Candow**

All the tortured white artists in the world
couldn't put you back together again.
Just think,
if you were alive today
you'd be second class citizens
dependent on government largesse
occasionally making headlines
with some pathetic act of protest
we could all laugh off or
get indignant about.
But dead
you fester in our psyches like maggots
as you are claimed by myth.
Baby, you never had it so good.

# dead Indians

**Mary Dalton**

dead Indians
are safer
in poems, museums,
archaeo-
logical pamphlets,
bone pendants and ochre

weeping walrus
we mourn the Beothuk
close the sky in
on Labrador Innu,
the land wired
and caribou fled.

# Reports and Letters by George Christopher Pulling Relating to the Beothuk Indians of Newfoundland

**Ingeborg Marshall**

(A Beothuk word list compiled by Pulling in 1792).

| | |
|---|---|
| Ou-bee | The name of the Indian girl who lives with Mr. Stone |
| Dew-is | Sun or Moon which they worship |
| Ha-the-may | a bow |
| Hur-reen, or Huz-seen | a gun |
| Poodg-be-a | an oar |
| Huzza-gan | rowing |
| Thub-a-thew | a boat or canoe |
| Hod-thoo | to shoot a gun |
| Ou-thaje-arra-thun-um | to shoot an arrow perpendicularly |
| Han-nan | a spear |
| Tis-ew-thum | wind |
| Now-aut | a hatchet |
| Push-a-man | a man |
| Pug-a-tho | throwing |
| Hodg-us-um | cutting |
| Tu-wed-gie | swimming |
| Mou-a-gee-ne | iron |
| Pedth-au | rain |
| Pe-to-tho-risk | thunder |
| Koorac | lightning or fire |
| Pug-a-zoo | eating |
| Peatha | fur or hair of a beast |
| Pau-shee | birch rind or paper |
| Hod-witch | foot |
| Hadda-bothy | body |
| Co-ga-de-alla | leg |
| Hods-mishiet | knee |

| | |
|---|---|
| Ebau-thoo | water |
| Who-ish-me | laughing |
| Ke-aw-thaw | head |
| Eve-nau | feathers |
| Poo-push-raut | fish |
| Posson | the back |
| Coosh | lip |
| Cush | nails |
| Me-men | hands and fingers |
| Moo-cus | elbow |
| Sham-ye | currants |
| Mo-me-za-bethon | shoulder |
| Mis-muth | ear |
| Ou-ther-may | teeth |
| Me-ma-za | tongue |
| Donna | hair |
| Dis-up | a fishing line |
| Me-roo-pish | twine or thread |
| Koorac | fire |
| Ou-gen | stone |
| Adiab | wood |
| Ou-ner-mish | a little bird |
| Po-pa-dish | a large bird |
| A-bush-thib-e | kneeling |
| Thub-wed-gie | dancing |
| Pis-au-wau | laying |
| King-abie | standing |
| Wo-tha-ma-sha | running |
| Wooth-yan | walking |
| Ha-dos-do-ding | sitting |
| She-both | kissing |
| Ob-osheen | warming yourself |
| Corra-soob | sorrow |
| Hedg-yan | stooping |
| Mudg-raw | hiccups |
| Tib-e-thun | a trap or gin |

| | |
|---|---|
| Shaub-ab-un-eshaw | to throw a trap |
| Tus-mus | a pin or needle |
| Ke-oun | the chin |
| Sus-ut | a fowl or partridge |
| Sou-sot | spruce rind |
| No-mus-rush-ke-aw-a-thaw | scalping the head |
| Me-men-mo-mas-rush | shaking hands |
| Arrow-bauth | blood |
| Midg-u-thew | sneezing |
| Mome-augh | eye brow |
| Chec-a-shit | groaning |
| Puth-u-auth | sleep |
| Mau-the-au-thaw | crying |
| Tu-au-thaw | singing |
| Peg-a-thee | a scab |
| Poss-thee | smoke |
| Mush-a-bauth | oakum or tow |
| Yew-oin | knife |
| Po-pa-de-aden | fork |
| Madg-u-a | leaves |
| Traw-na-soo | spruce |
| Ti-be-ath | yawning |
| Yew-why | dirt |
| Methie | coal |
| Pooith | thumb |
| She-ga-me | blow your nose |
| Ife-ween | thigh |
| Ob-ditch | a beast |
| Mom-au | a seal |
| Me-no-me | dog berries |
| Shau-da-me | partridge berries |
| Pug-a-thuse | beating |
| Han-a-mait | a spoon |
| Te-de-sheet | the neck or throat |
| Od-au-sot | rolling |
| Esh-bauth | catching fish |

63

| | |
|---|---|
| Te-diddle | breaking wind |
| Su-ga-meth | bird excrement |
| Shisth | grass |
| Cus-e-bee | a louse |
| Kess-yet | a flea |
| Yew-one | a wild goose |
| Me-a-woth | flying |
| Chu-thing | a walking stick |
| So-ush-zeth | the stars |

Two moccasins from a boy's grave

Mamateeks, Dennis Minty

# bedoret ahune

**Randolph Paul**

beathook mamset bedoret zathrook
mamset bedoret ahune
kannabuck mamset bedoret beathook
kannabuck mamset bedoret ahune

oubee mamset bedoret beathook
mamset bedoret ahune
kannabuck mamset bedoret oubee
kannabuck mamset bedoret ahune

thubwedgie osweet
yazeek gobidin
cockaboset washawet
thooret abusthibe ejew

deedrashow shebon wothamashee
bedoret beathook wothamashee
arrowbauth beathook wothamashee

noduera ebadoe barodiisick
marot pugazoa
awoodet whoishme bedoret

beathook mamset bedoret zathrook
oubee mamset bedoret zathrook
bedoret deedrashow shebon wothamashee
bedoret ahune

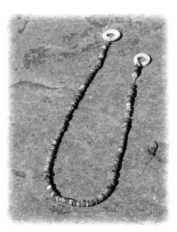

A string of flat beads made from
shell, pieces of clay pipe stem
and birch bark

# heart of the rock

**Randolph Paul**

the people live in the heart of a man
living in the heart of the rock
long life to the heart of the people
long life to the heart of the rock

oubee lives in the heart of a man
living in the heart of the rock
long life to the heart of oubee
long life to the heart of the rock

dancing deer
solitary eagle
fearless bear
come kneel look

the red river is flowing
heart of the people flowing
life of the people flowing

hear the water thunder
smell, taste
sing with laughing hearts

the people live in the heart of a man
oubee lives in the heart of a man
in the heart of the red river flowing
in the heart of the rock

A stone knife

Excerpts from

# Shanadithit: The Musical

Eleanor Cameron Stockley

## THE SCENES

### Act 1

| Scene 1 | Near Red Indian Lake 1800 |
| Scene 2 | Near Red Indian Lake 1806 |
| Scene 3 | Exploits River 1810 |
| Scene 4 | Wimbourne, England 1810 |
| Scene 5 | Marching up the Exploits River, Jan. 1811 |
| Scene 6 | Near Red Indian Lake, Jan. 1811 |
| Scene 7 | Near Red Indian Lake, Jan. 1811 |
| Scene 8 | Near Red Indian Lake, Jan. 1811 |
| Scene 9 | Near Red Indian Lake, April 1811 |
| Scene 10 | Near Rushy Brook, 1815 |
| Scene 11 | Lower Sandy Point, 1819 |
| Scene 12 | Near Red Indian Lake, March 1819 |
| Scene 13 | Near Red Indian Lake 1820 |
| Scene 14 | Near Red Indian Lake, Spring 1820 |
| Scene 15 | Outside a St. John's court house, 1822 |
| Scene 16 | Near Exploits, Spring 1823 |

### Act 2

| Scene 1 | St. John's Harbour Front, Spring, 1823 |
| Scene 2 | In a room in St. John's |
| Scene 3 | Wimbourne, England, Spring 1823 |
| Scene 4 | Outside Peyton home, Exploits, Summer 1823 |
| Scene 5 | Inside Peyton's home, Exploits, Summer 1823 |
| Scene 6 | Inside Peyton's home, Exploits, Fall 1823 |
| Scene 7 | In the woods, Summer 1825 |
| Scene 8 | Inside Peyton's home, Aug. 1828 |
| Scene 9 | Twillingate Courthouse, Sept. 1829 |
| Scene 10 | Inside Peyton's home, Sept. 1828 |
| Scene 11 | Outside Peyton's home, Sept. 1828 |
| Scene 12 | Outside Peyton's home, Sept. 1828 |
| Scene 13 | Inside Cormack's house in St. John's, March 1829 |
| Scent 14 | In St. John's Hospital, June 1829 |
| Scene 15 | Conclusion |

The following song, "Let There Be Peace Among Us All," is from Act II, Scene 8.

# Let There Be Peace Among Us All

## Eleanor Cameron Stockley

Children:
Sing in the mor - ning a song of love
Sing of peace and joy from a - bove

Al - le - lu, Al le - lu - lia Al - le - lu - lia

Englis: Let there be an answer to our prayer an answer to our prayer an answer to our prayer.

Let there be peace a -mong us all. Let us live to- ge - ther in har- mon - y.
Shanadithit:This man he wres - tles with such guilt; He has killed so many Be - o - thuk In - di- ans.

Let all God's Chil - dren be strong to o - ver come the prob - lems that they see.
Cull: If I a - pol - o - gize to her I de - ny ev - ery thing that I am.

All: Let the peo - ple of this I - land cher - ish what they have: fam - ily,
Shanadithit: I feel such pi - ty for his tor - men - ted soul. Cull: But

friends, wa - ter food and sun from God's al - migh - ty hand. No - thing
every one was kil - ling them; it was - nt me a - lone! Don't

more should we need, then to help us day by day. Keep us
look at me that way, for I've done no - thing wrong!

safe, Ho- ly fa- ther, oh we pray. Keep us safe, ho- ly Fa- ther, oh we pray.

69

**Children**:   Sing in the morning a song of love.
Sing of peace and joy from above.
Alleluia, Alleluia, Alleluia.

**Bishop Englis**:   Let there be an answer to our prayer, answer to our prayer, an answer to our prayer.
Let there be peace among us all. Let us live together in harmony.
Let all God's children be strong, to overcome the problems that they see.

**All**:   Let the people of this Island cherish what they have:
Family, friends, water, food and sun from God's almighty hand.
Nothing more should we need then to help us day by day.
Keep us safe, Holy Father, oh we pray. Keep us safe, Holy Father, oh we pray.

**Shanadithit**: This man he wrestles with such guilt; he has killed so many Beothuk Indians.

**Cull**: If I apologize to her, I deny everything that I am.

**Shanadithit**: I feel such pity for his tormented soul.

**Cull**: But everyone was killing; it wasn't me alone!
Don't look at me that way, for I've done nothing wrong!

**All**: Keep us safe, Holy Father, oh we pray. Keep us safe, Holy Father, oh we pray.

**All**: Can we put behind us wrongs that were started oh so many years ago?
Can we sing happier songs and include the people who were once our foes?
Can't we sing together, can't we hope for better days, as we come to join in the Lord's most holy praise? Help us, Holy Father, grant us peace.
Help us, Holy Father, grant us peace.

Concrete slab grave marker

Boyd's Cove Museum display.

# A Profile of Georgina Ann Stirling (1867-1935)

**The editors**

Georgina Stirling, the daughter of Ann Peyton and Dr. William Stirling, was born at Twillingate. She was educated at Twillingate and Toronto, and studied singing in Paris (with voice teacher, Mathilde Marchesi) and performed with a Milan opera company in Italy and the New Imperial Opera Company in New York.

Her professional name was Mademoiselle Marie Toulinguet (the original French name of Twillingate).

She gave several performances on short stop-over visits to St. John's. During a visit in 1897 she sang the National Anthem at the laying of the Cornerstone for Cabot Tower.

During an engagement in Italy she damaged her voice with a straining of her vocal chords. This prevented her from singing opera and later brought on periods of depression.

After the death of her sister, Janet Stirling, in 1928 in London she returned to Twillingate where she died on April 23, 1935. For twenty-two years her body lay in an unmarked grave in the Snelling's Cove cemetery, but in 1964 a six foot monument was erected to "The Nightingale of the North."

Amy Louise Peyton has written a biography of Georgina Stirling, *Nightingale of the North* (1983).

A Beothuk connection: Georgina's mother was probably one of the children Shanawdithit helped raise while she stayed at the home of John Peyton, Junior at Exploits. John Peyton, Senior (1774-1827) came to Newfoundland in 1770 with Captain George Cartwright. In 1819 he accompanied David Buchan on the expedition on which Demasduit was captured. John Peyton, Junior (1791-1879) came from England in 1812 to be the "youngster" on the Exploits River to guard and consolidate the Peyton salmon rights. In 1823 he married Eleanor Mahaney. Ann Peyton was one of their children. Shanawdithit stayed at the Peyton residence (1823-1828) and helped care for the children. Ann Peyton, daughter of John Peyton, Junior and Eleanor Mahaney, married Dr. William Stirling, a physician who was born in Harbour Grace in 1813. Georgina Stirling was their daughter.

Both John Peyton, Senior (Georgina's maternal great-grandfather) and John Peyton, Junior (Georgina's grandfather) were buried in the same grave at Exploits, Burnt Island in Notre Dame Bay. One horizontal slab marks the grave of the two men.

Georgina A. Stirling, Provincial Archives of Newfoundland and Labrador

To MISS TWILLINGATE STIRLING,
with a scarf of native colors,
presented by Rev. Dr. Potts, in the name of

"THE WOMEN OF THE METHODIST COLLEGE AID."

A token of admiration and love.

**Isabella Whiteford Rogerson**

Oh, 'tis only a scarf. Why, it should be a crown,
For our own "Queen of Song" is she,
And the glorious wealth of her voice of renown
She dispenses right royally.

Aye, and loyally, too, for she loves Newfoundland,
No matter how far she may roam;
And on earth there is nothing more touchingly grand
Than the love of a patriot for home.

In the courts of our God we are rapt in amaze,
Caught up by that voice into heaven,
Till entranced we can hear the bright seraphim praise,
Through the cleft air with melody riven.

Oh, this wonderful gift! for in heaven, with love,
It survives faith and hope—aye, and prayer—
Long may Twillingate Stirling praise God up above
With that God-given voice, rich and rare.

(1898)

# A Picture of the Past

Addison Bown

## A Romance of Newfoundland in the Days of French Occupation

 onsieur Le Comte D'Auxine spoke slowly, carefully, with a finger on the map of Avalon outspread before him. The young sous-lieutenant at his side had already begun to understand that this was a matter of no small importance.

"Henri," said the Count, "I have received a commission from De Frontenac, under the great seal of France, in which he bids me make ready for an attempt at the capture of St. John's. He leaves me free to make those preparations at discretion, but stresses imperatively the necessity of a successful assault. I am no less resolved that there shall be no failure. To that end, Henri, I am of a mind to send a brave and trusty agent to St. John's to spy out the defenses, and my choice has fallen on you."

Quarel, the sous-lieutenant, bowed in acknowledgment of the compliment.

"You pay me a great honour, Monsieur," he returned, "and one in the performance of which I trust I may justify your confidence."

"I have no doubt you shall," replied the Count kindly, "since I feel certain that my choice is wisely made. Come, Henri. Let us consider how best the mission may be carried out. Here is Plaisance: there, St. John's. Listen to what I propose. You are to enter St. John's: I think the best way of getting there would be to join Pierre Minot and his coureurs-de-bois, cross the peninsula in their company, and then allow yourself to be taken prisoner, alone you understand, in order to facilitate your movements while in your captors' hands. Hampered by the presence of others, you would be deprived of greater personal liberty, which you must endeavour to gain by complete submission to the will of your masters. I can count upon you to make use of such concessions to the best possible advantage—in the furtherance of your mission. Let me see. It is now late in the year. You must be prepared to spend part of the winter in the woods around the settlement, in order to spy out the lay of the country and to note the most convenient route for an attack by land. The rest of the winter you can spend in the town, thus permitting yourself ample opportunity for a thorough study of the fortifications. In the spring, make your escape. A corvette will be cruising near Rebou, to convey you to the harbour of Aquaforte, where I shall await your coming. What think you of the plan?"

The young sous-lieutenant made ready answer, testifying alike to his absolute comprehension and his admiring appreciation.

"Excellent, Monsieur le Comte, excellent! With skill and courage such a plan cannot but be productive of success."

"Which skill and courage, Henri," rejoined the Count, "I know you to possess, and am fully assured of ultimate triumph." He embraced the youthful soldier. "Mon fils!" he exclaimed. "Perhaps I send you to your death, you who are so brave, but these are the fortunes of war, and France, our glorious France, must be served." There was a sparkle in his eye, a ring in his voice, which showed perceptibly how wrapped up in his duty and calling was the Governor of Placentia. "But rather let us speak of the more pleasant alternative. You are now sous-lieutenant. Come you back successful and I will make you captain. But in the meantime the sword which you have ever wielded so well must be laid aside, and from the time you leave Fort Louis until you return to open service, yours must be the garb and language of a *coureur-de-bois*."

Henri had been embarrassed by the enthusiasm of his superior, especially when its warmth had extended to himself. There was something in his nature which disapproved of this intimate congratulation so essential to the French character, and it was with feelings of relief that he welcomed the change in the conversation occasioned by mention of the sword.

"Monsieur," he answered proudly, "I shall feel no regret at laying aside my sword, since in doing so, I discard it in the service of my country. And as for the fate you hint of, I possess, as you know, neither kith-nor-kin since my foster-father, Colonel Quarel, died, and so am free to risk my life, which is dedicated to France alone!"

"Spoken like a hero!" cried M. le Comte. "And yet," he mused, "heroic though your venture be, it is but a thankless task. I and the French nation honour you, for yours is a mission reserved solely for men of proved courage, ability and skill, but the penalty of infamy alone awaits you if discovered by the English. But there is no other course. We must make certain of our work, and justify the hopes of De Frontenac, whose mind is set upon the capture of St. John's, which he means to occupy permanently and convert into the powerful naval base its strategic position warrants."

"Ah yes, Monsieur!" put in the practical sous-lieutenant. "You have not yet told me of your own share in the matter. Have you decided on the course of action?"

The Count moved once more to the map and stood gazing down on it.

"That depends largely upon your report, Henri. Still, there are certain preliminaries which I have in view, one of which entails the removal of the fleet now in harbour to the Eastern coast before the coming of the ice. I have decided that a sea and land attack must be jointly made. Of the two, the more important is the land, and I am depending principally on you to discover for me the surest route. D'Iberville captured St. John's by land. I might follow his example and use Plaisance as my base of operations, but I have no mind for that long winter march overland, especially as we are without the aid of the Canadian Indians, whose familiarity with hardship is inseparable from success in such a venture. No. A shorter march, I think, would permit a swifter attack, and with the co-operation of the fleet, I may safely say that we are safeguarded against failure. However, we are somewhat premature in discussing details. Let that be done in Aquaforte. In the meantime, you do your share and I will do mine. By the spring all will be ready for the great attempt."

Henri Quarel, perceiving that the interview was at an end, bowed his way from the presence of the Governor.

Colonel William Fetherby, Commandant of St. John's, sat with wine glass and bottle before him in his quarters at Fort William.

A hard drinker was the Colonel, and a solitary, it being his custom to pass his nights thus with those never failing companions of his in secluded peace. There was sufficient in his daily round of duties to keep him occupied, but now when the shadows had fallen and the restless roar of the Atlantic surge was echoing from the rocks, he had retired to privacy. Pleasures there were none after dark to tempt him forth. A widower, and no longer young, it would have required some powerful inducement to drag him from his cups, even had there existed any such. In this wilderness of North America the recreations of the Homeland were nowhere to be found, and when the time hung heavily upon their hands it is not a matter of great wonder that the naval and military officers of the period were compelled to seek surcease from their loneliness in sherry, port and *aguardiente*.

A most explosive temper, too, possessed Colonel Fetherby, especially when disturbed in his lonely carouse. Such an outburst was now forthcoming, for a tap on the door had given notice of the arrival of an intruder. The Colonel stood angrily to his feet as the opened door revealed the sergeant.

"What in the devil brings you here at this hour, Pyme?" he flared.. "Have I not told you that I am not to be disturbed?"

The serjeant bowed his apology as he removed his hat.

"Pardin, sor," he volunteered in his broad Devon accent, "but thur be a prisner without. The scuts did capture un, and I thought as how ye'd like ter be informed."

"A prisoner? Officer—soldier?"

"Naw, sor. One of thim Frinch wood-rangers, I allow, ter take un by his dress."

"To the devil with him then! Bid them take him to the Battery and—" He was on the point of saying "Shoot him!" for the Colonel possessed an undying hatred of all things French, inanimate as well as living, but appeared suddenly to change his mind. "Nay Pyme, bid them bring him hither, I have a fancy to see this rogue and question him."

The serjeant departed, returning shortly with a file of regulars and the prisoner. Fetherby surveyed him keenly as he stood there in his deerskin garb, face dark with beard, restless eyes roving here and there. The Colonel shot a question at him.

"Who are you?"

At first the prisoner did not comprehend, and it was only the shouted repetition of the question and the heavy accompanying step forward which brought the answer trembling from his lips. He cowered back.

"I do no harm, M'sieu," he quavered. "I—Claude Derange."

"Harm?" roared the bellicose wine-bibber. "Your very presence is an insult. What brings you here?"

"Noteeng, M'sieu. I am brought."

The Colonel's rage waxed higher still as he noted the broad smile which transfigured for a startling moment the homely features of Pyme.

"Silence, you dirty half-breed! I'll have none of your impertinence. Do you know," he thundered, thrusting his inflamed face forward until it was within an inch of the bearded *coureur-de-bois*, "that I have the power, if I will, to throw you to the fishes?" He turned away in disgust. "Ugh!" he exclaimed. "He smells of vermin! I can well believe his statement that he was brought. Take him away!" he shouted. "He has been here long enough. Perhaps even now we are afflicted with other French abominations which brought him. Take him away and lock him up!"

And laughing heartily at his own coarse wit, the Commandant went back to his wine, and so was left at peace.

The months of winter slowly passed, each with its attendant quota of storm and frost and snow, but still they passed. "Claude Derange" made himself useful to his masters. A harmless fellow, noted among the garrison for his timidity, but withal cheerful and willing, he evinced a readiness for work which found him employment at every sort of manual labour in and about the forts, and in the foraging of firewood from the woods around. He possessed a mortal dread of the fiery Commandant, which was all to the good, since it served to amuse his captors and to increase their opinion of his harmlessness. The widening scope thus afforded him by increasing personal liberty found use and benefit to the end designed, and there was prepared for the perusal of M. le Comte d'Auxine a comprehensive report on the fortifications of Fort William and the earthwork defences of the Narrows which would have greatly astonished the competent, if intemperate, Commandant, Colonel William Fetherby.

There came a day when a sudden storm raged from the North West, while Claude Derange was skating on the Harbour ice. It was a favorite occupation of his, this skating, one which attracted little attention and no molestation, on the part of his captors. The storm was sudden, swooping down with a wild shriek to the accompaniment of driving snow which thickened quickly to a raging blizzard, and Claude Derange, upon the river, steered an uncertain way for shelter. He came upon another situated as himself, a girl as it chanced, and checked his own flying speed to aid her in her confused meanderings through the snow. They reached the shore and path in safety, but it was not until the confines of the Fort were gained that Claude Derange discovered the identity of his companion: the Colonel's ward, Nell.

At the door of her guardian's quarters, she thanked him graciously and invited him to enter to receive the Colonel's thanks.

"He will be anxious about me," she smiled, presenting a pretty picture as she stood there with her rosy cheeks and disordered hair," and I know that he wishes to thank you for the services you have done me."

The young Frenchman bowed in silence, regretting the while that his assumed lack of English forbade his assuring in adequate terms so fair a damsel that the little he had done was a pleasure.

Colonel Fetherby had been drinking harder than his wont that evening. There was a hot flush on his face and the menace of a storm of unusual violence in his eyes as he stood to his feet at their entrance. For a moment he said nothing; then before any explanation was forthcoming from his ward, who had hastened to his side, the battery of his wrath was levelled at the Frenchman, now that he had recognized him.

"So!" he shouted. "You are here again, and this time with my ward!" He pushed her roughly to one side as he spoke and came forward. "You have insulted me before, sir, but this last is too much. Were you a gentleman I would call you out. Since you are not, I will throw you out!"

There was that in Nell Fetherby's glance which told the Frenchman more plainly than if she had spoken that she considered her guardian in these besotted moods unaccountable both for words and temper. Derange comprehended instantly, and so was able to restrain his indignation. Strangely enough, he faced the angry Colonel fearlessly now and looked him squarely in the face. He cringed no longer.

"You mistake, M'sieu," he answered boldly. "M'selle there, she tell you I am gentleman. But yes! I make no insult!"

"Mention her name again, canaille, and I will choke the life from you! 'Tis ever thus with you scum of Frenchmen. Fair words and smiling lips, but treacherous hearts as black as Erebus! Listen and I will tell you what your race has done to me. Then deny me, if you can, my just cause for hatred of your nation. Fifteen years ago I was returning to Boston from leave in England on board the *Raven* sloop. With me was my only son, a boy of ten, whose mother had died in these arms two weeks before. In the night, when nearing the American coast, we were set upon by a French Privateer of twice our strength, and boarded. My boy was torn from me and I cast into the reeking hold. They took us into Louisburgh, from which I eventually escaped and rejoined my countrymen. I have searched, do you hear: I have sought unceasingly for years for news or trace of my son, but from that day to this I have never laid eyes on him. Revenge alone remains to me, for it seems that I am doomed never to discover him, and I have sworn—aye, by the most binding of oaths—that France will yet atone to me for the wrong that she has done me! I live only to see that vow fulfilled to the very letter. And now you—one of that accursed race who have already despoiled me of one child—you come hither to lure away the only treasure left me…."

His hand went out with a sudden jerk to the sword and scabbard lying on the table. With a fierce gesture he drew the blade half out; then, restraining himself by a mighty effort, he plunged it again into its sheath.

" …You are defenceless, a hostage, and for that reason I will not soil my hands by touching you. But get you gone from this as swiftly as you may. Another time and I will not be so merciful. I warn you that, if you approach my ward again, not even the immunity of your captive state will save you. Remember that and slumber on it tonight, Frenchman. Get you hence!"

Claude Derange bowed slowly to them both, and there was something so graceful in that bow, some trace of the courtier, that the Colonel's attention was arrested.

"Who are you?" he demanded suddenly on a note of suspicion; then, as if reassured by the other's outward guise, perhaps by the thought of the craven role so cleverly enacted during the past months by Claude Derange, he turned aside contemptuously and addressed his ward. "Come, Nell," he said kindly, "you have not yet told me what delayed you."

The young Frenchman lay long that night in thought. The time had come, he decided, to leave the Fort, and although the moment of departure was earlier than he had anticipated, it were wiser to go now, when the way was open, in case the hostility of the Colonel, dangerous enough already, should be carried to such lengths as to render fruitless any effort at escape.

A favourable opportunity arrived soon afterwards. When the shade of evening fell, Claude Derange made his way unnoticed up the river from the Harbour, and was quickly lost in the Southern woods. At daybreak the waiting corvette in the harbour of Bay Bulls took him off and trimmed her sails for the open sea.

On the morning of Holy Saturday, Capitaine Henri Quarel, with the three hundred men under his command, began his march from Bay Bulls.

M. le Comte D'Auxine, with two frigates, eight privateers, and three corvettes, had already weighed anchor and was standing out to the ice-free sea.

The object of the two parties, out of sight of one another, but nevertheless in cooperation, was the same: the strategic settlement of St. John's.

The newly-appointed Captain was in high feather that morning. Several things contributed to this elation. He was back in uniform again among his compatriots after an enforced period in unfamiliar garb; and again there was the prospect of the coming battle, which before the sun was set, would be waged for possession of the town wherein he had laboured in secret to make possible this great attempt. He could almost visualize the scene so soon to become a reality.... Under cover of the forest his men would creep to within musket shot of the bastions of Fort William. He could see the sentinel, blissfully unconscious of danger, pacing mechanically behind the row of cannons peeping through the embrasures. Then the sharp word of command and the flood-tide of attack across the open ground; the frenzied beat of drums within, the hasty, unsuccessful attempt to close the gate in time. A sudden boom to seaward heralding the Count's attack.... The plan was admirable. With Fort William in their hands, the French could turn their guns upon the defences of the Narrows, caught between Scylla and Charybdis, their surrender was a foregone conclusion, impregnable though they had ever been to attack from the sea.

But not all the Captain's thoughts were martial ones. Persistently there arose before his mental eye an entrancing picture of rosy cheeks and golden hair to urge him on towards his goal. Who knows but that his stern purpose of victory in today's attempt was not dictated by that lovely prize he hoped to win in the town he meant to capture?

So the leader mused pleasantly as the storming party threaded its way across the frozen barrens, through the snow-laden thickets, and over the rocky eminences of that broken country. Anon they would dip into the shadow of the evergreens, where the all-pervading blanket bore down the weighted branches; again they stood on higher ground, which afforded them a distant glimpse of ocean stretching away to grey infinity. Thus they marched till noon, to resume their way after a brief bivouac among the snows, onwards to the goal behind the Southside Hills.

Henri, confident of the secrecy of his movements, posted no scouts, and therein made a fatal error. He discovered it too late. A musket shot from among the rocks was his first inkling, and in a moment every boulder seemed to be raining fire. The French column stopped dead in a sudden panic. Here and there a gap showed in the ranks; those in front pressed back on those behind. A wild confusion followed, a medley of bewildered, startled men, in the mass of which the ambushed weapons of the assailants took heavy toll of life.

Unhurt, the leader shouted to his men to disperse. Those of quicker intelligence threw themselves under cover; the others turned and fled. Soon an answering rattle of musketry went rolling back in defiance, although as yet there was nothing to be seen.

The Captain, armed only with sword and pistol, both weapons of close combat, could do naught but direct the defence. A sorry task he found it. Above and all around him, shot was whistling through the air or ploughing furrows in the snow. The rocks were ringing with the sound of striking metal. Worse still, the ambush seemed to hem them in completely. The discipline of barracks and the experience of open tactics availed him nothing against the cunning of hidden foe.

The white flag of surrender fluttered unwillingly above the French position.

As the triumphant band of assailants—a motley throng of settlers, scouts and soldiery—closed about the crestfallen Frenchman, a dull boom sounded far away in the direction of the sea. It was the opening shot of the marine attack, and the knowledge of his failure came then in the nature of a heavy blow to Henri, as he delivered up his sword.

The nearer they approached St. John's, the louder and more insistent grew the sound of firing, echoing and re-echoing among the hills. On occasion a far-off glimpse of water was revealed to them as the column stood upon the higher points of land, and once the batteries on the Northen shore were seen, wreathed in swaying smoke clouds and tinged with swiftly fading streaks of crimson. They were now descending to the lower valleys, thickly wooded, and the forward march went on with that continuous bombardment ringing in their ears. At last the stream was forded, and anon the excited English and the gloomy, depressed survivors of the French landing party stood in a position whence they could view the combat beyond range of danger.

The fight was well-nigh over. Beyond the Heads, too well received to venture farther in, the ships of the French squadron were creeping slowly through the water under furled canvas, flinging their broadsides at the land. Under the great frowning mass of Signal Hill, ably supported by its sister earthwork on the other shore, the cannon of the Battery Fort were belching forth their leaden answer, encircling the enemy craft with spurting jets of spray. Upon the Hill itself—indicative of forewarned preparation—a battery of lighter guns was raining havoc on the enemy, protected as it was by the immunity of its elevation. So near were the onlookers on that shore that, when the eddying smoke permitted, they could see the lighted matches of the gunners behind the earthworks of the Battery, could perceive too the flashes of the pieces as the burning fuses sped those liberated missiles seawards. Around the French battle line that heavy, obscuring smoke wrack also hung, the taller spars and the banner of the Lilies showing clearly above it in bright sunshine. The French were drawing off. Canvas soared aloft to catch the breeze; little by little the fire slackened until it had diminished to intermittent volleys. Under a growing spread of sail the Frenchmen went about and glided out into the safety of the open sea, firing their stem-chasers as they went. A mighty shout of victory swelled up from the gallant defenders of the Forts, those hardy sons of Devon, whose deeds of heroism are written broadly across the marine history of that and many a succeeding period.

Colonel William Fetherby was in a very merry mood that afternoon. Returning from the Battery, where he had directed the efforts of his gunners, he received the uneasy leader of the French storming party in the gateway of Fort William.

"So!" The bow he swept him was ironical beyond measure. "We meet again, Monsieur. Permit me to express my deep appreciation of the high honour you have paid me by this unexpected visit!"

But the French officer held his peace.

The Colonel's play-acting dropped from him then like the mask it was. He straightened swiftly, and the humour was gone from his eye, the sneer from his lip.

"Your visit was NOT unexpected, Claude Derange. When you left this Fort, in the blissful delusion that you had cleverly fooled us, I missed you before you were very far away. My scouts pursued you through the night, but failing to overtake you, were yet in time to witness the manner of your escape. Forewarned is forearmed, 'tis said. My conjecture of what was coming closely ran the truth, for I am not the fool that you may think, and I strengthened the defences of the Forts as swiftly as I could. Yesterday a planter from Petty Harbour brought me tidings of your landing and of the presence off these shores of the hostile fleet. I think you know the rest."

This time Henri Quarel was too dumbfounded to speak.

"And so," went on the Colonel, assuming fresh his former tone of mockery, "you were naught but a stinking spy, Derange. It seems a pity does it not, that such cleverness as yours should go unrewarded? Your countrymen, I fear, will not appreciate it, but I, who perceive your true genius, will be more generous. Tomorrow, at dawn, a firing party will present you with a gift in keeping with your merits, one which I beg of you to accept as a slight token of my esteem—and you will have the satisfaction of knowing that your last look on this earth is to be directed on the scene of your deservedly rewarded labours." He roared an order to his men. "Take this dog to the battery and chain him up till morning!"

Henry Quarel, with head erect, was led away.

Dawn of Easter morning!

The sun of Easter has risen on many a scene of conflict, on many a day of peace. That same sun which rose o'er Calvary's consecrated height, kissing reverently with its first beams that towering Cross whereon the Son of God had died in agony and ignominy, shone too upon the grave wherein the resurrected Victim cast aside in triumph the bond of death. Through all the years between, those same contrasts of violence and majestic calm stand revealed. Today, when the warring strife is hushed, and "Nature with her thousand voices praises God," a brave man walks forth to meet a violent end at the hands of fellow-men.

A timely interruption came even as the fatal order hovered on the lips of Colonel Fetherby. Overhead, upon the Hill, a sudden cannon-shot rolled the echoes of its discharge down to the Battery Fort. As one man the entire garrison on the battlements, prisoner, executioners, and spectators alike, turned seawards. There, sailing majestically around the Northern Head, coursed a stately French frigate under a billowing cloud of snow-white canvas; next instant, a flash of fire leaped from her ports. Came the thunder-clap of sound, reverberating in myriad echoes in that narrow space between the mighty cliffs, and the round shot of the broadside whistled overhead. Shattered by a lucky ball, the standard which had proudly flaunted above, fluttered down, evoking a long-drawn shout of jubilation on the Frenchman's decks. A spark of hope glowed in the heart of Henri Quarel, to die almost instantly as he saw the *L'Aigle* yaw and go about, content with the damage she had done.

The Colonel's rage was terrible to behold. One of those ungovernable outbursts of temper had come upon him at the fall of the flag; he seemed as a man bereft of sense. Shrieking an order to his gunners, he swung to his victim, fiendishly intent on wreaking his vengeance upon an enemy who could not flee his grasp.

"By Heaven!" he roared. "Your time has come at last, you cursed spy! You die—now—now—but not in the uniform that you have lived in, Frenchman!"

He rapped out a command. The watching red-coats started forward and stripped the captive violently of his silken surcoat and his upper garments, leaving him standing there naked to the waist. The Commandant drew closer, was seen to stop, surprised, and then run forward in a state of agitation which seemed strangely out of place. To see him, one would think him anxious to delay the execution, rather than determined to enforce it. He reached the Frenchman, peered incredulously at the birthmark on the left shoulder, and then his voice went ringing through the Battery in accents that were laden with overwhelming joy and gratitude.

"Is it possible?" The watchers gaped in wonder to see the French spy whom he had so violently persecuted clasped tenderly now to the Colonel's breast. "My son!" The words trembled on the speaker's lips in the throes of his emotion.

"My long-lost Hal! My boy!"

The discovery of Hal Fetherby's true identity was as much a surprise to himself as to his father. Delivered into French hands while very young, he had come to regard himself in time as one of them, and the story told him by his dead foster-father, Colonel Quarel, of the loss of both parents at sea had been implicitly believed. A lucky circumstance removed the youthful officer from Quebec to the French capital of Terre-Neuve, a step which, though unrealized by him, was to change materially the whole current of his fife. The events leading up to that change have been set forth. It remains now to tell only of Hal Fetherby's decision in the choice offered him between the rival services—a decision which may be best summed up in his own words, spoken as he stood at evening with his sweetheart on the parapet of Fort William, within sound and sight of the mighty sea: "This day has been the most eventful of my existence, since it has brought me back from the very shadow of death to a life such as I have never known. I have no regrets, no repining, for that which is past. I have been a Frenchman, but willingly, joyfully even, I renounce my fealty. The living lilies of Easter are fairer to me than the gilded lilies of France."

Excerpt from

# Dictionary of Newfoundland English

## G. M. Story, W. J. Kirwin, J. D. A. Widdowson

…It is the purpose of the *Dictionary of Newfoundland English* to present as one such index the regional lexicon of one of the oldest overseas communities of the English speaking world: the lexicon of Newfoundland and coastal Labrador as it is displayed in the sources drawn upon in compiling the work, sources which range from sixteenth century printed books to tape recordings of contemporary Newfoundland speakers. Rather than attempting to define a "Newfoundlandism" our guiding principles in collecting have been to look for words which appear to have entered the language in Newfoundland or to have been recorded first, or solely, in books about Newfoundland; words which are characteristically Newfoundland by having continued in use here after they died out or declined elsewhere, or by having acquired a different form or developed a different meaning, or by having a distinctly higher or more general degree of use.

Thus, among the latter are articles on such words as **cod, haul, quintal, salt water**; articles on **bawn, belay, cassock, cat, dog, graple, lanch, room, strouter**, and **tilt**, for words which have been given a new form or meaning in the region; on **droke, dwy, fadge, frore, keecorn, linny, nish, still, suant**, as examples of the many survivals, or, equally common, dialectal items in use, or former use, in the British Isles; on **hawk, caplin, janny, landwash, nunny-bag, penguin, steady, sunker, ticklace** and **water-horse** among words apparently invented in Newfoundland or appearing first in books about the region. And to these are to be added a number of words which, while they are often in varying degrees part of the common English vocabulary, are nevertheless given entries in the Dictionary because they occur with important nuances in Newfoundland usage, displayed with unusual fullness in our data, or themselves stand at the centre of semantic fields of great regional importance: **barren, bay, coast, harbour, ice, salt, ship, shore, spring, trap, water**, and so on. These take their place in the Dictionary side by side with many other words the precise regional discriminations of which have often been hard won—subtle, but critical, terms such as **in** and **out, offer** and **outside, up** and **down**, which display a people's exact sense of place; terms such as **bank, berth, ground, fouly, ledge, shoal**, etc, which reflect a complex system of classification of water bodies according to the types of ocean floor perceived by and significant for a coastal fishing people; names for birds and plants, especially those of economic or other importance; the seemingly endless nomenclature of seals at every stage of growth and development (**bedlamer, dotard, gun seal, jar, nog-head, ragged-jacket, turner, white-coat**, and a score of others); words for conditions of ice (**ballicatter, clumper, quarr, sish, slob**); and names for familiar operations in the woods or on the water, at work or play, in the ordinary and long-established patterns of Newfoundland and Labrador life.

The Dictionary therefore has both a breadth and a detail considerably greater than we originally envisaged, and this realization has been forced upon us by the evidence at our disposal and has increased with the progress of the work. The levels and kinds of lexical record included might be displayed graphically as a series of concentric rings spreading out from the centre, these rings formed by successive stages of the historical experience of

English-speakers in Newfoundland; or as a series of isoglosses, marking the special lexical features shared by Newfoundland speakers with those of their principal points of origin, especially the south-west counties of England and southern Ireland, and, across the Western Ocean, with those with whom Newfoundlanders have been in language contact: the native peoples of the region (**adikey**, **oo-isht**, **sina**, **tabanask**), speakers in the Canadian North (**fur**, **stove cake**, **trap line**), along the Atlantic seaboard of North America from Nova Scotia to New England (**banker**, **dory**, **gangeing**, **scrod**, **trawl**, **tub**), and in a sea-faring world which has left a ubiquitous record of nautical terms and nautical transfers in the regional lexicon….

# Goin Hout
David Glover

Fine nuff now wear Ise at
no ciddy boy me

good ferda feesh dough
awls um een I do fases time
puntload no truble
win da widders good

strawng harms

sumtimes cums awn ard dough
no truble
stazeen eefes tu bad

Young feller liksit tu
wansa go hout awla time
ard ta keppin een

nuttin wrang wid feeshin e sed
ef yu knows wat yer up tu

E goze scool sumtimes
doan likit dough
tu ard awnin een
wansa be hout

hawlrite I spose

Guna burn down scool e sed

I tol en prawper ting
lit taycher go da work tu

wuna deze daze
we'll be awl doyed awf
no time fer feeshin den

# Dictionary Sam

**Geraldine Rubia**

*It is now believed that Dr. Samuel Johnson, the noted 18th-century British writer, lexicographer, and philosopher, suffered a severe form of Tourette Syndrome.*

Dictionary Sam
Is a big, ugly man,
With a scruffy little wig
Twisted sideways on his pate;
He eats like a beast,
An he don't care the least
If his fingernails are dirty,
And he's rude, uncouth, and late.

He whistles and he grunts,
There's no limit to his stunts:
Tracking squares and triangles
With the heel of his shoe,
He clucks like a hen,
Mutters "Mercy" and "Amen,"
Calls his odd condition "scruples,"
Peppers all with "too, too, too."

He roars down your talk
And persuades you to a walk;
Children mock his hops and bends
As he struggles down the street;
He counts to his door,
Puts the right foot in before;
If his calculation's lacking,
He'll return, recount, repeat.

He loves a hearty laugh;
Swiftly winnows wheat from chaff;
Castigates the best of friends,
And defends the reprobate
He thinks it not a sin
If a beggar spend on gin;
He indulges motley lodgers
And goes calling soon and late.

As talker and as scribe,
He unleashes many a gibe
At hypocrisy and jargon,
At ineptitude and pose.
A blessing fled his life
With the passing of his wife;
He's obliged to any caller,
Staving melancholy's throes.

Nearly deaf and blind,
Fearing slippage of the mind,
Wresting vict'ry over "scruples"
Hoping not to end in Hell—
He's taunted "Oddity,"
Yet, the world will come to see
The immense and open nature
'Neath the rude restless shell.

**newfoundland dialect**: any of the varieties of English spoken by Native Newfoundlanders; Newfoundland English.
[1836 [wix]² 143 The difference of extraction has occasioned, as may be supposed, a marked dissimilarity between the descendants of Jersey-men, French-men, Irish, Scotch, and English people. The people, too, with whom the first settlers and their immediate descendants may have had contact, or intercourse, have attributed much to the formation of the dialect, character, and habits of the present settlers.] 1922 *Sat Ev Post* 195, 2 Sep. p. 129...a babel of loud talk, inthe half-comprehensible Newfoundland dialect, troubled that dim, stifling air. 1967 *Bk of Nfld* iii, 560 It must not be thought that Newfoundland dialects can be described purely in terms of their British and Irish origins, or of the elements of those origins which have been retained in the new land. In many respects local speech has been conservative; but in others it has been immensely creative and innovating.

# To Whittle an Alder Whistle

**Gary Saunders**

If someone asked me right now who first showed me how to make an alder whistle, I couldn't say. My father? Probably not, because when I was ripe for such lore he was away a lot working. My mother? No; women didn't seem to whittle much when I was a kid. My brother? He was probably too busy chasing girls. An uncle—I mean the authentic, blood-related sort? That's a possibility. And it could have been any one of several peripheral uncles of the sort so common in those tribal days before the nuclear family and the old folks' home undermined their status, one of those Uncle Bobs or Uncle Rays of indeterminate linkage who seemed equally beloved by our parents and us.

But no; when I come right down to it, my guess is that it was one of my grandfathers. They were different as day and night. The gruff, shopkeeper one? Couldn't have been him, for with all his hurrying and worrying he hardly knew our names. (Or so we thought then. Later we found out different, found out the reasons for his worries, learned how many people he was carrying on credit with no hope of repayment.)

So that leaves the other one, the impossibly tall, stooped giant with the weathered face, twinkling brown eyes and beaked nose, the one who all his life had made fish barrels in which to ship salt cod to Spain. This gentleman did stay with us one winter. I remember him sleeping on the daybed in the kitchen, his wool-stockinged Size Twelve feet dangling over the end because it was too short for his lanky frame. And that spring, when the meadow flooded, he did whittle me a sailboat. Yes, it might well have been him.

Whoever it was, I wonder if he realized the significance of his act to me, the small human person seated at his knee on the doorstep, completely absorbed in the purposeful movements of strong, calloused hands and shining knife blade. I cherish the notion that such innocent rituals help keep human society from flying apart. Out of the strong came forth sweetness. Out of the common wood came a magical note, a bond with the past. So now I too carve whistles for small people.

The trick is to get the bark off and on again without cracking it. Spring, when the buds and catkins are swelling and the bark is slippery with rising sap, is the only time to do this. If you don't know alders by their bark or buds or new leaves, ask someone, or consult a book. Brook valleys and wet fields are the place to look. Choose a nice smooth sprout that is free of twigs or bumps for at least three inches, and as thick as a cigar. With a sharp blade, slice downward at an angle while holding the branch from above. Trim off any excess twigs until you're left with a manageable stick six or eight inches long. That will give you enough for a whistle at each end—in case the first fails, which is likely.

Before removing the bark you must shape the mouthpiece. A forty-five-degree cut with no rough edges is about right. (It may be that you cut it that way in the field.) Square off the sharp end a bit so the bark won't fray. Now score the bark all the way around the stem about two inches back from the tip. The best way to do this is to hold the blade against the bark with one hand, and roll the stem against the blade with the other. This gives a good straight line. Repeat a quarter inch farther along. Slit between the marks and peel off the resulting ring of bark. This gap will let you adjust for better sound later on.

Lay the piece on your knee and tap it gently but firmly all over with a rounded object like the handle of your knife (sharp corners will ruin the final product), going back as far as the ring of bare wood, and turning the stem as you go. Grasping the tapped portion in one hand and the untapped in the other, twist. The tapped part should come unstuck and turn, like a screw-top bottle cap. If it doesn't, tap and twist some more. When it does (as it will, if you don't crack it first), you can easily pull the bark off in one piece.

G. SAUNDERS/83

Just before you do that, line up the bark as it was and carefully remove a small lens from the top with the blade tip a half inch back from the lip, taking care to cut slightly into the wood. This lens-shaped hole will be the whistle's air outlet. (Had we cut it earlier we would have risked breaking the bark while tapping or twisting.) Fresh alder bark is fragile. It also dries and shrinks rapidly, so I make a habit of holding the sleeve in my mouth like a cigar and breathing through it to keep it moist while I finish the whistle.

The next step is to carve a chamber in which the air can resonate. Its length can be varied (the longer the chamber the deeper the pitch), but the end toward the lip should always lie right under the air outlet. This is where my hint about cutting the wood slightly comes in; it leaves a mark to guide you. Slanting the blade about 45 degrees and parallel to the lip, bear down (on a firm surface, not your knee) with a rocking motion until it reaches the center of the stem. An inch or so away, make a second cut facing the first but opposite in slant and half as deep. With the blade still in the wood, prise out the chip. Repeat until the chamber has an even depth. Trim off any loose slivers.

Now there is only one step before you slip the bark sleeve back in place. You still need an opening to get the air into the chamber. Make this by shaving off a layer of wood the thickness of a dime between the chamber and the lip.

By this time the wood surface will be almost dry. Before reassembling, wet it in your mouth (alders contain nothing poisonous, only tannin—like tea) so it won't stick to the bark. Slide the bark back on and adjust until the air-hole is above the near end of the chamber. Puckering your lips (taking care not to cover the air vent), gently blow into the whistle. A clear sweet note should sound. If it doesn't, fiddle with the bark sleeve until you hear something other than air escaping. If even that doesn't work, remove the sleeve and pare the air intake a trifle deeper. Wet the wood again and repeat the test, again adjusting if necessary. With luck you'll be rewarded. If success still eludes you, put it down to experience and right away make another. There's nothing wrong with the design. But even veteran whistle whittlers fail. Patience; it will come.

When it does, you'll be able to indulge in one of the purest pleasures of springtime, that of making a whistle for a youngster. From experience I can affirm that this coaxing of sound from an ordinary stick is one of the most satisfying of acts for all concerned. It can't be the music alone; there's only a single note. Yet I've known adults—even teachers—to exclaim with delight when finally they heard it. For the more inventive there are other designs and different woods to be tried. Willow is good, and probably some other species are too.

But for a start, try the humble alder. Follow my recipe, and take along a youngster or two. It will make the world a saner place.

# A Chant for One Voice

**Harold Horwood**

he magic ground lay far back from the village in a patch of wilderness backed by a mountain. A wooded valley, a stream with marshes and sandbanks and a chain of small ponds, some of them flanked by grass flats, stretched almost due east and west, hills rising to the north, forming a natural trap for the sun that poured its rays across the flat woodland to the south.

Boys went there to swim, or sometimes to angle for the small trout that inhabited the ponds. Otherwise the magic ground remained unvisited by human foot, for it was of no use to industrial man. Its soil was thin, its timber weedy, its rocks mere quartz and granite; no oil was known to lie below its mantle, the water ran as a small, sluggish stream, useless alike for power or power boat.

Eight-cylinder tourists came spewing to the big lake on the far side of the village where the paved highway curved smoothly around its outskirts. Faint and distant from the magic ground could be heard the revving of engines and the whine of outboards, so distant, they seemed only to underline the silence.

At most times the painted turtles travelled quietly between pond and marsh, and huge old snappers, their shells green with moss, dozed in the sun beside the stream. Only on summer afternoons was the quiet broken by splashing and romping and fighting, the mud churned with footprints, the air rent with yells of love and hate and self-assertion, as the invading children went through the prescribed dance that they had come to perform in this place they supposed to be sacred to themselves, where they could revert to the wild, imagining their tableau primeval, like the dance of fox and raven, never suspecting that their sensual play and the restraints they placed upon it had all been taught by the staid, straight people at home feeding and watering and gassing the tourists, and disposing of disposable diapers.

The turtles did not consider the matter at all. They hid in the safety of the water for three or four hours of the invasion. The foxes and the muskrats did not consider it either. They just stayed at home on summer afternoons when for a brief period the ground that they knew to be sacred to themselves supported a show of madness.

Then with dusk the magic ground returned to its true vocation. Weasels came out of thickets and began to hunt with ruthless hunger the song birds and the meadow mice. The almost silent dance of life and death that wove its intricate pattern above the magic ground resumed its course, punctuated by night and day, summer and winter, but single and whole for all that. The fox paced the trails that he knew; the trees, by taking thought, added a cubit, or even a cubit and a half, to their yearly stature; in the black ooze of the water's edge, larvae fed on larvae and grew fat, and far below them algae and protozoa performed their measures of the dance, already incomparably far removed from the simplest steps of the viral beings that occupied the complex border between the dance of the living cells and the dance of the molecules.

And the earth, pointing always to the North Star, made a dance of the sun in the heavens, a mass of hydrogen and other gas and dust, contracted upon itself, driven by light, drawn by gravity, until its own weight and heat ignited nuclear fires and it blossomed into living planets with birdsong and warfare and the limitless venture of the spirit and the evolution of mere matter into the very substance of God. And this great distant heart of the system danced for the people of the magic ground, bringing the swish of snow and the song of frog, laughter of the last loon and yap of fox cub in their strict and regular rhythm.

Into the magic ground, then, I obtrude myself, a phantom, feeling underfoot the yielding of the mudflat, smelling the dark scent of the water. Here I drop my clothes on a bush and walk toward the huge turtle that lies in the last rays of the sun beside the pond. Will this ancient creature wake and dive, disturbed by my approach? The sandpiper nodding nearby stretches and bobs and spreads its wings. To the sandpiper I am not invisible. Nervously, it twists and fidgets and prepares to fly.

The canoe comes downstream silent as a leaf, but swift, almost skimming the water. It moves with the sanction of the gods of the stream. The figures in it are dark and unformed. It follows their will around the bends, and vanishes along the bank of a small pond.

Only the ghosts of the boys are there, bodies flickering in the soft gloom, no chant of voices, no music of cloven water, no scream of killer chasing frog or snake or turtle to its silent terror. And the gods rise up and surround me, ancient and unchanging, speaking only in parables.

The canoe goes by, silent as a leaf, and the turtle stirs, bends its scaly neck, twists its snakelike head. The canoe vanishes, and the sandpiper returns, teetering nervously along the margin of the stream. The ghosts come by, flickering in the gloom, bodies like pale flames against black water and black forest and black marshland; there is no sound of laughter, no ribald shout, no calls of love and hate, as the gods rise up and surround me, ancient and tall as the firs, speaking the language of the forest and the rocks.

And the gods dance, gravely and slowly over the magic ground, treading the measures that the stars dictate. And the stars dance, circling the galactic core, a swarm of bees swinging in the night.

The ghosts come by singly, a procession of cold flames like darkroom images purified of flesh. I would touch them. I would hold them. I would talk with them. They pass through me in the gloom. The canoe, too, is a ghost, as it follows the bends of the current and disappears downstream. It has nothing to say. Nothing is said by the ghosts of the children. Nothing by the stars. Only the gods speak.

# Second Heart

## Michael Winter

They go in Lady Slipper Road and hunt with the truck, cab lifting over potholes. Because the father's feet are bad. Splash in wheel wells and tilt and lean into each other. It's an intimate, unintentional touch of shoulders and knees. They haul off by a small pond the shape of a knife and pull back the red vinyl seat and dislodge two twelve gauges and a Winchester pump and load up. The father instructs.

Only a bull, Gabe. If there's no antlers you leave it. If Junior's with you, let him shoot. I want this to be legal. You've got to be close to use a slug. Remember how far from the road you are. Don't go in miles. Keep the slugs separate. If you have a shell in the chamber, keep it breached. Your barrel needs bluing, Gabe.

A box of food from Mom all stacked to get the most out of a cardboard box, enough food really for three days but Junior is with them.

Junior: Meat pie looks like it's going off.

Dad: Yeah, better eat it now. Sausage rolls, too.

You're right. That roast chicken, don't forget that.

It's Junior first as he has eyes that see into the periphery always, he sees black lifting wings near the pond. They eat the pie and walk to it, Junior with the rifle and the crows hop and lift and are annoyed. They haul away heavy from the bloated guts and front half of a moose. The carved white hind quarters, flayed.

Someone in a hurry.

The poacher took steaks, roasts. Carved them quick off the bone.

The father tries to turn the carcass with his boot but it rocks back into its own hollow. What a waste.

About a hundred pounds of meat.

There's disdain in his tight mouth.

Junior's eye now, roving, frozen on a cutover. Gabriel follows the eye to a mound of dead alders. But the branches are moving and as he concentrates the branches slowly separate into finer branches and antlers and the heads of three moose. There is only one with antlers. Junior already with the sights on him. The white bone of his cheek pressed to the stock. A shot hard on the air and the bull reels, his neck lowers and swings.

The cows.

Leave them, June.

Junior hesitates on the two cows. He sights, says quietly, Bang. He pivots the rifle three degrees, again says, Bang. But his trigger finger doesn't squeeze. He looks for the bull, but can't find it through the scope.

Is it down?

Dad: It went behind the rise. You got him, now just leave him be.

The two cows stare straight at them, downwind, calm, lifting their noses. Now turn and trot quickly, shoulders full of alarm but almost haughty.

93

Junior is running through high brush, rifle at the top of his arm, he sinks out of sight. There are three more shots. Gabe and his father make the rise and see Junior sizing up the strain and falter.

Dad: Don't go hitting the meat, June.

One cow on the knoll looking back. Hesitates.

Could get her, Dad.

You leave it.

The bull in deadfall.

Junior: They love to get into that. You shoot one in the open and he runs for the alders.

If you'd let him be.

Junior paces around the shoulders of the animal. He takes his time looking for a spot. Well, that was quick, hey? He positions the muzzle of the rifle to the ear and fires and all four legs lift a little then strike the ground and relax. Junior pulls a knife from the back of his belt and tucks it under the throat. He rummages until a red gush pours over his hand.

The cow still lingers, nostrils flared, understanding all through her nostrils.

Remember the time when the eyes popped out, Dad? I was putting one through the ear, Gabe, and the force. Junior laughs. Held on by stringy things to the sockets.

Dad: That was ugly.

The cow turns and leaves.

They wait over the throat of the animal. They pass time by looking at the truck with its high cap on the woods road and the gap on the hill where the cow was last and understanding the lay of the woods road, which weaves through pulp mill cutover and heads to the highway. Then they begin the paunch. The father says I wonder where that second cow got to. He knots a length of seat belt strap around one hoof and pulls it wide so the moose is splayed. He ties this to a stump left by the Company. Junior punctures the belly and works the blade along, piercing a white membrane but not the stomach. A steam rises. His blade runs smoothly through the hide like a zipper. Blood sloshes into the cavity. Junior counts the ribs, Here, Dad.

They carve sideways between the third and fourth ribs. Hot blood leaks out the sides. They rock the moose to empty it of blood. The stomach like an island in the blood, the yellow of chanterelles.

Junior approaches the head again. He cuts through backbone and slices the gullet. He works off the head and tosses it on some low bushes. One brown eye staring back at the body. If the eyes are closed it's still alive.

They return to the cavity, chopping through the boiled egg of sternum to pry open ribs. They coax the vast stomach down, slicing hitches that anchor it to bone.

Let's get him on his side more.

They roll out the guts. The father ties off the dark intestine with a rope and then separates the anus.

Where's the scrotum?

It's out already.

You should have left it on.

You don't want that, Dad.

You do want it, June.

I tossed it off in some bushes.

He wheels around, points with the knife.

Over there somewheres.

Gabriel checks the bushes and finds a strip of hide and the loose orange balls. He holds it up.

That's it.

He puts it up by the head.

Junior reaches into the chest, his shirt sleeves pushed up. The motion indicates he is cutting something, hoses. His hands appear with the heart. It is bigger than the platter of his hands. His silver watch smeared in blood.

In my bag, he says.

Gabriel finds the newsprint and Junior lays the heart on it beside the scrotum. He is careful with the heart. He wipes his hands front and back in the gorse and then up and down the thighs of his jeans.

I'm just going to see what's down there, Junior says.

Dad: You're not taking the rifle.

Junior: I emptied it. I just want to use the scope.

The father wipes out the ribcage with grass. Take a shotgun.

I'll take a shotgun too.

Well, make sure the action's empty.

It's empty. I'm waiting for some shotgun ammo, man.

The father hands him shells, for birds.

They rest while Junior investigates the knoll. He is holding the rifle to look through the scope. Gabe and his father fall back onto the spring of alders. Look around. The father takes out a flask. He says, He's not supposed to do that.

It's dangerous.

There could be a cartridge. Don't do that, will you. Want some?

Gabriel takes the flask, but it's ice tea.

Good isn't it. I can't abide pop.

They have the pond to get round and then a bog to the road. From this angle the bog and pond are only long slivers of what they are. The wheelbarrow is in the truck. And Junior returns.

You see anything?

The mill got it all logged. Not a feather anywhere. You'll have to figure out a good route for us, Gabe.

June notices the head and picks up his axe. He puts his foot on the nose to steady it. Then he hacks into the skull. When he swings, the butt of the axe nearly touches Gabriel's ear. The axe leaves blunt wedges in the skull, white showing through like coconut. They are sprayed with skull and brain.

Sorry about that. I should be doing this over here.

Junior drags the head by one antler to the side.

Gary wants the rack, he says.

The father waves Gabe back and they wait until the antlers are free. It's a small set of antlers, about eight points.

The bull last year was huge, hey Dad. Had four sprigs coming down over his eyes before the plate even started.

Junior puts his thumb to his cheek, fingers stretched out, to indicate the plate.

Gabriel finds a grown-over trail from a tree harvester, right to the road. He brings up the wheelbarrow. And watches his father carve out the lower jawbone. He has trouble getting through the hinge.

Let me at that, Dad.

Junior aims the axe at the hinge.

Watch the back teeth, June.

You want it here?

Just back.

When the jawbone is off Junior wraps the scrotum around it and reserves it by the heart. So they won't lose any of it.

The scrotum to identify the sex. You keep that in the freezer for if the police come. The jaw for Wildlife.

There is a blue dumpster outside the Irving gas station, a heap of skinned lower jawbones.

They saw off the legs above the talus and place them in a row. The father scalps a strip of hide off the spine. Gabe picks up the saw.

Junior: An axe is faster, Gabe.

Dad: Sawing is preferable.

Junior: You can tap an axe through and not splinter.

I like a clean cut, June.

They hold the front half while Gabriel saws. They pry open the quarters as the teeth descend, so the brace of the saw doesn't catch. Gabriel wipes the backbone clean to make sure he's straight. The bone is warm. He wouldn't have thought bone had heat.

Dad: That's a fine animal, June.

Yes, fine animal. Those cows were fine too.

Each quarter a hundred pounds easy. The father takes out the silver tags.

Now Dad not yet.

It was supposed to be first thing.

Sure Dad we almost got this animal out.

June. We're tagging it.

He punctures a leg between tendon and bone.

Okay Dad. Thread em through but don't click em.

We've been through this, June.

Dad, it's only ten minutes to the truck.

And twenty to the highway and an hour to home. In my truck.

On my licence.

The father stands. Looks Junior in the eye. With your mother. That licence is between you and your mother, and your mother won't have it.

Sure, Mom don't need to know.

First thing she'll look for when it's hanging in the building. How come there's no tags.

We'll hang it over at Gary's.

June, I'm not having anything to do with Gary. If there's no tags involved, you're alone.

As Gabe and Junior carry out a quarter in the wheelbarrow, Junior: Dad, boy. A man of details.

In the dark of the truck, a beer each, sitting on the wheel wells. The moose quarters jiggling, the meat warm. They hold on for potholes. Junior says, If I come home I can work with Dad. I can make daybeds and baby cradles. I'll get Dad to show me. Because he needs a hand, Gabe. Like this truck. He didn't understand the gas consumption. It was eating gas. And I showed him the pollution gear. Marked all the hoses and gauges with chalk and we hauled out the works.

They are sitting in the back of the truck, the father driving. The night highway moving backwards, framed by the truck cap. A car passes and the tags glint on stiff legs above the tailgate.

Dad: We'll let that hang a week.

Mom: It wasn't lying in its own blood again, was it?

Junior: It was lying in someone else's blood.

Junior slit its throat first thing.

Because if it's like that, Al, I'm not having it.

The meat's well cased.

The brothers share the bunkbeds. Junior stretches his legs and makes the frame crack and fifteen years vanish. Teenage years of Junior home late, drunk, opening the window to pee and it splashes over the desk. Urine on the blankets.

They watch headlights of cars arc over the bedroom wall.

Christmas, Junior says. If I come home I'm coming home then. I'm getting a tree and really celebrating.

What about Mom.

Gabe, I'm having a tree. I know she calls that pagan. Well, to say that is like me telling her to shut up. It's Christ's birthday and I feel like enjoying it. And if she don't, then I'll live in Dad's building.

A little later: Gabe, eventually I want to build a little cabin with twelve-volt lighting in Mount Moriah. I want to occupy the land and I don't care what happens. I'm gonna keep the land the way I like it and have a son who can take it over. I want you to do me a favour.

Pause.

Can you do me a favour?

What.

A favour, boy.

I heard you, Junior.

Look up the rules on building codes and old Newfoundland laws on occupying land. If you could get some books on it or show me where it's to.

Junior would get out of bed, leap down, and drive Gabriel with his leg. In the thighs and ribs. Gabriel vowed to hate him. I hate you. No, you don't, he'd say. I'm your brother, you got to love me. You can't help it.

And Gabriel realizes this is true.

In the morning, Junior:

Gabe. Come on.

What's up.

We're getting Dad a load of wood.

He's got lots of wood.

Come on, Gabe. He's got bad feet. I got the saw in the truck. I got gas and oil. I even made you a little sandwich. Just half a load. We'll be done by one.

Is Dad going?

Dad can't be at that any more.

I'm too stiff.

Just you and me against some trees.

They take the truck and go in Lady Slipper Road again.

That deadfall stuff is rotten, June.

Are you catching on?

Junior parks where they were parked before. And get out. It's cold and low light. Grey rolling nimbus. Junior takes an axe from behind the seat.

Okay.

Junior: You can't guess?

A sweat creeps into Gabe's armpits.

There's a moose in there.

Junior points the axehead to the knoll.

Man oh man they're long gone, June.

I'm not talking about the one that got away.

They walk past the bog and around the pond and the crows now at yesterday's remains. Dew wetting their jeans. The butchered head and swollen stomach. Four cut-off legs in a row. Four legs with no space between them. The respectful thing would be to give them space.

Gabriel follows Junior to the knoll. Where Junior had looked for birds. Gabe pans the clearcut. Then he sees the cow moose lying in full run in the clearing. Its throat cut.

Man oh man, June.

Got her when I shot the bull. I was too quick for Dad. Ain't it beautiful? Had to find it yesterday, cut its throat.

Jays are perched at the eyes.

You know what Dad does when he hits a moose, Gabe? He boils the kettle. That's what he wanted to do, boil a kettle while that bull died. Moose sees you after him he runs. If you hang back he'll lie down. He's hurt, see? Wouldn't have got this cow if we'd boiled a kettle now would we. Got to watch out for wardens, okay?

A quarter rolls off his back.

Junior: The meat is some alive, hey?

We should've taken the barrow.

Dad would miss it. He'd say, you took the barrow for wood?

They take a quarter each, Gabriel carrying the lighter, front quarters. Resting at the remains of yesterday's bull. Then all the way to the truck. At least there's the path the wheel barrow made. But Gabriel stops with his second quarter.

Gabriel: I say we leave it.

Okay, we leave it. But I'm getting the heart.

Junior jogs through the cutover, to the knoll, and down to cut the hoses that hold the heart to the lungs. He shuffles the heart under his arm and jogs back to Gabe.

Take the heart.

Junior hoists the last quarter over his shoulder. He strides hard for the truck.

Gabriel wraps the heart in newsprint and tucks it safe on a shelf in the cab. Junior rolls the quarter into the truck bed.

That's seventy-five dollars' worth of meat, Gabe. Couldn't let that go to waste.

Okay, the deal is you drive and I sit in back with the moose. You're to rap on the rear window. If you see anything at all.

Gabe can spot Junior through the rear view mirror. Junior with his hands ready under a quarter. And up on the hill where the road winds down is a white jeep. Gabriel slows. The jeep disappears into the green. Junior lifts the meat over the tailgate. He has to lift and throw the meat to the side so it makes the ditch. He lifts a second quarter and hurls this too. Gabriel keeps it moving. Junior pushes down the legs on the other two quarters and drapes himself over the moose.

The warden passes. Gabriel nods to him but the warden's eye is on the back of the truck. The jeep halts in the side mirror. The warden is studying the truck. Gabriel tilts carefully through potholes. He wants the warden's brake light to wink out. He wills the red light to dampen and it does. The warden drives on. And Junior bangs on the window.

They back up and bring up the meat. The fresh bone and cut muscle stained in dirt. When they get to the highway Gabe pulls over. They cover the meat in a blue tarp and Junior gets in the passenger side.

I'm beat.

There is a nasty cut across his wrist from a bone.

Couldn't get it all out in time. Dad got the tailgate on. Tailgates, Gabe, are crap.

Gabriel drives into town, up past the house and down into Curling. Junior asleep against the door post.

Junior reaches over to press the horn. Stop here, Gabe.

He jumps out and opens a screen door and disappears. He comes out with Gary. Gary is wearing a shirt that goes with a tuxedo.

Best to back her in, Gary says. Hi, Gabe.

Gary puts on a red jacket and they take a quarter each down some stairs to a garage with a basketball hoop over the door and lay the quarters on spare tires. Junior returns for the last quarter.

Meat looks bloody. And dirty. Man, d'you drag it behind the truck? You run it down first?

Junior: It's good meat, Gary. Anyway, look, let's settle up. I need some birch. Got a load of birch?

In the yard. Don't take my dry stuff.

We want lengths.

Lots of lengths.

Okay, Gabe. Move over.

Gary pulls down the door and doesn't even look at them. The yard next door. A heap of stacked eight-foot lengths of birch.

Junior: We're late, but this is good wood.

They take over a cord.

Gabriel packs for the airport. He has a cheap flight back. He's stacked frozen cuts from last year's moose in a cardboard box padded with newspaper. Another box has pickled onions, pickled beets, mustard pickles and tomato chutney.

Mom: Got room for spuds?

In the basement in a barrel of sawdust are the blue potatoes. Gabriel fishes out about forty pounds.

Mom: When I was going grey, I told your Dad he wouldn't love me any more. He got upset. Which means he must've thought it a little. Anyway I've written you all a little something and for your Dad I've said, if we both make it to heaven, look for someone with red hair.

She says, I won't be hovering in heaven, as some people claim. And if you win an Academy Award don't say you know your mother's watching. I won't know anything until the resurrection.

Seeing Gabriel off. Junior: You should buy my Dart, Gabe. Go back in the Dart. I'd have to take the stock car mirror off though, I want that. Parts are dirt cheap. Only problem is it's rear wheel drive, so you got to have weight in back in winter on those hills in town.

But he wants five hundred for it.

Dad, sizing up the wood. So where'd you go for that?

Junior: In off Georgetown Road.

See Anthony?

No. No one in there.

Funny you didn't see Anthony. On a Sunday.

We were in a little further along, hey Gabe.

Gabriel nods.

It's good yellow birch. You didn't have trouble with the saw.

It cuts good.

I've found it losing power.

I was gonna tell you about that, Dad. I can have a look at it before I go.

I'd appreciate that, June.

And Gabriel shakes hands with Junior. Then hugs his mother, who's come down. It's good to have you, she says.

It's on their way to the airport. His father says, I hate to guess what you two were up to this morning.

Pause.

All I know is. That wood wasn't cut today.

But he helps Gabriel with the potatoes and shakes his hand at Departures. He hands him a piece of wood. Written on it with today's date is,

I, Al English, gave to my son Gabriel, a quantity of moose meat. Tags # 02946. He will be transporting said moose to St John's where he lives.

The woman swipes his feet. Steel toes, she says.

Are they?

She nods.

When the boxes go through she halts the conveyor. She scrutinizes the x-ray. You got moose steaks in there?

Yes.

Lucky you, she says. And hits the switch.

Gabriel sees his father waiting behind the glass; he mouths something but Gabe can't understand it. He nods anyway. His father now in pantomime, and he sees it: the police coming to arrest Gabe. His father encouraging, and they both know he could have been angry.

Two weeks later, in a letter from his mother:

Your Dad said there was a smell coming from the back of the truck. He says he found a second heart.

# The Hunt

**Larry Small**

You did not know
that night on Rushy Pond Road
when the moon and stars touched the earth
and you and your companions
gathered among the first snows of winter
caressing each other's bodies
feasting on buds from last year's birch
twentieth century man
lurked with his deadly arsenal.
This would be your
last night of love
your last winter's dawn.
At eight you stood alone at bogside
separated from your friends of two years
when you entered the cross-hairs
of the hunter's scope
and became a victim of
man's massacre for meat.
Lying now in the quiet snows
of a late November morning
your blood gave cinema to
the silent bog
hanging on half-dead trees
seeping into young snows
oozing from your fatal wound
as if your heart was still working.
All that day men would
celebrate your death
drink to their health
dissect your body
with the skill of a surgeon's scalpel
freeze the flesh of your body
and then give grace.

# Seasons

Neil Murray

I

Steered by the sun,
a bee follows
a bright thread of purpose
through the sizzling maze.

Ahead,
ghostly dancers
converge in a violet glow:
nectar concealed
within the fourfold cup.

2

Afternoon,
a chalk amphitheatre.

In a finned sky
stream torn
flags of a windy picnic.

Ripples rock
a blown white rank of birds
riding the bleak lake.

3

Here at the antlered gates
the wind spumes
over hooded snows.

An astonished white face,
the moon
recedes, half hidden
by a dark nautilus of cloud.

All night long
the foghorn has roared
like a wounded mammoth
dolefully through the sleet.

The morning light
kindles the silvery bushes
after the last
glitterstorm of winter.

**mauzy** a also **maus(e)y, mawzy** Cp *EDD* mosey adj¹ 3 'damp and warm, muggy, close; foggy.' Of the weather, damp, foggy, misty or close, sometimes with very light rain or condensation on objects and a cool, gentle wind off the sea; cp CAPLIN (SCULL) WEATHER.

1897 *J A Folklore* x, 207 Mausey day, one dull and heavy, with no wind and thick mist. 1937 DEVINE 33 A*mausey* day is a cloudy, foggy day with no wind and a little rain at times. 1957 *Daily News* 16 Oct, p. 4 Old-time seal hunters...expressed the opinion that the long, hard winter, the heavy ice and the 'mauzy' weather of early March were just right for a bumper season. P 105-63 It's a mauzy old day, sir. 1968 KEATING 13-14 'Breeze comin' from duh sudard,' the skipper said. 'Always blows up mauzy weather.' And the fog did indeed roll over the deep as the warm south wind hit the chill air of the bank. 1969 HORWOOD 166 The Caplin Scull is not just a phenomenon of nature, but also a period of the year, and even a special kind of weather—'mausy' weather, with high humidity, frequent fogs or drizzles, easterly winds.

# Elemental Poem

Roberta Buchanan

**East West North South**
**Earth Air Fire Water**

We turn to the East: AIR
Blue space—breathing—the kiss of life
The wind driving sails and waves across the ocean
Impelling clouds across the sky.
Blowing away the cobwebs at Cape Spear
We take deep breaths and laugh.
Meditation on the breath
I watch your breathing as you sleep.

*Otherwise:*

Difficulty in breathing, the poisoned air
Tear gas, poison gas in the trenches
Coughing up one's guts
Emphysema, asthma, bronchitis
Choking, throttled, the breath stopped
The air that kills.

We turn to the South: FIRE
The singing kettle on the hearth
Cooking: the bubbling pot of beans
The barbecue that friends and neighbours share
The camp fire, sitting in a circle
Glowing coals, warmth in winter
Making love by firelight
Candles burning before the shrines
Solar energy
The fiery sunset flowing red
The stars dancing round the sky.

*Otherwise:*

Smoke from the death camps: Auschwitz
The burning of people
Witches burned alive in the burning-times
The mushroom cloud at Hiroshima
Bombed houses catching fire in Philadelphia
Napalm burns on screaming children
Caught in cross-fire
Fire that destroys.

We turn to the West: WATER
First element, the waters of life
The sea womb of the Mother Goddess, giving birth
To strange creatures, bearing exotic cargoes
Aphrodite rises from the foam
The waterfall tumbling over cliff
The holy well, the sacred spring
That heal our spirits
Swimming in the sunset
Immanence is light on water.

*Otherwise:*

The flood that destroys, the burst dam
The raging sea, sailors drowning
The Ocean Ranger gone, bodies never found
The water cannon on the protest march
Polluted lakes killing fish; mercury poison
The poisoned water that kills.

We turn to the North: EARTH
Gaea, Mother Earth, the Deep-Breasted One
The nurse of seedlings, infusing the blossoms
Forming the fruit
Digging our gardens
Manuring, tilling, sowing seeds
Until the bean hangs on the vine
Until the lettuces fan out their delicate leaves
Carrots, potatoes plump and swell
The fertile earth, abundantly feeding her children
At the last our final resting-place.

*Otherwise:*

The parched earth, desert, famine
The rain forests cut down
Defoliation—stripping the earth
Chemical warfare where nothing grows
The earth poisoned with PCBs
Eroded soil, the waste land
The bomb—nuclear winter
The poisoned earth.
EARTH AIR FIRE WATER
Essential elements, natural sources, resources:
Extract, extort, exploit, rape, destroy, kill
Or reverence, worship, conserve the sacred grounds of being?

Excerpt from

# Suspended State: *Newfoundland Before Canada*

Gene Long

## THE PURSUIT OF SQUIRES

The merchants who had organized public meetings against the government a year
earlier, now directed their energy toward an unprecedented demonstration of
gathering public sentiment. A public meeting was called for Monday night, April 4th,
[1932] to adopt a resolution for presentation to the House of Assembly calling for a
"full, final and conclusive inquiry" into the charges made by Cashin. This meeting,
which went on for four hours and featured "over sixty citizens" on stage, was held in
front of a packed hall of about 1,500 people at the Majestic Theatre, with an overflow
crowd hooked up by speaker at the Longshoreman's Hall and broadcast to the city on
radio. Led by members of the merchants' Citizens Committee (the unemployed held
no monopoly on this moniker), the meeting was turned over to a variety of speakers,
and featured several incendiary addresses, including one by a Rev. W. E. Godfrey.
Introducing the resolution, Godfrey said that the people had a "solemn, undeniable"
right to know whether the charges were true, a right that "in almost any other country,
would be to court riot and bloodshed in a determination to find out."

Gordon Ask, described by the *Telegram* as a "well-known citizen," made the
obvious point: "Politicians can rob thousands of dollars and get away with it, but if the
common man stole a flour barrel it meant he had to go to jail." Ask suggested all
constitutional steps should be taken, but "if it has to be a revolution, let it be a
revolution." A war veteran, J. H. Adams, spoke directly to his comrades in the audience
and said that if an officer on the battlefield had been accused of "misdemeanours of
such a serious character," and was found guilty, he "would stand before a firing squad
and be shot." No one needed reminding that the Prime Minister was accused of
stealing from funds that were an entitlement of the veterans. The resolution was
adopted unanimously and notice given of a "parade" that would take place the next
day to petition the Assembly. A motion was passed to send copies of the resolution to
every outport newspaper in the country. The meeting closed with the singing of the
national anthem to the accompaniment of the Guards band.

The next morning's edition of the *Daily News* carried a front page advertisement
from the Citizens Committee addressed to the "employers of the city" asking that leave
be given to all employees who "desired to take part" in the afternoon's parade. The
paper contained a detailed account of the previous night's meeting and an extensive
excerpt from a speech given in the Assembly the day before by Peter Cashin. Cashin
said he wanted to "cut the mask of hypocrisy from the faces of the Prime Minister and
those associated with him." After re-stating the immediate outstanding charges for what
he said was the benefit of Sir William Coaker, who had not been present during their
previous airing, Cashin proceeded to level new allegations of bribery and corruption
relating to the 1928 election. He accused Squires of having illegally imported two

hundred cases of scotch whiskey from a Montreal distiller and accepting donations of $15,000 toward his campaign in return for promises of future business. For Cashin, the worst part of the "scotch orphans" story—one he admitted was widely rumoured but he had not revealed for four years—was that Squires did not make any "earnest endeavours" to return the favour to the distillers. Instead Squires tried to pass himself off to the electorate as a prohibitionist while secretly campaigning with illegal liquor. Screaming headlines of yet more scandalous revelations likely persuaded additional numbers to leave their workplaces and join the day's parade.

The population of St. John's at the time was about 40,000 people. If the crowd count in the *Evening Telegram*—between 8,000 and 10,000—was correct, then virtually every adult male in the city was in attendance. Existing film footage shows a foggy day and a massive crowd, led by the Guards band and the Union Jack, making its way through the winding downtown streets on its way to the Colonial Building. Most of the faces are men, although a large gathering of women and youth waited on the grounds of the legislature. Anticipating the crowd was also a squad of about thirty police, including four on horseback. Arriving for the public opening of the House at three thirty, the Citizens Committee sent a delegation to the Bar of the House seeking to have the prayer of its petition acknowledged. A procedural argument ensued, during which the Speaker declined to accept a motion of referral to committee from Squires, as the Prime Minister himself was the subject of the petition. Just as agreement to establish such a committee was reached, a disruption occurred in the gallery and all hell began to break loose. Stones rained in through the windows in all directions.

The delegation retreated to the front of the building and called for the parade to reassemble and return to the Majestic Theatre. A sizeable portion of the crowd evidently left the grounds. Those who stayed, apparently numbering about three thousand, began an assault on the locked front doors, behind which was the squad of police. A classic case of misjudgement followed, as the police "divested themselves of their greatcoats" and launched a baton charge on the front steps. They smashed heads "left and right" and momentarily succeeded in clearing the front of the building.

Unfortunately, their colleagues on horseback had no such luck. "Like a flame, a desire for revenge took possession of the crowd," according to the *Telegram* report. "There were no leaders but the crowd appeared to divide into sections to prevent the exit of the police and the executive heads of the government." Two of the mounted police were pulled from their horses and sent to hospital with serious injuries. Entry to the legislature was gained through the side door basement and pandemonium followed as most of the building was trashed. Fires were set, and the police and others barricaded the Speaker's chamber where Squires and a group of supporters were holding out.

While Cashin and a number of clergymen, including the Reverend Godfrey, tried to restore order, the crowd sent forward a delegation of about forty men who entered the building. They returned with Squires through the front door and proceeded to escort him through the grounds to a waiting car. The crowd had other ideas. Night was falling and the situation was extremely tense. For an hour the escort made its way across the couple hundred yards to Military Road in front of the grounds and onto Colonial

Street. From there the Prime Minister was "by some manoeuvring," according to the *Telegram*, put into Mrs. Connelly's house at #66, where he was able to exit through the back. Here he jumped a fence, went in through the back of another residence on Bannerman Street and slipped into a waiting vehicle. The people gathered on Colonial Street could not believe he had escaped. They would not relent until a delegation was sent to inspect Mrs. Connelly's house. A slight shower of rain began to disperse the crowd, but it was not until after midnight that the Assembly grounds were vacated. At that point, having lost the pursuit of Squires, liquor stores became the desired prize. Through the night bands of angry men roamed the streets, raiding both downtown liquor stores and smashing shop windows.

The next morning the Great War Veterans Association published a front page notice in the *Daily News* calling all ex-servicemen, and other citizens, to immediately report for duty in patrolling the city. More scattered looting occurred that day. Over the next several days, the papers reported that more than two thousand men had been sworn in as special police. No doubt some of these special constables were among the many unemployed in the city who would have been pleased to get regular work. Not a few of them would have been at least witnesses to the great riot of Tuesday afternoon. The papers were full of postmortems and related arguments. Twenty people had been treated for injuries. Squires was said to be in hiding and Coaker was rumoured to have resigned. The committee of the unemployed published an advertisement seeking "the full co-operation of the unemployed in helping to preserve law and order in the city." Alderdice published an appeal to fellow citizens, telling them they "could do no good by force," to "go quietly" to their homes, and offering a guarantee that justice would be done. The opposition would exert all efforts to ensure the resignation of the government.

The head of the constabulary wrote a letter to the *Telegram* stating no order had been given to lead a baton charge. Peter Cashin sent one saying that contrary to rumour spread by the government, he was not behind "mob rule," and was retiring, "temporarily at any rate," from public life. Front-page advertisements taken out by the insurance firm Outerbridge and Daly assured coverage against losses from riot and civil commotion, at "very low rates." And there was great objection taken by correspondents to a cable sent to the outports by a government member claiming that the crowd had been "primed with rum" before demolishing the House of Assembly. In its weekly edition after the smoke had cleared, the *Advocate* ran an editorial under the headline "A warning uttered seven years ago." It claimed there were many men in both parties "who feel strongly that the parliamentary system of government by elected representatives has failed badly in recent years." It also re-printed an excerpt from Coaker's 1925 address calling for a commission government.

# Newfoundland's Dream

**W. P. Williams**

I dreampt I met a maiden fair
    With maple leaves around her brow;
I spoke to the maiden, and I said:—
    "Pray, answer me a question, now.

"The question is: 'What shall I do
    To realize my people's dreams,
To hitch their wagon to the star
    Of Hope, which through the darkness gleams?'

"Their fathers ate the sour grapes,
    The children's teeth are set on edge;
And now they see, with failing faith,
    The shattered dream, the broken pledge.

"My people seek a fuller life,
    With social justice for them all;
To face the Future free from fear,
    Which seeks to hold the soul in thrall."

She gazed at me with charming smile,
    And clasped my hand in greeting,
And e'er since then I oft recall
    The pleasure of that meeting.

"Your problem, Newfoundland," she said,
    "Is now well-known in my own land,
For isolation e'er retards
    The progress of your thrifty Island.

"There's but one answer, I can give
    To you for your consideration:
Your governmental gods have failed,
    Now why not try Confederation?"

She pointed to a sun-lit-road,
    O'er which a rainbow, bending
Gave promise of bright, new dawn,
    My people's troubles ending.

MORAL

Let's spread our wings toward that Dawn,
    Forsaking isolation,
And find in Canada our dream—
    The status of a Nation!

# The Announcement of the Rooster Tax

**Gregory Power**

L ast night, the Guffs and the Bluffs had another get-together. Pete still occupied the chairman's stool. Opening the meeting, he confessed that he was at his wits' end to know how to deal with the new turn of political events. The situation had got completely out of hand, and he was convinced that the patriotic approach adopted by the Guffs had begun to sound a bit corny. He saw no hope of correcting the situation, or of improving the story with regard to Federal taxes. He stated that he had closely studied the campaign in 1869, and expressed deep respect for the anti-Confederate campaigners of that day, adding that his hat was off to the unknown people who first informed the people of Newfoundland that under Confederation their babies would be seized and used as gun wads in Canadian cannon, and their bones left to bleach on the desert sands of Canada.

He admitted to a feeling of humility when presented with this evidence of sheer genius, and when he compared this powerful anti-Confederate argument with current masterpieces, such as the pious cry that the terms were unnegotiated, he had to confess that the anti-Confederate giants of the past were head and shoulders above the anti-Confederate giants of the present. However, when it came to presenting the bogey of property taxes, he took a back seat to no one, and asked the boys to put on their thinking caps and suggest some new item or thing which he could say would be taxed after Confederation.

The boys put on their thinking caps, and Geoffrey was the first to come up with an idea. Clapping his hands, he enquired: "Did you tell them that under Confederation every hen in Newfoundland would be taxed?" Pete informed him a bit wearily that he had already foamed at the mouth about the tax on hens.

"But," said Geoffrey, "if my memory serves me correctly, you omitted to include the roosters, thereby conveying the impression that after Confederation, roosters would continue to strut around as if nothing had happened."

Pete was quick to realize the gravity of his omission, and promised to go to town on the Federal rooster tax in his next broadcast. Getting into stride, he explained that under Confederation, roosters would be taxed to such an extent as would rob them of all initiative. He failed to see how the owner of any enterprising rooster could be so false to his trust as to vote for Confederation. He warned his fellow Newfoundlanders that all roosters would be taxed to the quill under Confederation. Offhand, he estimated that under Confederation, the Federal rooster tax would cost the Newfoundland people $165,236.11 a year.

Rising from his stool, he shouted: "Look at the roosters in Prince Edward Island, where the Federal freight subsidies have reduced these once proud birds to the status of capons."

He felt sure that Rear Admiral Bailey could substantiate this. He appealed to all patriotic Newfoundlanders not to let down our proud breed of roosters. He felt absolutely certain that the Newfoundland roosters would turn up their bills when the

Confederates tempted them with freight-subsidised feeds under Confederation. Newfoundland roosters were not asking for Canadian dole. The boys cheered. In the absence of Ches, Donald Duck pledged the support of the Comic Union troupe in this particular drive to protect our farmyard friends. He promised to place a picture of Ches in every hen-house in the country.

Gordy then rose and informed the boys that after a close study of the Canadian tax system, he had discovered that under Confederation every Newfoundlander would have to pay an oxygen tax. All Newfoundlanders would have to wear a register on their chest for the purpose of registering the number of breaths per hour. This tax would naturally fall heaviest on miners, loggers, fishermen, and all those who worked hard for ten or twelve hours a day. Those who failed to pay it would have their wind shut off by the Canadian Government. He was moved almost to tears by a contemplation of the fate of his fellow Newfoundlanders under Confederation.

Pete was pleasantly surprised by this flash of intelligence from Gordy. He warmed to him noticeably, repeating "Excellent, excellent." He felt that the idea could be used to tremendous effect in the second referendum campaign and indicated that after turning the idea over in his mind, he might be able to improve it somewhat.

Donald Duck promised to have the *Sunday Herald* publish an enlarged picture of the actual register used, and intimated that it might be possible to make recordings of the noise made by the victims when the Federal government shut off their wind. He congratulated Gordy and stated that it was indeed a pleasure to be associated with such patriotic gentlemen, adding that unless Newfoundland could keep producing politicians of such calibre, we would never be able to keep standing where our fathers once stood.

Mr. Wayfarer then asked permission to speak. As he got to his feet, the boys braced themselves in anticipation of another verbal haymaker, but apart from clipping them with a couple of split infinitives, he didn't attempt to overtax their mental processes. He warned them, however, of the consequences of getting caught posting places of worship with sectarian propaganda, and made a stirring appeal to keep the campaign clean. Here Geoffrey interposed a precocious question. He asked if it were permissible to hint that the Confederate leaders were Communists, or otherwise slyly imply that they were doubtful characters. Mr. Wayfarer spluttered for a moment but, quickly recovering his self-righteousness, he ignored Geoffrey and went on to say that it was not his intention to unduly provoke the Confederate leaders. He had only wished to point out their lack of worldly goods.

Pete then moved that the meeting be adjourned with the playing of "Yankee Doodle."

**Excerpt from**

# As Loved Our Fathers

Tom Cahill

> As loved our fathers, so we love
> Where once they stood, we stand
> Their prayer we raise to Heaven above
> God guard thee, Newfoundland
>
> > "The Ode to Newfoundland"
> > Sir Cavendish Boyle
> > Governor, 1901-1903

## PREFACE

Unable to raise new bank loans to meet interest payments on a debt of five million dollars, the Dominion of Newfoundland faced bankruptcy in June, 1932, and its government was making plans to default. Fearing the damage to its own credit and a bad example to the Empire, the government of Great Britain offered to assume responsibility for the debt of its oldest colony if Newfoundland would, in turn, agree to abide by the recommendations of a Royal Commission sent to investigate the reasons for the financial collapse.

Citing longstanding mismanagement and widespread corruption, the Amulree Report suggested the affairs of the colony be taken over by a team of professional administrators recruited from the British civil service. In November 1934 the Newfoundland House of Assembly met to unanimously approve a motion to surrender an independence granted one hundred years earlier, "until such time as the colony became self-supporting again, when Responsible Government, at the request of the people, would be restored...."

By 1946 Newfoundland enjoyed a booming post-war economy and a forty million dollar surplus, along with constant agitation for return of self-rule, and Great Britain agreed to the election of a National Convention to discuss a political future. After two years of acrimonious debate, the 43 members defeated a motion by the delegate from Gander, Joseph R. Smallwood, that Confederation with Canada be considered an alternative, and adjourned with the recommendation that a referendum be held to decide between retention of the Commission of Civil Servants for another period, or immediate return to Responsible Government.

Ten days later London announced that, in answer to a petition from its adherents, Confederation with Canada would be added to the referendum ballot, scheduled for June 3, 1948. The results were: Responsible Government, 69,400; Confederation with Canada, 64, 066; and Retention of Commission, 22,311.

Seeing no majority sufficiently established, Great Britain ordered a second referendum for July 8, with the choice of Commission dropped. The Results were: Confederation with Canada, 78,323; and Responsible Government 71, 334.

Newfoundland became the tenth province of Canada April 1, 1949.

T. C.

## THE CHARACTERS

**Cornelius 'Con' Hartrey:** A master carpenter; he works at the American military base at Argentia. In his mid-fifties.

**Theresa Hartery:** His wife, known as Trese; about 40. She is a housewife; her children have grown and moved away.

**Gord Roberts:** Her brother, about 25; a mechanic.

**The Old Woman:** Trese's mother, Mrs. Roberts.

**Imelda:** 'Mel' Roberts, Trese's sister, just turned 45; a teacher.

**Jack:** A crony of Con's; in his fifties.

**Sooley:** A widower who lives next door, and "has it bad" for Mel.

The men wear work clothes, plaid shirts, work boots. Trese wears a flowered dress and apron. Mel is more stylish in a short coat of the period; she smokes a lot. The Old Woman wears black; she is confined to her wheelchair.

## THE SETTING

The kitchen of Con's house in a small outport about fifty miles from St. John's, Newfoundland. A woodstove sits against one wall in the upper left corner. Snuggled close to it for warmth, the Old Woman is snoozing peacefully in an ancient wicker-backed wheelchair. On the wall above her head is pinned a picture, torn from a recent newspaper, of her hero, Joseph 'Joey' Smallwood, the leader of the party campaigning for Confederation with Canada in the referendum. A framed picture of former Prime Minister Sir Edward Morris hangs on an opposite wall. This one is turned to face the wall; its dusty back is covered with a piece of flowered chintz with a frilled border. The upstage wall has a window, a sink and kitchen cupboards; on the wall hangs a framed and garish representation of the "Sacred Heart," a large black rosary hangs from the same nail. Beside it there is a political poster with black block letters reading, "This House Is Responsible Government." Along a side wall there is a settee for afternoon naps, a sewing machine with a foot-pedal, and a floor-to-ceiling china cabinet with two drawers at waist level, and cupboards underneath.

**ACT I: EVENING, JUNE 3, 1948.** The day of the referendum which will decide the political future of the oldest British colony.

**ACT II: EVENING, JULY 8, 1948.** The day of the second referendum.

## ACT ONE

*GORD ROBERTS is seated at a table, centre, fiddling with the tubes and insides of an old battery radio. His sister TRESE is at the sink, transferring some newly-made bread dough to baking pans and the oven. His sister MEL stalks around the room in an agony of excitement, not particularly shared by the other two.*

*MEL stops pacing and turns to shake GORD's shoulder.*

**MEL**: Gord, for the loving honour of God will you try and get something on that bloody radio. It'll be all over soon.

**GORD**: How can anybody be expected to fix the likes of this, for cripes' sake. (*He holds up a battered knob.*) Look what's off now!

**MEL**: Oooh, I only wanted to hear the first few counts to know how the tide was running. Why did I have to choose this place with that damn thing gone.

**GORD**: You chose this place so's you and Con could have somewhere to hide away in case you don't win tonight. That's why you chose it.

**MEL**: Hmmph! Fine place to hide…in the chairman's home!

**TRESE**: Gord, will you shut up antagonizing the woman and go fix the radio.

**MEL**: Come on, Gord. I'm missing all the excitement. It's after eight thirty and the returns are coming in. (*She paces about in frustration.*) Oh God! I fought all the battles and I'm missing the war!

**GORD**: Why in hell didn't you buy a new radio if you knew it was going to end up like this? You and Con are not exactly starving.

**MEL**: Who ever thought it'd be this bad? Is there a sound in it at all, or have I got to go somewhere else to listen?

(*She shakes his arm; he laughs at her impatience.*)

**GORD**: Take it easy, will you?

**MEL**: (*Turning suddenly to TRESE*) Trese, how about going over to Sooley's and asking for the lend of his?

**TRESE**: Me go over? Sure, you're the one he's cracked about.

**MEL**: Oh come on, Trese. He'll want me to go in if I go. I don't want him to know I'm here.

**TRESE**: Yes, and he'll be damn soon over if he finds out.

**MEL**: (*Urging her toward the door*) He didn't see me come in and don't tell him. Now go on over.

**TRESE:** (*Pushing MEL away with an elbow, her hands full of dough and flour, she joins GORD's laughter at MEL's excitement.*) Get away, look, or you'll be full of flour. Mel, you know everyone and his dog is locked up with their radios tonight listening to the returns. There's no one going to lend out a radio, least of all old Sooley with an election this important on.

**MEL**: (*Turning away in frustration, to stand over GORD like a hawk*) It's not an election, I keep telling you, it's a referendum.

**TRESE**: What's the difference what they calls it, it's all foolish politics anyway.

**MEL**: You shouldn't be out voting today if you don't know the difference. People who don't know shouldn't be allowed to vote.

**GORD**: It's a wonder they let anybody out then.

**TRESE**: Ah, you crowd make me sick, always putting the ordinary people down just because you're mixed up a bit with the politicians. Trying to tell everyone what to do and how to vote. You might get a fright one of these days when you find out they can make up their own minds.

**MEL**: Someone's got to tell 'em what to do. After four hundred years on this rock they still can't tell the difference between an honest man and a rogue.

**TRESE**: I do so know the difference about today, then. We got a chance to vote for three choices. We either keep the Commission of Government sent over from England to look after us, get back our own we gave up to get **them** here, or join Canada!

**GORD**: Hurray, go to the head of the class, Trese.

**TRESE**: Yes, Miss Teacher, I been doing my homework after all.

**GORD**: I still think there should be a fourth choice, and we should be voting to join the Yanks!

**MEL**: Ah, stupid Canada missed her chance to grab Alaska when the Russians sold it to the Yanks, and she's not going to make the same mistake on this coast, old bitch-mother England will see to that, and there'll be no Yankee voting in these woods this year!

**GORD**: (*With an evil grin*) I though you liked the Yanks so much yourself, you might be out campaigning for them instead of the Independents.

**TRESE**: Now, Gord!

**MEL**: You mind your own business, now, that's what you'll do. And be careful you don't find out what your precious Americans are really like when you and your buddies get fired for trying to start a union on their Navy base.

**TRESE**: (*Turning to him in shock*) Gord! You're not at that again, you'll lose your job, boy.

**GORD**: You're still the snotty older sister, Mel, got to go and spill the beans.

**TRESE**: And so she should spill the beans. Wait till Con hears.

**GORD**: I'm not going to lose me job, Trese. That's her fancy friends telling her stories.

**MEL**: I saw Commander Smithson's letter last week, buddy, that said Newfoundland bases are considered overseas posts and anybody who tries to start a union on them will be blacklisted. What's that if it's not losing your job?

**TRESE**: Gord, you'll never get work anywhere on the island again?

**GORD**: Look…there's no reason why they can't pay Newfoundlanders the same as their own men doing the same work, side by side. It's just a matter of putting a little pressure on them. Besides, the war is over. And so, by the way, is this conversation!

**MEL**: Okay, but don't be surprised if you find out your favourite people aren't as democratic as they pretend to be. I wish Con would come home, he might have got hold of a radio, or will he stay down to Bennett's half the night, I wonder?

**TRESE**: He'll stay down there till he starts to lose in the voting, then he'll come up here and take his spite out on us. That's what he'll do, if he don't win!

**MEL**: Ah, he'll win this one, Trese, no fear of that. By midnight we'll have our own government back for the first time in fifteen years and be the proud Dominion of Newfoundland again!

**GORD**: (*Faking a trumpet call as he perceives life in the radio*) Tatatatatatataaa! Hold everything. Hold everything!

(*They creep close as he makes a final dramatic connection, reaches for the knob and turns it with a flourish.*)

There!

**TRESE**: (*Suddenly remembering*) Sure, the battery's still in the oven!

**GORD**: Oh, shag it. I forgot about that.

**TRESE**: Get it, Mel. Me hands are full of dough.

**MEL**: How stunned. How stunned.

(*She streaks for the stove, grabbing a dishtowel from a line behind it, extracts a battery from the oven and carries it carefully to the table.*)

It is going to work?

**GORD**: If it dosen't, it's all going in the stove. Put it down.

**MEL**: Stunned! That's not the word. Putting a battery in the oven to charge it for an hour, and then forgetting to put it in the foolish radio!

**GORD**: (*Working to make the connection*) Shut up for once, will you.

**TRESE**: Imagine if it come on and told us we were all Canadians!

**MEL**: Ah, be quiet, they're only voting on a choice, we haven't joined anybody yet!

**GORD**: (*Addressing the radio*) Speak, or forever hold your peace!

(*We hear the voice of the RADIO ANNOUNCER*)

> …The first count just received from the district of St. George's reads as follows: In favour of retaining Commission of Government…thirty seven votes. In favour of the return of Responsible Government to Newfoundland, eight hundred and forty-six; in favour of Confederation with Canada, two thousand nine hundred and thirty-four. To repeat these figures…(*As the announcer repeats the bulletin they all talk at once; the radio fades out, unnoticed, during the scene.*)

**MEL**: (*Shocked at the news*) Merciful God, not St. George's!

**TRESE**: (*Running to shake the OLD WOMAN awake*) Mother, wake up, did you hear it? Your man is winning, girl? Oh! I got her covered with flour, poor soul. (*She dusts off the OLD WOMAN with her apron.*)

**GORD**: (*His ear pinned close*) Will you shut up so I can hear the bloody thing!

**MEL**: Oooh, Gord, it's not gone again! Here, look, shake it or something.

**GORD**: (*Pushing her hands away*) That won't do any good!

**MEL**: My God. I wonder is it true about St. George's?

**GORD**: You can be damn sure they weren't making it up, Mel.

**MEL**: That's unbelievable.

**TRESE**: (*Shaking and hugging the OLD WOMAN*) Joey won St. George's, Mom. He won, girl! The whole west coast is gone solid for Canada.

**MEL**: Who said the whole west coast was gone, he was talking about St. George's.

**TRESE**: Well, that's on the west coast, isn't it, Mom? Mel, she'd love to win the last vote she'll probably ever have, and I'd love to see her win it, it'd make her so happy.

**MEL**: Well it won't make Con very happy, reminding him when he comes home she voted Confederate, Trese. Especially if the count's going against him, so have a grain, will you? (*Almost frantic as GORD pokes at the radio*) Can you get it back, Gord? Here, Trese. The battery—back in the oven.

**GORD**: No. To hell with that. It's got to be something else.

*(The door bursts open, and SOOLEY runs in.)*

**SOOLEY**: Where's Con? Did you hear about St. George's? Oh, Mel. I didn't know you were here. Did you hear about St. George's? The first count was just…

**MEL**: *(Cutting him off abruptly, she slumps in her chair.)* Yes, I heard it.

**SOOLEY**: *(Looking about)* On what?

**MEL**: On that thing if you can believe it. It went again after ten seconds.

**SOOLEY**: I thought Con was getting a new one.

**TRESE**: He was trying to get one from the PX all week. Mel's gone mad to hear the returns but can't find anywhere to listen.

**MEL**: Shut!

**SOOLEY**: Sure, you can come over to my place, Mel, I got a fire in and everything.

**MEL**: No thanks, Sooley. Gord's going to get this one working soon, now aren't you, little brother… *(She give GORD an elbow behind SOOLEY's back. He gasps and exhales loudly.)* Besides, I promised Con I'd wait till he came home.

**GORD**: I'm going to find out why it won't work if I have to stay here all night. There's no reason why it shouldn't.

**SOOLEY**: And St. George's is gone, Mel. Are you surprised at that? Gone this early in the night?

**MEL**: It's not gone, Sooley. It's only a first count. It was close and it could change. Don't start getting dismal.

**TRESE**: *(Going to the oven with a bread pan)* Speaking of getting dismal, if that count don't bring my darling husband roaring home, nothing will.

**SOOLEY**: If he didn't manage to get a radio, he'll have nowhere to listen to the counts.

**GORD**: If he's losing he'd rather sulk than listen anyway.

**MEL**: I'd say he's staying where he is. He won't want to take a chance on missing a count now, with that St. George's racket on.

**SOOLEY**: Strange for them to go and do that, 'ent it now, Mel? 'Specially after the Archbishop himself telling 'em to vote for Responsible Government.

**TRESE**: He didn't tell 'em anything of the sort, Sooley! That's not nice. You're worse than Con and the crowd, dragging religion into everything. Why can't you leave it out of your politics?

**SOOLEY**: He came out in the church paper last month and said the Catholics might lose their private schools and get public ones if we joined Canada. What's that if it's not telling 'em to vote against Confederation?

**MEL**: It's damn smart politics for the Confederates to spread stories like that around, Sooley, that's what it is, and get a few votes on the backlash.

**TRESE**: Now don't you two get going on about any religion here tonight. For God's sake just keep it to politics and that'll be bad enough as it is.

**SOOLEY**: I'm not starting any religious racket, I got the editorial in my scrap book if you wants to see it, over at the house right now…

**TRESE**: I never missed mass a Sunday this four years and I never saw any Archbishop's message about an election, then.

**GORD**: Referendum!

**MEL**: Attaboy, Gord!

**SOOLEY**: Well it was in the *Monitor* the week, Joe Dean gave it to me, dated and signed and all by the grace of God and the Holy Apostolic See!

**TRESE**: Well if it was, he's entitled to his opinion.

**SOOLEY**: Nobody said he wasn't. But it's like Mel said, there's a Catholic backlash against him trying to tell them how to vote, and there's liable to be a Protestant one against him coming out to do it in the first place.

**TRESE**: If Con comes home and hears you blaming the Archbishop for losing his election tonight, there be a backlash around this place.

**GORD**: Yes, Sooley, right up your rear end!

(*As they hoot with laughter at TRESE's sally, the door opens and CON HARTREY steps into the room. He tears off his jacket and throws it one way, his cap another, and advances to the table, panting from his run up hill to the house.*)

**CON**: Is the damn thing still gone, Gord? Oh no! Can't you get anything at all on it? I couldn't get me new one off the base, they were searching people at the gate. Mel! Did you hear about St. George's?

**MEL**: Yes, boy, we got that thing working for the few seconds it took 'em to give the count. Is the rest of it going so bad?

**TRESE**: It's no use going on about it, now Con, 'tis over and done with. Me and Mom gave our votes to Joey.

**CON**: But you knows this is a Responsible Government house. Everyone in town knows I'm chairman of the League…

**TRESE**: It's a free country, Con, and I can vote for who I like.

*(CON jumps up and, racing over to snatch the Smallwood picture from above her chair, startles the OLD WOMAN awake. He tears it to shreds, and throws it in her lap.)*

**CON**: By God, you can vote for who you like, all right, but you're not going to turn this house into a Confederate headquarters, the two of ye! Here, take your bloody leader. 'Tis little enough he'll do for you if he gets in and you believing his tripe about your Old Age Pension. (*He stamps back to the table and sits in a sulk.*) I've been feeding that old thing now since she came with us ten years ago. What's that if it's not giving her a pension? Don't you think she should have the decency to thank me for that, and honour what I stands for in this community?

**TRESE**: (*Flying to the OLD WOMAN's side, she picks up the scattered pieces and presses them into her hands.*) How bloody crazy are you getting at all, man, frightening a poor old soul half to death. Are you all right, Mom? Yes girl, don't mind him. Here, gather them…here's another piece. Bloody crazy man and bloody crazy politics. I wish to God they'd never started about the damn Confederation.

**CON**: Well they have started. And I've probably got to spend the rest of my life going around this harbour explaining how me own household voted with the quislings.

**GORD**: (*He has stood up to see if the OLD WOMAN was all right, now sits again.*) She did it to humour the old woman, boy.

**CON**: To humour the old woman. We're trying to save a country, not humour old women. Why doesn't she realize that and try to humour me for a change?

**TRESE**: I just told here I'd try and help her get her pension like she heard on the radio from Joey every night, didn't I, Mom? A little bit of money for you, girl, who cares where it comes from?

**CON**: What for? Why does she need it? She's looked after here, isn't she? She's fed here, isn't she, as much as she can stuff in her gullet? Why does she want to go selling her vote for a pension from Joe Smallwood or anyone else?

**TRESE**: (*Patting the OLD WOMAN's hair back into place*) Because she doesn't want to be beholden to you or anyone else, that's why. Because she wants her independence like you do and has the same right to try and get it. Because she thinks thirty dollars a month is a fortune and will vote for anyone who will give it to her. (*She softens her voice and bends to hug the OLD WOMAN gently.*) If you saw her face when the poll clerk let me go into the booth with her today, you'd understand. I showed her where to mark her "X," and she watched to see if I marked mine in the same place. I wasn't going to vote at all, but when I did the same as her, it made her smile, really smile for the first time in years, and that was good enough for me, wasn't it, sweetheart?

*(CON slumps in his chair in utter frustration and disgust.)*

# The Black Tie

**Grace Butt**

*On the day in 1949 when confederation with Canada was proclaimed
many Newfoundlanders opposed to the loss of their country's independence
wore a black tie as a sign of mourning.*

"Why the black tie?"
you, a Canadian, ask.
"Why the long face,
why the mourning?
Losing a sovereign name isn't such a tragedy:
aren't we all on the map together
designated by the same Imperial shade
linked by the same traditions
washed by the same blood-waters?

Why the black tie?
to be one with us isn't such a terrible thing:
we're not hateful creatures
but people
just like you
with wars to face
and some of us with hunger
and all with uncertainty
seeking the strength that lies in unity."

Why the black tie?

Listen:
we don't mourn nationality—as a piece of earth
our hospitality has never let us hate
and we've known hunger, and will again.
We mourn
something more permanent than lines drawn on a map,

we are saddened
by a frailty worse than fear,
we are thinking of other things
than ways and means to keep a stomach full, an empire safe.

We grieve for our lost self-joy

a joy not lost the other day
(the day of referenda, of outward signs)
but slowly lost
like youth
down through the years.

The joy that once impelled us
to explore the unknown seas
gaze into unknown skies
embrace the unknown risks
of ships
and souls and government.

The joy that clambered up the mast
mocking the timid ones left safe on shore
scoffing at the squabbling ones below decks
grabbing, as always, in the name of justice,
the best grub
or clinging, in the name of right,
to the best bunks.

The joy that swayed with the wave
up, dizzily, and down, dangerously,
but always in motion
till the day the wind died
and the ship
becalmed
settled into a glassy lethargy
with the seams opening
and the ropes rotting
and at last the sails too limp to catch and hold
the freshening breezes of hope.

We mourn not an empty name—a name is but a legality
nor the dead husk of sovereignty, promised or earned
but the vision of what we could be
the pride that we were.

Why the black tie? you ask.

This is no time for arguing
this is no time for shouting with the loud voice:
the spirit that once was lingers with us
we are still whispering in the house
something of us has died.

# To Mark the Occasion

## Bernice Morgan

In the last morning in March 1949 1 woke up a Canadian. For months—forever it seemed—I had been falling asleep to the sound of two politicians doing battle over whether Newfoundland should enter Confederation or not. I could not remember back to the time before it started; it had become the background sound that in memory dominates my childhood. The radio voices were known, soothing, almost loved. They were part of me, like my parents' voices drifting up to my dark bedroom with the click of teacups and the smell of the kitchen fire. Often my brother, who worked, would be having lunch with them and he would bring me up a warm raisin bun or an apricot square. As I lay nibbling crumbs into the flannelette the sounds of all their voices and the sounds of the house would blend like smoke into a low haze and I would fall asleep.

My parents were "Anti-Confederates," they wanted Newfoundland to stay independent, they dreaded a turning away from England, the mother country, a country that no one in our family had seen for generations. Confederation would separate us from England, my father said—make us American, "Canadians are just Americans with some of the varnish rubbed off," he said. My father disliked Americans.

I loved Americans. People like June Allison and Jane Powell. In American high schools children were called teenagers (I would be thirteen in two years), they had huge gyms where they produced musicals that would have put Ziegfield to shame. My friend Joan and I went to Saturday matinees every week, our stomachs full of pea soup and our arms full of comic books. I wished my family was like the families we saw on the screen, living in big white houses on tree-shaded streets, with boyfriends who drove cars and sisters who had weddings under perpetually sunny skies on perpetually green lawns. My teachers were for Confederation, too—they explained to us that little countries could not survive in the modern world, that Newfoundland had a history of bad government. We needed Canada, to protect us.

Tom, my brother, was undecided about Confederation. He was seven years older than I, and worked in the grocery store on the next street. Tom made deliveries pushing a long-handled wooden cart around the neighbourhood. It was a blue cart with curly gold letters on the side saying "J. B. Davis, Groceries and Provisions." Sometimes, coming home from school, I would meet him and if the cart was empty he would give me a fast ride down the street. Tom usually agreed with my father, if we got Confederation we would just become a captive market for Canada. He felt more strongly about England than I did. But one day he told me that the store might get a truck if Confederation came. Tom loved mechanical things and I knew he was imagining himself driving up the street behind the wheel of a big shiny truck.

So we argued, but not bitterly as some families did. We argued with much feeling and little fact. Reason did not sway us, neither did the long tirades of Mr. Smallwood or Mr. Cashin, although we always listened to them, nodding when they said something we agreed with. Their function was to back up our position, not to change it.

There were families where the argument cut deeper. Down the street Mr. McNeill had turned Meg's boyfriend off the front porch when he found out he was for Confederation. My father's cousin had packed up and left home after a loud argument with his parents about Confederation. Our street was split about half and half and everyone knew how everyone else had voted except for Mr. Batten who lived alone in the house adjoining ours. No one ever knew anything about Mr. Batten.

I often wondered about Mr. Batten, sitting in his lonely, quiet house on the other side of our kitchen wall. What did he think of us? Especially on Saturday nights when our house overflowed with sound. On Saturday night I took a bath in the big galvanized tub in front of the stove, discreetly screened from the rest of the kitchen with a circle of chairs draped in towels. My mother peeled vegetables for Sunday and my father would sit on the sofa under the radio, polishing shoes and listening to a shrill soprano sing "Kelly the Boy from Killan" on the Big Six Radio Program. We sometimes played a game of 45's when Tom came home. Although my mother frowned on cards she loved the competition of the game. Our house was very noisy Saturday nights.

My mother thought of Mr. Batten then, too. "We should have the poor man over some time," she would say as she dropped the peeled vegetables into the big brown bowl. Once I'd said, "Well, why don't we then?" My mother had blushed and looked flustered. "Well…he works on Water Street, you know." My question was unexpected, unfair; by asking it I had destroyed part of the Saturday night ritual; she looked to my father for help. "He's got a very good job, he's a floorwalker," my father said. It was settled then, my father wore overalls to work but Mr. Batten wore a blue serge suit and a white shirt—Mr. Batten was a different social order and in St. John's such barriers were not to be ignored.

Besides being austere, remote and a floorwalker, Mr. Batten had another distinction. He had the only front yard on the street. A scruffy scrap of black earth, but in it stood the only tree on the street, a stately maple that reached over to my bedroom window, and when the leaves were red gave a lovely glow to my cold room. Mr. Batten spent most of his off-work hours caring for the tree. In summer he sprayed it, pruned it carefully and guarded against the neighbourhood boys who tried to hang swings from it and climb it. In winter he built a little fence around the tree and in the early morning knocked glitter off the branches with a long pole.

It was a lovely tree. A Canadian Maple. Tom, who had once made a leaf collection, told me. I looked through its branches and fat green buds as I studied the street to see if there was any difference that morning. I should feel different, everything should have been different—yet here I was getting dressed for school, just like any other morning. The street was empty—the only change I could see was a black ribbon tied onto the stick of a Union Jack and nailed to the McNeill's front door. It looked damp and mournful.

How strange that they hadn't made today a holiday—after such an epic battle surely some celebration was in order but no, they were afraid, my father said, there might be riots if people were given time off. He had ruffled my hair on his way downstairs at seven o'clock, comforting me, or perhaps himself, for I didn't need comforting. "It may not be so bad…anyway it's done now and we're Canadians, we'll have to make the best of it!" He'd gone off to work, wearing the same overalls and carrying the same scraped, black lunch tin. What would change for him, I wondered.

For me everything would change, we would be able to get all the wonderful "mainland catalogues" and order things without paying duty. We would be teenagers—an unknown word in Newfoundland—it had come just in time for me. I was lucky, I'd always suspected it, now I knew. I hugged myself and started to dress in my ugly school uniform that would, I hoped, be outlawed in the Canadian educational system.

I went down the stairs and saw Tom on the front porch, a strange place to stand at 8:30 on a damp March morning. Something about the way he stood, very still and leaning slightly forward, made me go out to see what he was watching.

Mr. Batten was in his front yard. It was the first time I'd seen him without his suit jacket; his blue-white shirt glowed in the grey morning light. I was astonished to see that he wore red braces and I looked at Tom, expecting him to turn and wink at me. He only frowned and shook his head, not taking his eyes off Mr. Batten who stood looking at his tree. He walked around it once and reached out to run his hand over the trunk, like a man reaching out to touch a woman's hair. The maple tree was beautiful, a graceful curve against the sky—the only beautiful thing on the narrow, mean street. In the instant before Mr. Batten raised the axe I realized how important it was to me. The stroke was swift and hard, it cut a gleaming white gash into the trunk. The axe hit again and again, slowly, surely, methodically taking great gouges out of the tree. Tom and I stood as still as cats, watching. Tears dripped off my chin and I bit hard on the top button of my sweater so that I wouldn't make any noise. I think Tom was crying too, but I was afraid to see.

It seemed like a long, long time before the tree groaned and fell into the street with only a small sound. He looked at us across the ugly jagged stump, nodded and went into his house. We just stood there. A few moments later he came out with his jacket on; not even looking at the dead tree he turned down the hill towards Water Street where he was a floorwalker.

# Text of an Address

*Delivered over the Newfoundland Network of the CBC*
*at 9:30 p.m., February 12, 1959*

## J. R. Smallwood

My talk tonight is addressed especially to all the loggers of Newfoundland; not only those who are on strike, but all loggers wherever they may be, the 20,000 of them, full-time loggers and part-time loggers.

Now the first point I want to make is that I am absolutely sure and certain that our loggers must have a strong union to protect their interests and help them forward in the battle of life. It would be madness or suicide for our loggers to be without a strong union. They never got anywhere in Newfoundland until they got their first union twenty (20) odd years ago. If they found themselves without a union, they would go down hill very fast. Without a union they would wake up some day to find that their last state was worse than the first. The loggers would not be fair to themselves if they failed to have a strong union of their own. It is absolutely necessary for our Newfoundland loggers to have a strong union to guard their interests, to protect their future and to represent them in dealing with the employers.

It is not enough for them just to have a union. The union must be strong, it must be honest, it must be honourable and it must be independent of the employers. It would be better to have no union at all than to have one that was only a company stooge.

The loggers must have a union, the union must be strong, honest, honourable and independent of the employers and the union must have a written agreement with the two paper companies, AND Company and Bowater's or their contractors. This written agreement with the employers must settle wages, rates of pay, rates of board, camp conditions and everything else affecting the lives of the loggers.

I speak to you tonight as the Premier of Newfoundland, the Leader of Her Majesty's Government in this Province. And as Premier of Newfoundland I say that for Newfoundland's sake, for the sake of peace and contentment in Newfoundland, the loggers must have a strong union, a union that is independent of the employers and a union that is able to make written agreements with the employers covering wages, conditions and everything else touching the lives of the loggers. There never will be peace or contentment in the logging industry without such a union. My task in bringing a third great paper mill to Newfoundland would be made much harder than it is if there was no strong independent union of loggers that could represent the men in dealing with the employers. Without such a union I would see nothing ahead but discontent and unhappiness amongst the loggers and their families for many years to come.

But it is not only as the Premier of Newfoundland that I say this, I say it as a man who has favoured trade unions and labour unions all my life. I have myself organized many unions, at least a dozen of them in my time, have helped to organize other unions as well, I have reorganized still other unions. The last union I organized was at Gander not many months before I became Premier and I have helped to form another union since I became Premier. I believe just as firmly today in good strong decent unions as I ever did in my life. As a lifelong labour and union man I tell the loggers tonight that the one thing they must have is a good strong union. But it is not only as the Premier of Newfoundland and a life long union and labour man that I tell you this tonight. There is another reason. In a few weeks from now Newfoundland will be ten years old as a Province of Canada. I did my part to bring that about and the great majority of you loggers helped me to do it. If it were not for the loggers of Newfoundland, we probably would not have Confederation today and our people would have been forced to do without the great blessings of Confederation. All Newfoundland owes you and your wives a great debt of gratitude for the noble part you played, often right in your camps, on the day the referendum was held in that glorious fight for Confederation. I can never forget the part you played at that time nor can I ever forget how you have stood by me from that day to this. I want Confederation to succeed in Newfoundland, I want it to be a success. It can never succeed, it can never be a success so long as there is discontent and unhappiness amongst the loggers, their wives and their children. This is something that must be understood. Not only by the loggers, but the employers and everybody else in Newfoundland tonight. We cannot have a happy and prosperous Newfoundland if the 20,000 loggers and their wives and families, if they are unhappy and suffering under a sense of injustice.

The IWA strike is a failure and the IWA itself is a failure. The IWA has failed the loggers of Newfoundland and failed the loggers' families. In my opinion the IWA never will and never can win in Newfoundland. That organization has not led our loggers, they have misled them; they have not given leadership to the loggers, they have given the loggers misleadership; they have not won the friendship of the people of Newfoundland, they have turned the people of Newfoundland against them. The vast majority of our Newfoundland people tonight are shocked and horrified by what is going on.

Some weeks ago I sent a considerable number of level headed Newfoundlanders traveling through the big stretch running all the way from White Bay to Trinity Bay. They had strict orders from me to keep their mouths closed and their ears and eyes opened. They were to act as my ears and eyes in traveling throughout the section where 98% of the AND Company's loggers come from. The instruction I gave them was simple. They were to learn what the people were thinking about the IWA and about the strike. It was my duty as Premier to try to learn how people were thinking.

In addition to these persons that I sent out as my ears and eyes I wrote a great many clergymen, pastors and officers of the different religious denominations on that big stretch of coastline and other quiet decent citizens as well asking them to give me strictly confidential reports of how people are thinking about the IWA and about the strike. In addition to this I arranged to have many other reports brought to me all the time from people living or traveling in the section between White Bay and Trinity Bay. It was the feeling and thoughts of the people out on the coast, out in the bays, in the coves and settlements that I wanted to know about. I will tell you what the people are thinking in those hundreds of settlements—the loggers and their wives, the general public, ordinary men and women, ordinary Newfoundlanders. Here is what they are thinking.

1. The loggers must have a good strong union.
2. It would be a disaster for the loggers to be without a good strong union.
3. The IWA is a failure and this strike never should have been called.
4. The great majority of the loggers want to get back to work.
5. The Premier should step in and try to do something to help the loggers in their plight.

This is the opinion of the vast majority of all the people including the loggers and their families, all the way from White Bay to Trinity Bay. Oh, I know very well indeed that there are a few places in that big section of coastline where the loggers are very strongly in favour of the IWA, but there are only a few such places in all Newfoundland tonight. Thousands of loggers have lost their faith and confidence in the IWA. Of course they would still support the IWA, if the IWA was the only union they could have. The great majority of the loggers are so determined to have a good strong union to represent them, so determined that they would still have the IWA if this was, if this was the only union they could have. Thousands of loggers who in their heart of hearts feel that the IWA has misled them will still support the IWA as long as the IWA is the only union that they can see to represent them. If I myself were a logger, if I were a logger and if I had to make a choice between the IWA and taking the risk of going back 15 or 20 years then I would be just as strong for the IWA as any other logger.

And now I am going to outline a course that I think the loggers should take and take without a moment's delay. If they will follow my advice, this is what the loggers will do.

1. Send the IWA about their business, send them out of Newfoundland, tell them never to come back here again, write, or better still, telegraph at once to the IWA telling them that you are no longer a member of that organization.
2. Form a brand new union for all the loggers of Newfoundland. If the loggers who are still in Mr. Thompson's union want to join up in this new union, give them a hearty welcome. If the loggers who are still in Mr. Fudge's union want to join up in the new union, give them a hearty welcome, give all loggers a hearty welcome to your new union. If you want help from me to form this new union, I will be happy to help you with all my strength and all my heart.
3. In a very few days it would be possible for you to have the new union formed and negotiations started with the AND Company.
4. The men could be back in the camps working within the next week and within the next fortnight or so a new working agreement can be signed between the new union, and the AND Company. I would be very willing to help bring this about.
5. Give careful consideration then to banding all the fishermen and all the loggers together in one great Newfoundland union. You could go then to the Federation of Fishermen and ask them if they would unite their Federation with the new union of loggers.
6. With the IWA driven out of Newfoundland and a much stronger union organized to take their place, you could then decide if you wanted to affiliate with the

Newfoundland Federation of Labour. They would probably be very glad then to have you because you would then have as many members as the Federation has itself.

I have talked all this business over with a man who is highly respected in Newfoundland by thousands of fisherman and thousands of loggers—Max Lane, the General Secretary of the Fishermen's Federation. Max Lane is, as you all know, a true-blue Newfoundlander, an outport man, a man who is educated, experienced, fearless and with enough grit for five men. I said to Max Lane that I thought it was his duty as a Newfoundlander to get into this thing and launch a great new loggers' union. Mr. Lane has agreed if the loggers want him, he has agreed to throw himself into this great task without a moment's delay to organize a great new union of loggers. He is already known to thousands of you because of course thousands of loggers are fishermen and every fisherman knows Max Lane. I myself would be delighted to give you every bit of help in my power and I would be able to bring many good helpers with me. Mr. Lane, as you know, is a member of the House of Assembly. Now the loggers might want him to resign from the House of Assembly and if they did, he would be quite willing to do so, but if the loggers felt that it would be good for them and for the new union for him to keep his seat in the House of Assembly, he would be perfectly willing to do that also. It would be all the same to him. The House of Assembly would lose one of its best members if he resigned, but we would be willing to take that loss for the good of the loggers.

Now let me sum up:

1. You must have a good, strong union to represent you.

2. You must have a signed agreement with your employers, fixing the conditions and the pay you are to receive.

3. The IWA has failed and never can be a success in Newfoundland.

4. You should send the IWA packing and tell them never to show their faces in Newfoundland again.

5. You should at once, tomorrow morning, notify the IWA that you are no longer a member.

6. You should immediately invite someone to form a new loggers' union, to include all the loggers of Newfoundland. If you want Max Lane to organize the union, he is ready and prepared to do so.

7. In a fortnight or little more from tonight the committee of the new union can be sitting down with the AND Company negotiating and signing a new contract.

8. Within a month, at least, at most, within a month from tonight that new contract can be signed.

9. You could then decide with your new union if you wanted to, to bring in all the fishermen to your ranks and make the biggest union that Newfoundland has ever seen and this union could decide then if they wanted to affiliate with the Newfoundland Federation of Labour.

I offer you my help and my services to get this new union formed and to get your new union contract with the AND Company. I would be willing to drop all other work for the next fortnight and give my time, day and night, to help bring all this about. Besides myself, I can bring a great many others in to help you. The full weight of the government of Newfoundland will be thrown in on your side to help you and will be there at your back after this Civil War is over. The government doesn't want the IWA, the government will never work with the IWA, will never talk to them, will never answer a letter or telegram from them, will never have anything to do with the IWA We think, and a great majority of our Newfoundland people think, that the IWA are the greatest danger that ever struck Newfoundland. We think that they are the greatest danger that ever came to the loggers and their families. There is not room enough in Newfoundland for the government and the IWA at the same time. One or the other must go. It is not a strike they have started, it is a Civil War.

"By their fruits ye shall know them," and what bitter fruit from this terrible outfit. The IWA since they came to Newfoundland have brought nothing but trouble, trouble, trouble, bad feelings such as we have never known before. Lifetime neighbours have been torn asunder. Father torn from son, fisherman from logger, settlement from settlement, union from union. There is hate in Newfoundland tonight, bitter and ugly. There is more lawlessness, more violence, more lies, more falsehood, more cheating, more deceit in the past four weeks than we ever saw in Newfoundland before. We see hate and suspicion and fear and falsehood, this is what the IWA has set loose in our beloved Newfoundland. How dare these outsiders come into this decent, Christian province and by such desperate, such terrible methods try to seize control of our Province's main industry. How dare they come in here and spread their black poison of class hatred and bitter, bigoted prejudice. How dare they come into this province amongst decent, God-fearing people and let loose the dirt and filth and poison of the last four weeks. The very presence of the IWA in Newfoundland tonight is an insult to every decent Newfoundlander. Every decent Newfoundlander should feel that he has been made dirty by the presence of this wicked and mischievous body of reckless and irresponsible wreckers. As long as I live on this earth, as long as God gives me breath, I will denounce this vile outfit for what they have done to our decent Newfoundland people.

Our House of Assembly will be called together in the very near future. We would be ready to meet the brute force and wicked violence of this unspeakable body with all the majesty of British law. Ninety-five or ninety-six or ninety-seven out of every hundred loggers are decent, respectable, law abiding, God-fearing, Christian men. Thousands of loggers and their wives tonight are broken in heart and tormented in spirit by the terrible way in which the IWA has misled them. A few young hotheads, a few young hotbloods may think that this is a great bit of fun, but not so the decent family men who want to live decent lives and want a decent union to help protect their living in the future. Thousands of decent loggers who know that this strike has already cost them a million dollars and more don't look upon this strike as anything but a disaster. In the hearing tonight of hundreds of thousands of my fellow Newfoundlanders I pledge my strongest support and the government's strongest support to our loggers in their fight for justice.

Send me your telegrams starting first thing tomorrow morning, tell me that you want to be rid of this black nightmare that goes by the name of IWA. Tell me in your telegrams that you want a clean, decent, strong union to represent you and to protect you. A strong union that will have the backing of your government, that will not bring your young men and even your women out to fight against the law. Save Newfoundland you loggers. Save Newfoundland from the awful danger that faces us all. Send me telegrams in thousands tomorrow. If you want trouble, and ever more trouble, trouble without end, if you want lawlessness, violence, lies and ever more lies, lost wages, unhappiness and failure, follow the IWA. If you want peace and work and wages, if you want a strong, safe, civilized, successful union that will quickly get you a union contract with the AND Company, follow the advice I have given you tonight. If you want civil war and bitter defeat, bitter defeat, follow the IWA. If you want peace and victory I have shown you the way.

May God guide you in your decision.

**woods work**: (a) the cutting of timber for household use; (b) pulp-wood operations. Cp WINTER WORK.

1953 Nfld Fish Develop Report 21 This conclusion would not apply, of course, or would apply only with substantial modification, to areas where fishing is unusually successful or where supplementary sources of cash income (such as woods work) are unusually accessible. T 43-64 So every spring, 'twould be handy about the last woods work would be done [and we'd] get the flake boughs. T 49-64 There was no woods work there done, an' people get their own firewood an' their stuff for fencin'. 1966 FARIS 39 'Woods work' usually starts soon after the first snows in October or early November and lasts intermittently until April. To haul wood out by slide it is necessary that the bogs and ponds be frozen deep enough to support the weight of a horse and fully-loaded slide, and that there be enough snow to enable the slide to function.

# The Bowl

## Lillian Bouzane

The bowl was large. It was a gift. It had a deep chocolate glaze. It could hold a dozen and a half delicious reds. It stood on the counter and held the day's fruit: apples, oranges, bananas and, in season, a persimmon or two. In my white and wheat coloured kitchen it caught the eye.

Its full lustre was on display, however, only on the occasion of Halloween, when I filled it with apples and placed it on the floor under the light in the front hall and waited for the bell to ring.

As I opened the door to the first goblin of the night, the light over the door and the light in the hall streamed together and produced dancing stars on the glaze of the chocolate rim and they, in turn, bounced off the gleam and glimmer of the apples; the goblins—dazzled—squealed with delight.

As the children came and went, I found myself waiting for the uncovering of the aubergine waterfall that started at the rim of the bowl and circled half way around and down the inner side. The last few apples picked off the bottom uncovered the creamy froth stippled in spray and foam.

I often wondered why in all the years I owned the bowl I didn't give it its proper place on the floor in the living room, or in my study, for it was only when it was empty and I looked down into it, did the midnight waterfall that cascaded its inner side guide my eye to the burst of spray at the bottom. It never ceased to delight.

The last Halloween I owned the bowl, more children came to the door than usual, and I had refilled it a number of times. Finally, the bell fell silent, and I was standing contemplating the design and sheen when a ripple around the rim, that I hadn't noticed before, caught my attention. I was standing there in that forgetfulness of self and surroundings that an object so lovely instills when my father came up behind me on his slippered feet; I was startled by his question.

What do you see?

I believe that ridge at the lip of the bowl might have been made by the thumb of the potter.

My father bent, picked up the bowl, put it in the crook of his arm, and traced his thumb around the ridge.

Yes, I think you're right.

I have been given other pieces of pottery over the years, and some that stand here and there in my house I have purchased, but it's the bowl: the high gloss of its chocolate sides, its aubergine waterfall, the spray rising at the bottom, and the signature of the potter's thumb, that I remember on a day.

*Stoneware Bowl*, stoneware clay and glaze with gold lustre, 13" x 2 1/2" (33 x 6 cm), 1995, Bonnie Leyton

# Raku: Sod

for Sharon Puddester

**Mary Dalton**

*Fire cannot bee hid in the straw, nor the nature of man
so concealed, but at last it will have his course.*
                                        — Thomas Lodge, *Rosalynde*

Wodge. Lump. Clod.
Riddle me.

Riddle me. My mothers:
Clay and fire and straw
And the shaper's hands.

Hands on/of sod.
Seething of earth
Out of, into, up from
The clay mother, her turfy
Enticements. Let me out.

Let me out: knead, slap, tear—
Knobs, hollows, gouges—
You caving, I am forming myself,
You are finding me, I am bubbling up,
Yeasty ferment twisting in your blood.

Twisting in blood out of bog and inferno
I am dragging myself up dragging you are
You being that surges
Out into, along with
The breathing, you breathe, I am breathing—
Who is roiling here into birth?

Who roils along my clayey flanks
Swelling them to muscle bulging
Great hams and calves, the taut
And eloquent feet, clenched into, against
The pull downward, the mother I must
Wrestle out of, the mother I must
Know, my own spores, while writhing out of her?

Writhing out of her, my back a gleaming furrow,
Mica glints on field, my potato beginnings,
And the lifting, I am shaping myself
Out of my own being, the hand, yes, my hand
Poised to augment, augment. Moving into a

Face out of that cracked glaze, broken time.
The infinite, taut moment: creating, dissolving.

The taut moment: here Adam, Antaeus
And Caliban gather. A ghost in the future,
Rodin's thinker beckons. My mother laughs,
Calls me home, down. Her mud-crooning
Bathes me in the warm dark. Still I go on.
The pulse of fire burns in me now.
My hand will rise slowly to the hacked and broken mosaic,
There where my eyes will glimpse their own image,
There where my mouth will pour out its song.

*Sod*, raku fired clay sculpture, 9 1/2" x 11" x 5"
(24 x 28 x 13 cm), 1989, private collection

*Ash Wednesday: Portrait of Poet, Al Pittman*, Gerald Squires

# Portrait of the Artist as a Young Mortician

**Al Pittman**

I had seen some of Gerry Squires's portraits before. And I had admired them as I had the rest of his work, some of which I had viewed at various stages between conception and completion as he brushed them into being in one or another of his studios. By then he had committed to walls his own angel's eye version of Ted Russell (the writer), Arch Williams (the painter), Gail Squires (the potter), and God-only-knows-who-else.

But I had never been there to watch while he went delving with his brushes into anyone's soul, went lopping off layers of facial flesh in search of that elusive mechanism that makes someone sink or swim, float or fly, or drown. Until one night he had a go at me.

I was living in St. John's at the time, having recently arrived from Fogo Island via Kelligrews. Gerry and I had been friends for some years by then. Ever since Shoal Brook and the flashing mackerel we caught in Bonne Bay and devoured with grace beforehand after meals in the landwashed and sea-swept house he then called home.

My father had come from Corner Brook to visit and Gerry had come from Ferryland to paint my portrait. And he did.

After the inaugural several drinks of over-proof rum, Gerry Squires, the artist, got down to business. He insisted I put on my winter coat; a red plaid sheep-wool lined coat that would roast you outdoors in February on top of the Gaff Topsails. I did, and sat where he sat me, on a stool across the width of the kitchen table where he stood opposite with his assembly of scalpels; several buckets of paint, some number of brushes (the size you'd use to paint clapboards or palings), a knee-high stack of old newspapers, a forty-ouncer of London Dock, and his bluer than sky blue eyes, like two propane torches, aimed at me.

It was a most marvelous and excruciating many hours. Gerry would look, blink, look, dab, sweep, look, swipe, sip, and tell me to have another. On and on it went.

And this is what was all so upside-down about it. The way he did it. The portrait.

There he is. All hair and eyes. Broad brush in hand. He smears the empty rectangular space with broad-sword swipes at the enemy, blankness. Up with a page of newspaper. He puts it down, almost nonchalantly, over his mess of colours. He presses the heel of his hand to the paper and smudges off the smudges he's painted. This he does again and again, and again. It is going to go on forever. It is madness without method. My father, the innocent bystander, isn't as innocent as he pretends to be. He's painted many a thing in his lifetime: boats, fences, houses, stages, stores, window boxes, wheelbarrows, birdhouses, oars, rake handles, and once, for no purpose at all, a piece of driftwood resembling nothing under the sun. He's not scouring. But I know he is skeptical of all this. And yet, he knows, as I do, that Gerry is, after all, an artist. And, until now, has been a very good artist. A very fine painter.

Some hours and many overflowing glasses of London Dock later, he's still at it. Sweep, smudge, erase. Layer upon layer of paint to no purpose. Until, not suddenly at all, there's something emerging there among the mess of incoherent colours. Gradually, vaguely, distorted perhaps by some original sin or other, I am being born before my very own blind-faith eyes. I am beginning to believe I know nothing about this artist's art. Nothing about any art at all. It ought not to be a startling revelation to me. But it is.

My father has gone to bed. He's come a long way to see me and I haven't yet so much as given him the time of day. Or night.

Gerry, finally, as the dawn sweeps its own bright brush over the western edge of the Atlantic ocean, says, "Pour yourself another and come see." And I do.

And there I am on the kitchen table looking up at myself as ugly as sin. Beautiful.

I wrap my arms around my friend for what he has done. He hugs me, and forgives himself for what he has had to do. He puts the portrait in the armchair in the corner of the living room to dry. There it is. Sitting upright in the chair. Me, scalped down to the last layer by this soul-surgeon, this very good friend of mine.

We finish off the last of the London Dock and go to bed, determined to sleep in our diverse and separate worlds. Perhaps to dream of worlds swirling with mackerel and mermaids. I don't know.

I didn't know then either. What I remember is that I didn't sleep at all. Couldn't. In time, I gave up tossing and turning and went downstairs. I was in the kitchen tempestuously trying to pour myself a cup of instant coffee when my father, wide awake, with that same early morning alertness that had been his affliction all his life, descended from on high, turned abruptly into the living room, took one look out of the corner of his eye at the chair, where sat the portrait of his first-born son.

From the kitchen, while hunting for sugar, I heard him address the thing sitting in the living-room armchair.

"Al," he said, with all his fatherly might, "you haven't gone to bed yet! Turn in, for Godsake. Get some sleep. You've been up all night. Now you'll be in bed all day. And besides, you don't look well."

From around the corner, between the elusive sugar bowl and the impenetrable can of Carnation milk, I dared to stammer a bold "Good morning, Dad!"

My father damn near died. Such a strenuous effort to conceal embarrassment could have killed a less healthy man.

In an effort to get us both back on track, I gave up on my inadequate attempts to open the can of milk, poured another cup of awful coffee and spiked both servings with whatever was left over from the endless hours past.

While Gerry slept downstairs on the basement floor, dreaming perhaps of the Ferryland Downs or some woman unknown on the planet Earth, my father and I sat there in the dim light of early day, each of us trying hard to pay no attention at all to the portrait, the portrayal of the son he'd hoped for so long with such futility to be so proud of.

Years later, one near fatal afternoon I'd rather not recall, Gerry's portrait of me burned along with almost everything else I treasured. The sudden destruction of things irreplaceable, things that mean more than what they are, is hard to take at times. And those things aren't easily forgotten. On the other hand though, I have no desire to forget them.

My father used to tell a comical version of the morning he gave my portrait a dressing down, one of the few tongue-bangings he had ever given me. He's long gone to memory now, but Gerry and I still smile about it all when we meet. Anyway why wouldn't we? I still don't look all that well. And I could still do with a good night's sleep.

In that sense only, nothing much has changed. In every other sense almost everything else has changed and "changed utterly" since then. Gerry Squires, with all his embalmer's art could not make anyone indelible. He could not preserve his subjects, rescue them, enlighten them, or enliven their lives. He painted them as he saw them, for what they were. To know how close he came to accuracy in my case you'd perhaps have to ask my father. But of this I'm certain. Neither Gerry's vision nor my father's admonishment had anything to do with eyesight. Recognition maybe, but nothing to do with eyesight.

**fetch**: n *OED* ~ sb²1 (1787-1871), *EDD* sb¹ for sense 1; cp *EDD* 13 'quantity fetched or carried at one time' for sense 3.

1 An apparition or double of a living person, the appearance of which often portends death or disaster; ghost; TOKEN.

1924 ENGLAND 219 'Fetches,' or spirits, are annoyingly familiar at sea. They wander about vessels and try to get the crew to chat with them; also with ghostly hands they essay to remove human ones from the wheel. If the living steersman will only keep cool and quiet and hold fast, the fetch will presently disappear; if not, and the fetch gets possession of the wheel, woe to that ship! 1937 DEVINE 21 ~ An apparition of an acquaintance that the observer knew to be in a distant locality. 1968 DILLON 138 If I didn't meet you on the road last night, 'twas your fetch. C 68-16 A fetch is something seen which resembles a human person. It may be seen at night or day usually before or after a person dies. A person may see his own fetch. C 71-95 To see someone's fetch from midnight to noon was a sign that person would soon die, but to see a fetch from noon to midnight was a sign that person still had a long life.

2 A phantom ship.

T 55/7-64 Lots o' people see her beating in here under sail, you know, this schooner—the fetch or whatever you call it.

3 A cargo (of seals) (1925 *Dial Notes* v, 330).

**fetch** v *OED* ~ 10 naut; *EDD* ~ 11 esp s w cties. To reach, arrive at.

1937 DEVINE 21 ~ To reach a point steered for in a boat. P 113-56 We should fetch the point on this tack. 1966 SCAMMELL 78 Not hardly, grandpa, with this wind I think we can just about fetch to the nets. P 108-70 He didn't fetch home till dark. 1971 HORWOOD 22 The wind hauled farther ahead and the schooner could not fetch Baccalieu Tickle.

# With Love from the Andes: Some Multicultural Facts about Jiggs's Dinner

Kathleen Winter

One of the hallmarks of a culture has always been its food—but we are often so familiar with our own dinner tables that we don't realize the food upon them does not belong to us alone. In Newfoundland, "Jiggs's dinner"—a boiled dinner of salt beef, cabbage, potatoes, carrots and turnips—seems to us to be the traditional Newfoundland meat-based dish. Newfoundlanders on the mainland long for it on Sundays, and Newfoundland men or women who marry spouses from "away" long to go back to their parents' houses where they can get Jiggs's dinner without heavy negotiations. Until recent years, every Newfoundland outporter had a "cabbage garden," where the vegetable ingredients of the meal were grown, and even with the demise of traditional outport ways, Newfoundland vegetable markets always offer cabbage, potatoes, carrots and turnips. Because they grow in our soil and climate which support few more exotic vegetables without intensive care, we equate these four vegetables with our windy, rocky, salty habitat. We think of them as sturdy and hardy; in this we even equate them with ourselves as a people. In doing so, we are linking ourselves with cultures in South America, Europe, Asia and Africa, because these are the lands from which these plants come. While the multiculturalism of some mainland areas may be more readily visible than here in Newfoundland, just one look at these staple foods can remind us how basically we are connected with the peoples of parts of the world that we think of as exotic or distant.

Humble potatoes, for instance, came originally not from Ireland where we might place them, but from the Andes mountains in South America. The first record of the white potato comes from Juan Castellano, who wrote of Inca campfires and potatoes abandoned when conquistadors invaded the little mountain village of Sorocota. Sophisticated by European agricultural standards of the time, Inca gardeners used crop rotation and irrigation in their potato fields. They preserved the harvest of potatoes by freezing them in glacial drifts, sun-drying them, and storing them in cool caves. It is believed that Francis Drake brought potatoes from South America to Ireland, where they were planted on the estate of Walter Raleigh and slowly gained the reputation of being able to save poor families from starvation at very little expense. Gradually their reputation spread throughout Europe, and in the 1800s, missionaries introduced the potato to the Far East.

The cabbage, a popular vegetable in Eastern Europe, especially Poland, Bohemia, Germany, Austria, and Russia, is thought to have derived from wild cabbages found growing among rocks by the seashore in numerous distant lands. Wild cabbages grow on the isle of Laland in Denmark, the island of Heligoland, the south of England and Ireland, the Channel Isles, and the islands off the coast of Charente Inferieure. They also grow on the Mediterranean's north coast, near Nice, Genoa and Lucca. This wild cabbage was gathered and used by people before it was cultivated. But even cultivated cabbages have a long history. Introduced to Britain by the Romans, the English have eaten them for at least 2,000 years.

Carrots still exist in their original wild form, known as Queen Anne's Lace. Native to Europe, Asia and North Africa, the wild carrot was used by Greeks and Romans as a medicine for various purposes that included protection from poisonous bites and love potions. In its wild state the carrot was extremely bitter, not like the sweet version we now know. This change came about during the fifteenth century when the carrot was introduced to Holland. During wars of the Middle Ages, the Dutch had had to substitute vegetables for meat. They took the bitter wild carrot and improved its size, flavour and colour, before exporting it to England with fruit and other vegetables.

The turnip is believed to be a native of temperate parts of Eurasia, where it has been cultivated for centuries and valued as an important food source, both for its root and its vitamin-rich leaves. Another, more slender-rooted, form of turnip originated from the Scandinavian peninsula and spread towards Siberia and the Caucasus. It was likely introduced to China and Japan through Siberia some time just before the epoch of Greco-Roman civilization.

Already we have traveled—just by eating the boiled vegetables of traditional "Newfoundland" Jiggs's dinner—through Siberia, the Andes, Bohemia and Heligoland. Think where you could find yourself should you explore the origins of the little cucumbers and mustard plants that make up the mustard pickles essential to a good Jiggs's dinner, not to mention the salt, the pepper, and of course, the beef. Even the name, "Jiggs's dinner," does not come from Newfoundland, but was adopted by its people from a world-wide syndicated comic strip in which corned beef and cabbage was the favourite meal of Jiggs, the main character. We might think, in Newfoundland and Labrador, separated by geography and climate from the mainstream of the Canadian kaleidoscope, that we are not as culturally diverse as much of the country. But to learn about the food of our people—the most basic element of our physiology—is to think otherwise. If, as some believe, there is a connection between our physical and inner selves, we could say that our island nature in Newfoundland, and our cultural separateness in Labrador, are only illusions.

# The Brule Men

Peter Leonard

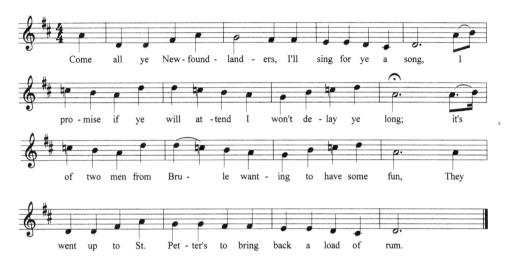

Come all ye New-found-land-ers, I'll sing for ye a song, I
pro-mise if ye will at-tend I won't de-lay ye long; it's
of two men from Bru - le want-ing to have some fun, They
went up to St. Pet-ter's to bring back a load of rum.

The day had been a fine one, and the sun was shining bright;
When those two men from Brule arrived there just at night.
They took on board a heavy stock, and then the wind veered down;
They then set sail for Brule, leaving St. Peter's town.

The wind did last us to St. Lawrence and the sky looked kind of black.
Our skipper said now we'll go in where we can take a nap.
We anchored 'round the point of the beach and put a line ashore.
Our skipper said now we can sleep while the wind and sea do roar.

That night the storm kept raging, but we came through all right.
And when the water smoothened down, again we put her out.
And late up in the evening the sky looked kind of clear,
But very shortly after the wind began to veer.

The wind veered off about nor' nor' west and the sky fell thick with snow;
And now the storm is raging and now where can we go.
We had no compass for a guide no means to make a light.
The waters still washed over us on that cold winter's night.

We must give up and pray to God our skipper he did say.
For we can't live no longer, for this is our last day.
They thought of friends and loved ones who they had left on shore;
And took each other by the hand to part for evermore.

Oh, who can tell the feelings of those two Brule men?
Tossed on the stormy ocean, no one to comfort them.
The blood was frozen in their veins the salt tears in their eyes.
They raised their heads to heaven above and uttered mournful cries.

They drifted before wind and sea all that long cruel night.
And when the daylight cleared away no land or strand in sight.
But very shortly after a vessel hove in sight;
The captain's name was Harvey, out that long winter's night.

When Harvey saw them coming he called all hands on deck.
"Oh, come and look to win'ard and see that little jack.
Have we no means of saving them?" he said unto his crew.
"Get ropes and lifeboats ready and we'll see what we can do."

Those men got near that vessel hailing with all their might.
Crying, "Save us, captain, save us; do try to save our lives."
There was not time for talking, he told them what to do.
"Just run around our quarter, and then heave her head to."

In the shelter of the vessel drifted that little jack.
When they got hold of those two men they dragged them in on deck.
And took them to the cabin where they were treated fine;
And placed them by a hard coal fire and gave them hot claret wine.

Now Harvey he gave orders unto his men did say:
"The wind is on the drop, me boys, so get her under way.
Go trim your canvas by the wind, and then well reach her down."
And on the following evening we arrived in Marystown.

Oh, telegrams were soon dispatched unto their friends and wives;
And said how Harvey picked them up and saved their precious lives.
Theirselves, will tell the story on some cold winter's night,
In praise of Captain Harvey who saved them from their plight.

It was the hand of Providence that brought him in this bay,
And saved those men from Brule all for a longer day.
They thought their time had come to go their friends to see no more;
But now they're safely landed once more on Brule's shore.

Before that I do finish for Harvey I must say:
May the great God protect him while sailing on the sea.
And grant him all the pleasures in every port he'll find,
For saving those two Brule men and acting very kind.

Come all you men from Brule, I'll have you to beware;
Don't you go to St. Peter's in the springtime of the year,
While winter storms are raging I'm afraid you'll get a fright.
And Harvey won't be always there waiting to save your life.

Excerpt from

# The Broadcast: The Story of CBC Radio's Fisheries Broadcast

## Jim Wellman

They said it wouldn't work. They even had a label for it. "Ghetto programming" they called it. Afraid that a radio program about a single industry would be so narrowly focused it would not attract an audience, everyone said it would not last.

They were wrong. It did work, and now, going on fifty years later, it is still working.

For years, CBC Radio's *Fisheries Broadcast* has not only been working but is considered an "authority" in the fisheries constituency it serves. Even Newfoundland's law courts accept the Broadcast as a matter of public record, acceptable as evidence. Hosts of the *Fisheries Broadcast* are often required to tell the court whether a certain announcement, usually from the Department of Fisheries and Oceans (DFO), was broadcast. The announcements usually concern opening and closing dates of fishing seasons. Circumstances often dictate that DFO is unable to announce an opening or closing date until a day or two before the day in question. When that happens DFO depends, almost exclusively, on the Broadcast to publicize the announcement.

Fishermen, charged with setting a net or trap in a closed season, may argue they didn't know the season was closed. If a fisherman challenges the charge in court, Fisheries Broadcast hosts are usually subpoenaed to sign an affidavit stating whether or not the announcement was broadcast. That affidavit often makes the difference between a conviction or a dismissal of charges because the court accepts the Broadcast as a sufficient notice to fishermen. As one listener put it, "if it was on the *Fishermen's Broadcast* it was not only the gospel, it was also the law."

The "Fishermen's" Broadcast, as it was called, went on the air in March, 1951. The name changed to "Fisheries Broadcast" in the more politically correct days of the 1980s. But whether it is "Fishermen's" or "Fisheries" is almost irrelevant because the vast majority of listeners affectionately know it simply as "The Broadcast."

The Broadcast is the longest running program in Canada. It is probably one of the longest running daily programs in North America. There are radio programs that have been on the air more than forty-seven years, but most of them, if not all, are broadcast just one day a week. The Grand Ole Opry in Nashville, still popular after seventy-two years, is broadcast live on Saturday nights. The Detroit Symphony, now hosted by Dick Cavett, has been on the air for seventy-seven years but is broadcast just one day a week. There may be radio programs somewhere that are older than the Fisheries Broadcast, but there are not many.

From March 5,1951 to this day, the Broadcast has enjoyed a loyal following. Despite early doubts and fears of "ghettoising," that loyalty should not have been surprising. After all, the Broadcast deals with subject matter that directly affects and touches the essence of what tens of thousands of Newfoundlanders have been for hundreds of years—sea people.

Surprisingly though, the Broadcast holds a special attraction for thousands of people who have nothing to do with the fisheries. It surprised many people, including most hosts of the programs, that thousands of so-called "townies" and other urbanites listened to the Broadcast as faithfully as fishermen. I have often wondered why bankers, nurses, lawyers or salespeople from urban centres listened so intently. I'm still not sure. Some said they were simply interested in knowing what was happening "around the bay." Others, salespeople for example, said they listened to the Broadcast to get a feel for what was happening in outport areas before they went there on a sales trip.

"If I heard that the cod fishing was good or the lobster season was bad, it gave me an idea what my sales meeting might be like," one salesman said. "But more than that, knowing what was happening in the fishery always gave me a confidence that I could carry on a conversation with people in the outports about the issues they wanted to discuss. I could only get that information from the *Fishermen's Broadcast*—it gave me some appropriate small-talk before I started to do business."

A lot of the Broadcast listeners had relatives back home who were fishermen or plant workers. In many cases, they themselves had grown up "around the bay" and had fished with their fathers and mothers or brothers and sisters. Others worked in the local fish plant when they were young; some financed their way though university on summer employment at the plant. One doesn't have to dig far into the history of most urban dwellers in this province to find a direct link to the bay and the fishery.

Several urban centres have a fishing presence right in their backyards. Corner Brook is best known for its pulp and paper industry, but the Bay of Islands is home to hundreds of fishermen who fish from both small and large vessels. The province's largest herring fleet is based in Curling, on the western fringe of that city. The Barry group of companies in Curling operates a fleet of five herring seiners, all of which are more than a hundred feet in length.

St. John's, the province's capital and largest city, has been described as the biggest outport of all. That's not just a reference to the fact that St. John's is built around a harbour; it is also factually true in fishing terms. St. John's has always been home to a large inshore fishing fleet. For generations, family names like Critch, Wells, Alcock and Meadus have been synonymous with some of the most prominent trap fishermen in the province.

Like his father and grandfather, St. John's fisherman Lloyd Critch trapped cod all his adult life. "I remember a time when there were more than forty trap crews here," he said.

With five or six members per crew, that means St. John's had more than 200 inshore fishermen fishing from the Battery, the South Side, and Quidi Vidi. Just around the corner from St. John's is Petty Harbour, a community of several hundred inshore fishermen.

Large fishing operations based in St John's dated back many years. Companies such as Baird's, Job's, Bowring's and Steers were part of the cityscape for years. In more recent times, National Sea Products had a large fish plant on the south side of St. John's. That plant operated a fleet of large steel trawlers until the cod moratorium in 1992.

Today, St. John's harbour is perhaps the busiest fishing port in Newfoundland.

Dozens of longliners and fishing vessels of just about every description land there, almost daily, with catches ranging from crab to monkfish. In 1992 the federal government spent seven million dollars on a landing and off-loading facility on the south side of St. John's harbour at Fort Amherst.

While fisheries make up a large part of the urban identity, there are other reasons why so many urbanites listen to the Broadcast. It's a different kind of radio program. It's not just different because it deals exclusively with the fishery—it's different in sound and it's different in its style. Guests on the Broadcast are not always the head of a company or the president of some organization or a spokesperson for a group. For most of its existence the *Fisheries Broadcast*, almost daily, talked to what we called "real people"—ordinary men and women who harvested fish or worked in fishplants. It didn't matter what their status was—they didn't have to be anyone "special." It didn't matter what accents they had either.

I remember an interview with a plant worker from the south coast. The interview was about the delay in reopening his fish plant that spring. When I asked him when he expected the plant to be operating, he said "we were opin' to be hopen on Monday." Like all of our listeners, I knew he said "we were hoping to be open on Monday."

Dr. Peter Narváez, a folklore professor at Memorial University, once described the Broadcast as "Folk Talk and Hard Facts." He was referring specifically to one of the most famous features of the Broadcast, "The Chronicles of Uncle Mose," but his description applies to the Broadcast in general terms as well. The Broadcast talks to all kinds of folk about all kinds of facts.

Ged Blackmore has some insights into the special nature of the *Fisheries Broadcast* and why people with no direct attachment to the fishery are attracted to it. Ged is one of the main driving forces behind "Folk of the Sea," a group of one hundred fishermen and fisherwomen who have celebrated their culture on stage through song, storytelling and dance since the moratorium on cod fishing in 1992. If Ged were not so modest I'd say he was the driving force behind the group but I know he would chastise me for writing it that way, so I won't.

Ged faxed me a few of his thoughts on my last day with the CBC:

> Jim, you know of course, you are not departing just a radio station or just a radio program—you're leaving "The Broadcast," a kind of reserved and sacred place in this singular culture of ours. For wherever we go with the Hibernias and Voiseys Bays and Hydro and Governments, we began with fish. This is why so many people in this province who were not fish harvesters, who did not come from fishing communities, who did not know a haddock from a halibut "listened in," betimes, to the Broadcast; we kept in touch with vessel reports, the list of lights, the marine forecasts, the stories of the fisheries and the oceans. And we listened in most of all, because of the voices—voices whose shape and sound and words define where we came from and who we are.

I only wish I could have said it so eloquently.

# Let Me Fish Off Cape St. Mary's

**Otto Kelland**

Take me back to my Wes-tern boat, let me fish off Cape St. Ma-ry's, where the hag-downs sail and the fog-horns wail, with my friends the Browns and the Clea-ry's. Let me fish of Cape St. Mar - y's.

Let me feel my dory lift,
To the broad Atlantic combers;
Where the tide rips swirl and the wild ducks whirl,
Where Old Neptune calls the numbers
'Neath the broad Atlantic combers.

Let me sail up Golden Bay,
With my oilskins all a-streamin'
From the thunder squall, when I hauled my trawl,
And my old Cape Ann a-gleamin',
With my oilskins, all a-streamin'.

Let me view that rugged shore,
Where the beach is all a-glisten,
With the caplin spawn, where from dusk to dawn,
You bait your trawl and listen
To the undertow a-hissin'.

When I reach that last big shoal,
Where the ground swells break asunder,
Where the wild sands roll to the surge's toll,
Let me a man and take it,
When my dory fails to make it.

Take me back to that snug green cove,
Where the seas roll up their thunder.
There let me rest in the earth's cool breast,
Where the stars shine out their wonder,
And the seas roll up their thunder.

# Eighteen

**Janet Fraser**

A florist brought me your gift of eighteen roses,
blood red buds on stems full of thorns.
I gave him a tip and said "Danke schön."
The post came with your gold heart on a chain.
I put it in my pocket and ripped the envelope,
then piled up your blue air-mail letters
and lit the lot.

I smoked Gitane cigarettes,
drank Turkish coffee that kept me awake
as I lay under a rose eiderdown
and stared at glass jars full of weeds
picked in the hillside vineyards.
I slept only as the sun through half-closed shutters
put thick strips down through the dusty room.

I was glad to see the end of my birthday—
toasts to youth, wishes for joy.
At that moment I thought I was sick
not just of you but of me, too
I could have made plans
but instead prayed for a long sleep.

I could not imagine a torture more complete
than life in this foreign country
full of ghosts of war and crimes
where a brassy blonde Grandmama, bracelets jangling,
whispered, "We should have won, you know,"
and the corner greengrocer had only a pillow to talk to
about his coming of age in a Hitler Youth suit.

# Jeans

**Peggy Smith Krachun**

Smoke is pouring from every crack and seam in the charred walls of the nightclub. A fireman is hacking at the door in a heroic effort to rescue the one man still trapped inside—the manager of the ill-fated club. Finally the door gives way and the fireman stands in the entrance, peering through the thick clouds of smoke. The man is lying on the floor just inside the door, coughing and crying weakly for help. As the fireman spots him and starts to rush in, the man raises his arm and, with the last bit of strength left in his body, pulls open the fireman's coat, revealing trousers of blue denim material underneath. "Get out" the man gasps with his dying breath. "You're not allowed in here with jeans on!"

Ridiculous, you say. Of course. But so is the rule forbidding blue jeans in many of our nightclubs. Some places have it, some don't. In the case of those that do, beware: You might as well try to get in wearing prison stripes and a ball and chain.

I went to a union meeting one night with a friend. A union meeting is not usually a dress-up occasion, and we were both wearing blue jeans. We decided to stop in at one of our favourite watering spots on the way home. This particular club has two rules: You have to be age 25 or over, and jeans are not allowed. We were overqualified for admission on the first count, and we never dreamed the second one would be strictly enforced on a Tuesday night. We were sure no one would notice or care.

We were about halfway to the bar when the bartender came out from behind it and started walking toward us. He stopped in front of us, hands on his hips, his eyes moving up and down the length of our bodies. Feeling a little embarrassed but flattered by the attention, I smiled and said hello. My friendly greeting was rewarded with a stony stare, and in a tone I would have thought reserved for child-beaters and sex offenders, he said to us, "You'll have to leave right now. Jeans are not allowed in this club."

So it wasn't our shapes he'd been interested in at all—only the material they were covered with. We slunk out, tails between our denim-clad legs. Something in his voice had surprised me. Not the pleasure he'd gotten from exercising his small bit of authority—years in the work world had accustomed me to that. No, what took me aback was the hint of fear in his voice. It was as if he actually thought we might start a racket when he told us we couldn't stay. Those blue jeans had obviously given us, at least in his mind, an air of toughness we didn't really possess. The funniest thing about the whole incident was that except for the bartender, my friend and myself, the club was absolutely empty. Still, the poor fellow was only following orders laid down by a higher authority. As he explained to us the next time we went in properly dolled up, a rule is a rule.

But why the rule? Exactly what is wrong with blue jeans? Another pair of pants can be exactly the same style, with the same feature—fly front, back pockets, studs and double stitching—but if they're not made of blue denim, they're okay. This would lead to the conclusion that it's the denim material itself that's disreputable. But on closer examination, this theory doesn't hold up. I can walk into nightclub wearing a blue denim skirt, jumper or vest, and not be harassed. So it seems to be the combination—pants made out of blue denim. Now, denim jeans of another colour might also be chancy, but the closer you get to blue, the more you increase your likelihood of being tossed out.

So *why* are blue jeans unacceptable in some places, to some people? Could it be a holdover from the days when blue denims were the mark of the working class? The labourer could walk into his neighbourhood bar for a drink after work, wearing paint-spattered or grime-caked "overalls," and he and his money welcomed with open arms. But he wouldn't think of walking into some "respectable" establishment dressed the same way, for fear he might offend the more upper-class patrons as they sipped delicately on their daiquiris.

Jeans, however, started to spread out from the ranches and construction sites into the mainstream of society. Men had little trouble integrating them into their wardrobes, since they were already wearing pants, and in those days females weren't, except for the naughty, "mannish" ones who wouldn't play by the rules. But sometime in the fifties, teenage girls discovered blue jeans, rolled them up to their knees, and accessorized them with bobby socks, saddle oxfords, and their fathers's shirts, and a new era began. I still fondly remember my first pair, fresh from Eaton's catalogue and about six sizes too big. I'd waited so long, I couldn't bear to send them back and wait another month, and besides, everybody else already had a pair—so I tugged them up under arms, pulled them together with a piece of rope, and wore them proudly.

Over the years, jeans began to catch on with a few of the more progressive oldsters, and eventually wriggled their way into the affections of all but the most diehard dandies. Although it's taken a while, they've finally gained a great degree of respectability as a "go anywhere" garment. Even in the sixties, when the "hippies" adopted them as their uniform and wore them bleached, tie-dyed, frayed, and decorated with psychedelic patches, they still remained popular among the more conservative elements in society. And since the mid-seventies, jeans have ridden the crest of fashion, changing their lines slightly to go along with whatever silhouette is "in" at any given time, but remaining basically the same. Their popularity has spawned a host of other garments and fad items made from the same material. As well as the more ordinary skirts, vests, jackets and jumpers, we have hats, purses, sneakers, watch bands, earrings—well, the list goes on and on, with smart entrepreneurs cashing in on the denim craze by adding new items every day.

It's no wonder that jeans are so popular. They're serviceable, durable, comfortable, and the tightly-woven material has a girdling effect that's flattering to almost every type of figure. And if there's still any lingering doubt that they deserve a place of honour in civilized society, let me assure you that they are not cheap. A pair of designer jeans will net a neat sum of money for the seller, and even at a discount store you'll be hard-pressed to find a pair of jeans for under twenty-five dollars. I've heard that in the Soviet Union, our Western jeans are sold on the black market for the equivalent of well over a hundred dollars a pair. In the famous TV commercial we've seen Brooke babbling about how "nothing comes between her and her Calvins," although I personally find this a little hard to swallow. Can you imagine your tender skin right next to a pair of tight jeans, with their heavy, stiff denim material and hard, thick seams? It's a chafing thought.

Still, for people with sense enough to wear underwear, jeans are marvellous. They are constantly being praised in songs. Neil Diamond vows to stay forever in blue jeans; Conway Twitty rhapsodizes about a lady who's a tiger in tight-fittin' jeans; and I heard a song recently which announces that there's an amazing girl somewhere who can actually make her blue jeans talk.

University professors wear them, they're permitted in many offices, they're acceptable in most schools, and I'll bet that if I ever had the nerve to check, I'd find that priests wear them under their cassocks. But still many nightclubs persist in the rule: Proper Dress Required—No Jeans. When pressed for an explanation, a club manager will tell you that he personally has nothing against jeans—some of his best friends wear them, and he may even admit to owning a pair himself, although he keeps them in the closet—but the rule helps to keep riff-raff out. This leads us to deduce that "riff-raff" are frequently clad in jeans, which is no doubt true—but so are many of us law-abiding citizens. Surely there must be a more reliable way to recognize trouble-makers, and any bartender worth his salted peanuts should have a better gauge than the material in a person's trousers. As a matter of fact, the last fight I witnessed in a club was started by a white-haired man of about sixty, wearing a black and white houndstooth check polyester double-knit suit—with a red necktie.

Now, it's not that I have nothing else to wear. I love to dress up on a Friday or Saturday night in my most dazzling duds, silks and satins, frills and flounces, handkerchief tails and such, and go out on the town. I'd even go along with the "proper dress" rule in some clubs, on weekends, as it does help to create a certain "Saturday Night Fever" atmosphere that can be lots of fun if you're out with that kind of a time in mind, but on week nights, when you're weary from your gym-and-swim workout or your philosophy class or your union meeting, all you want to do is soothe your muscles, mind or ruffled feathers in a quiet club with a cold beer. If you have to go home and change first, you might as well stay there.

The places that book 'heavy metal' rock bands and cater to the young crowd don't, as a rule, forbid jeans, because they know they'd lose most of their business if they did. Instead of worrying about what the customers are wearing, they employ bouncers to take care of the riff-raff. I think next time I feel like stopping off somewhere for a drink on my way home, I'll just make sure I have my earplugs with me, and my jeans and I will patronize one of those places. Perhaps if everyone did that, the fussier clubs would eventually get the hint. After all, there's nothing lonelier than the ring of an empty cash register—and no crowd more poorly dressed than no crowd at all.

# Greenhair Goes for a Smoke

**Randall Maggs**

Flashing lights and yellow buses
crunching over ice, kids holding hands,
little blimps in snowsuits in the way—Christ! he wants
a drag or two, a word with friends, before the bell begins
another dreary day. No hat, no gloves, his hands balled up
inside his sleeves, he's bound for the gate where they gather
like bags and wrappers blown into the alders.
They hunch together against the wind. One
spots his new green hair. One with sufficient stature
slinks toward him like an assassin. They meet and grapple
carefully. All's forgotten for the moment, the fight with his father
over the hair, the bloodshot eyes turned away then *this* dump, the bell
and Mondays that lunatic Mrs. Donne with her rubbers and dongs
and basic math, except what he heard last week, half-known all along,
*something divided by one is itself.*

This is their high ground, their Golan Heights.
The boys talk percent, proof and over-proof, extolling
this brand of cigarette over that. The girls chew gum and try
a puff—they smoke straight on, their eyes turn in.
This is their Check-Point Charlie. They glower into
the other side's lights. They boo the Townsite bus, kids
in the choir, and taunt with mincing voice the minister's son
who figure-skates. One turns away elaborately, pretending
to retch, another favourite topic, the vocabulary
of vomit: *flash, barf, hurl, honk, the dry-heaves, tossed his cookies,
the technicolour yawn—Jesus, where'd you get that one!
Australia—I saw this cool movie.*

The alders are their signal palms, the jokes and talk
their cooling waters. One or two I've known since kindergarten
pageants: no Joseph from this crowd, of course, no Kings
or master-minding Angel. These were the cattle
with floppy horns, the comical sheep.
Half audience, they crowded around the cradle,
forbidden to scratch or squeak until Miss waggled her finger.

Then you could moo, though few of the fathers of cows
were there to hear. But, thinking then,
how did the Angel decide? And that Joseph.
Thinking even then how he pissed you off
with his holy fit when the Angel walks into the barn.
Just because his father was a minister.

The bell goes and groaning, they butt their smokes.
Greenhair's the last to go. Inside, he smells the smells
and hears the snickers at the lockers.
*Something divided by one is itself.*
Who had to tell him that?

**green man**: on a British migratory fishing
vessel, one of a specified number of inexperienced
men required by regulations to be carried on
the voyage; a novice; cp FRESH 1 YOUNGSTER.
[1661] 1954 INNIS 99 It was commanded that every
fifth man taken [out on a West Country fishing boat]
must be a 'green man.' [1963] 1793 REEVES ix That
every master or owner of any fishing ship going to
*Newfoundland* (after the said twenty-fifth day of
March), shall have in his ship's company every fifth
man a green man (that is to say) not a seaman, or
having been ever at sea before. [1701] 1895 PROWSE
228 These bye boat keepers...were most of them
ablefishermen and there was not one fresh man or
greenman amongst them as the Act requires. 1712
*West-India Merchant* 7 That will amount at a medium
to 16000 Men employ'd annually in this Trade; and on
fourth of those being usually green Men, it proves a
Nursery of 4000 Seamen *per ann.* for their Men of War
and Privateers. [1794] 1968 THOMAS 109 Her Husband
came over from England about Fifty-Five years ago
as an Adventurer—what is called here a green man,
which means a man that has never been in a Fishing
Boat on this Coast before. 1934 LOUNSBURY 130 In
order to provide a more continuous supply of sailors,
the proposed rules required that one out of every five
men engaged for the Newfoundland voyage should be
a green man, 'that is to say not a Seaman.'

# Adam and Eve on a Winter Afternoon

**Carmelita McGrath**

Adam comes in from sawing wood
with a chip on his shoulder.
And grunts. And heaves the wood down,
a heavy drop filled with creeping, unsaid things,
to the woodbox.

And Eve is trying to imagine it not there,
that slow and trembling thing within his breath
that lives between inhale and exhale. This
must be just exertion, and yet it feels
like a weapon, not quite secret but concealed.

She has words for such days—*wood hyacinth,*
*aurora borealis, Harley Davidson*—either
ethereal beauty or a fast-flying escape.
But the kitchen is a trap baited with supper cooking
and the imminent arrival of children.

And Adam says, "Whas for supper"?
And Eve says, "Soup."
And he says, "Any meat in it?
I hope you're not off meat again. Growing
children need their protein. And this
is no climate to be eating like rabbits."

And then the old clock rescued from a house
where pouncing bargain hunters drove deals
at a death sale
hammers four o'clock home.

And Eve thinks that four o'clocks are old-fashioned flowers,
and she stirs the soup and plunks down
in her bentwood rocker with her seed catalogues,
thinks *crocosmia*
thinks *branching tulip*
thinks *Apricot Beauty*
thinks *hemerocallis*

And the ragged thing between breath and breath
is there again, just for a second, a thing of air
with claws and teeth.

And Adam goes out for another load
before the early dark sinks in on him,
and while his saw buzzes
the language of massacre on wood
thinks *tomorrow's Friday*
thinks *pint of Guinness*
thinks *at least she dyed her hair*
thinks *I can hear the children*

Their footsteps saw over frozen grass, their voices
high, inadvertently calling everything back together,
one of them playing a blackbird's call on a recorder.

*Basket with Pears*, oil, 20" x 28" 1980, Helen Parsons Sheppard

*I enjoy painting in my own environment the things that I am familiar with
and like. I feel pure enjoyment when interpreting the objects I see around
me every day—the way light plays on white, the contrasting yellow of a
pear, how light filters through glass.*

— Helen Parsons Shepherd

# In the Chambers of the Sea

Susan Rendell

The air on the ward is hot and dry, and tastes like sand. Not that I have ever tasted sand, at least not since I was a child in a soft, sandy country, far from here.

In the cruel days of August, when the city became an asphalt oven, my mother and my sister and I would go off to the pretty little beaches, the domestic beaches of my childhood country. We would lie on the backs of their tame dunes and scuff along in the deep bone-white sand that was farthest from the sea, bending now and then to retrieve the half-buried remnants of dead sea babies: solemn little periwinkle cases, tiny bumps of limpet shells, stiff pieces of pink starfish. And bits of mother-of-pearl from the big mussel shells, which my sister and I pretended were solidified mermaid pee.

My favourites were the sand dollars. Every sand dollar, from the largest to the smallest, had a perfect flower etched on it, and I used to imagine that God's wife spent the long summer days making them in her shop in Heaven. At night She came down and tucked them, one by one, into the soft brown sand just under the lip of the sea, for me to find. (Like stars, sand dollars make it easy for a child to believe in God: look, there is a pattern, and another, and another. He must be!)

I took dozens of sand dollars home every summer. But after a few days they would start to rot, and by the end of the week they would have been consigned by my mother to the big aluminum garbage can. This made me bitter, as bitter as a child is able to be; I felt betrayed. I didn't know then that the sand dollars had been alive when I picked them from the sea, and that the flowers of the sea will not, cannot, take root in a suburban backyard.

The air in the hospital burns our eyes and flakes our skin. No one wears their contact lenses any more, and bottles of skin cream are handed around like whiskey at an Irish wake. The air is so dry because they nailed all the windows shut two weeks after I got here, when a young man jumped to his death from one of the other floors. He landed on a ledge outside my room, about a yard or so up from it. It was early in the morning, just before daybreak. Two nurses ran into my room and nearly ripped the blinds down from the window. "Sweet Jesus," said one to the other. "Can you see it?" And then they turned around. I was sitting up, groggy with sleeping-pill sleep, but already aching for a cigarette. "You'll have to get up, my duck," said the red-haired one. "We'll open up the smoking room for you." I asked what was going on, but they wouldn't tell me. I didn't really care anyway; the smoking room was to be opened, and I could sit and look out its east-facing window and watch the sun come up, if it was going to.

While I smoked I leafed through old copies of *Reader's Digest* and waited to be allowed back into my room. (It Pays to Increase Your Word Power; in the Beginning was the Word, and the Word was God. But what was the Word: Was it *Love*? *Om*? Was it *Good-bye*?)

Early that afternoon they summoned us to a grief therapy session. It was conducted by some nurses and a specialist in grief, a large woman in a suit; her hair was also wearing a suit, and her eyes were buttoned up tight. She introduced herself and then told us that a man, a young man, had "suicided." He had jumped from the seventh floor, she said,

157

and had landed, dying on impact, on the ledge projecting from the west side of our ward ("Westron wind, when will thou blow?/The small rain down can rain?/Christ, if my love were in my arms,/And I in my bed again!"). The grief lady talked about the need for us to come to terms with the "terrible thing." I recited Leigh Hunt's poem "Rondeau" over and over in my head while she talked. "Jenny kissed me when me met," Jenny kissed me, Jenny kissed me.

The grief lady said we should share our thoughts and feelings, and "vent if you need to." We patients are always being encouraged to "vent"; indeed, we are ordered to vent, at least biweekly. This process of venting is as intricate as a minuet: it must be done in front of a group, it must be done one person at a time, it must never contain anger or sarcasm or be directed at another person in the group, and, ideally, it should involve a copious amount of tears. To vent, to cry, to take a sea against an armful of troubles; to vent, perchance to heal; beat, beat, beat against thy cold grey breast, o patient; vomit up the sorrow that nourishes the worm of depression, flush it away with tears, idle tears. Weep, weep, weep; it seems odd to me that the air in here is as dry as it is.

When it was my turn, I said that at least the boy was at peace now, and that perhaps we should think of that and be glad for him. The doctor was waiting for me when I got back to my room. The nurses had told on me: Death was the enemy here, and I was a traitor. "You should not say such things," said the doctor angrily. "What about his family, and all the people who must suffer now because he has done this thing? And how do you know that he is at peace?" "How do you know he is not," I said. "What do you know, actually and really?"

The doctor reminds me of Toad of Toad Hall in *The Wind in the Willows*, only he is not as much fun. He doesn't like me. In the beginning, when he flicked out his thick tongue for my responses to his probing, I kept putting words on it that he couldn't digest. These days, I don't give him anything at all. He has told my husband that I won't listen to him, that I am stubborn. Now that I am eating three times a day, Dr. Toad mostly leaves me to his medical clerk, although he would be happier if I would cry in public, just once. Or even in private, as long as it was reported and noted on my chart.

Once, Dr. Toad's clerk asked me what my pain was like. I told her that I would rather go through childbirth every day than have this pain. But the pain is not in your body, it is in your mind, she said; no, I said, you are wrong, it is in every cell of my body, it bites at every nerve ending, it is immortal and omnipresent and omniscient and omnipotent. That was last month, though, before the pills kicked in. I can live in my body now, if I want to. It's a nice, safe, dead shell.

We heard later that the boy who jumped would have died within a day or two anyway. He was too young and impatient to wait, I guess, so he made the great leap into the arms of the Dark Angel. I imagined It carrying him out of his defeated body, up, up through the autumn fog, past the gulls that look like the silvery ghosts of birds and cry like ghosts, too; they sound so plaintive and eerie and anguished, although I can't hear them any more since they nailed the windows shut. But where did Death take him, I wonder. Somewhere? Anywhere? Nowhere?

There is a girl in here who sounds like a gull sometimes; she is fifteen, and she is here because she took a lot of LSD all at once. Last night I heard her keening in her room, like a gull with a broken wing. It made my stomach churn, but it is no good going in to her, because she doesn't know you are there when she is like that. One afternoon in the smoking room I saw her get up and claw at the air. She went up on her toes like a dancer *en pointe*—was jerked up, almost—and her head fell back, and she made a terrible noise in her throat. One of the other patients went for the nurse, and two of them came and led her away. She is never left alone, not even when she uses the bathroom. Her name is Deirdre, and she is elegantly slim and strong like a dancer, and shy and rude by turns, like most fifteen-year-olds. Unlike most fifteen-year-olds, she wants to die.

They tell me I am here because I said to my husband, quite calmly, that I intended to commit suicide. I don't remember saying that, but he wouldn't make it up. He has never made anything up in his life.

Before my husband could get me to the hospital, he had to coax me out from under our dining room table. Apparently, I had been sitting under it for an entire night and day, propped up against one of the four great carved mahogany legs, rocking myself and moaning. I hadn't eaten for five clays, my husband said, although I don't remember. I don't remember, I just don't remember; I remember the things I should not remember, and I leave unremembered the things I should remember. And there is no health in me.

I read Deirdre's palm the other night. It was difficult, because no one is allowed to touch her except her mother. Deirdre's mother reminds me of our old arthritic Lab, Mickey. Like him, she is short and dark and round and worn at the edges, and moves stiffly. Her anxious dog's eyes watch her daughter in the same way Mickey used to watch my husband and me when we went where he could no longer follow, such as into the North Atlantic at Salmon Cove. ("It's okay, Mickey," we would yell above the noise of the breakers, but he never believed us.) Deirdre's mother is waiting for her daughter to return from the sea of madness, waiting for the waves to throw up her real daughter, all bright and shining like Aphrodite on her shell in Botticelli's painting. But the nurses whisper and shake their heads when Deirdre passes, a bad augury.

The other night Deirdre's mother got Deirdre to hold her right hand out so I could divine her future; it moved slightly back and forth in the dim, aquatic light of the smoking room like a frond of the ferny seaweed you find in tide pools, and it was hard to make out the lines. She is so young, after all; even the major lines—the heart, the head, the line of life—are faint at her age, and Deirdre has fine skin. I never read my daughter's palm. I thought it would be too soon; her hands were only the size of sand dollars.

Deirdre's head line indicates that she may stay mad. But at least Deirdre's mother will always be able to touch her daughter's soft brown hair and hold her long, thin hand, and breathe in her essence. I do not pity her.

My closest friends in here are Mary and Lenora. Love is everything to Lenora; she must have it washing over her like a wave constantly; it is air to her, the gills of her heart are drying up for lack of it. I feel as though I am in the presence of a beached dolphin when I am with Lenora. I run my fingers over her back like rain until they ache, and then I let her lie in my arms and I try to brush some life into the brittle strands of her bleached-out hair. No one ever comes to see Lenora except her son, and he looks like he just stepped out of the shower when he leaves here; she soaks him with her tears.

Mary is tiny and wiry and somewhere around seventy, I think. I won't ask her how old she is because she takes great pains never to be seen without lipstick on, although it looks queer in her old oyster-shell face. She is the only person I remember clearly during my first week here, except for my husband and one of the night nurses. Mary sat with me a lot, without talking or expecting me to talk. Most people don't know how to do that.

Before he left me that first night, my husband took off the T-shirt he had on under his sweater and put it on me as a life jacket against the torrent of pain that was drawing me under. I went to sleep with his smell in my nostrils, a sweet, strong, acrid smell, a smell more intimate than my own smell. I love my husband, even though we are chalk and cheese. Because we are chalk and cheese.

Mary lost her husband last year. For forty years, she and Frank never spent a day apart, she told me. They were a lot alike, she said, and from the way she talks about him, I can tell that they swam through life together perfectly synchronized until he died. Her children are still close by, but all of them work, including the girls, and they all live in small houses, and none of them have enough time, or room, for their mother. But they are all good children, Mary says, and think the world of her, especially Francine, the youngest. That's just the way it is nowadays, Mary says; they've got to think of their youngsters first, after all.

When Frank died, Mary moved into a senior citizens' complex. Although she had her own apartment, they wouldn't let her have a dog, or even a cat, and if her children or grandchildren came to visit they had to leave by midnight as there was a strict rule against overnight visitors. One day Mary fell and broke her shoulder. When she got back from the hospital she found it hard to cook and clean, and she ended up in the hospital again, this time on the psychiatric ward. "I don't know what I am doing here," Mary said to me. "They says I told Francine I was going to do away with myself, but I can't remember saying it. Anyway, if I did, she should have had the sense to keep it to herself."

The nurse who put me to bed the first night I was here was a man. I had never had a male nurse before, but then I'd only been in the hospital twice in my life, at sixteen to have my tonsils out and at thirty-one to have a baby out. I read a lot of Sylvia Plath when I was pregnant with my daughter, because you can read her when you are happy. When they put sweet, bloody, blue and red Jenny on my stomach right after she was born, I thought of the opening line of "Morning Song," which is "Love set you going like a fat gold watch."

When I first looked into Jenny's eyes, I was startled, then awed; I saw an ancient one looking out at me, the oldest thing I had ever seen. Later, after she had been washed off and swaddled, her eyes had the unfocused gaze associated with infants. My sister is a doctor, so I asked her about it. "Yeah,' she said, "I know what you mean. They look right at you, and their eyes are like that creature's in *Star Wars*—Yoda, right?"

I read "Morning Song" again recently. It is in the *Norton Anthology*, which my husband's niece brought in to me. The end of the poem goes like this:

> All night your moth-breath
> Flickers among the flat pink roses. I wake to listen:
> A far sea moves in my ear.

The male nurse was very kind; he was short and stout and had a guppy's mouth and friendly eyes. He asked me a lot of questions, but I only remember one of them, which was whether I was having my period. I didn't answer right away. "I have to ask," he said, apologetically. "We've had cases where the nurses checked a female patient at night and they noticed some blood on the sheets, and they assumed it was menstrual blood, when in actual fact the patient had cut their wrists." "No," I said. I wasn't on my period, but all of a sudden I felt like screaming at him. Screaming what's wrong with you, surely to God you must know the difference between the blood of the womb and the blood of the heart, between strong, thick, sullen menstrual blood with its sea smell and fresh, thin, bright arterial blood spraying from a shocked heart. But I didn't say anything; what did it matter?

Two years ago, my mother died of breast cancer at seventy-seven. Last year, my seven-year-old daughter drowned. Seven, seven, seven, seventy times seven, unto the seventh generation. Sometimes I think God is math and math is God.

My husband teaches math and physics at a high school. I learned about Fibonacci's numbers from him, and about atoms and quarks. Quark really rhymes with *lark*, or *snark*, although most people give it the sound of *quartz*. (We used to call our daughter the Boojum, from Lewis Carroll's poem "The Hunting of the Snark.") Besides the *Norton Anthology*, I am reading Stephen Hawking's *A Brief History of Time*. The physicists now say that the smallest element in the universe is the superstring. If you could blow up an atom to be the size of the universe, one superstring would be the size of a tree. Superstrings loop around the eleven dimensions of the universe, holding it together like a cat's cradle. I wonder, who is holding the cat's cradle? Someone? Everyone? No One?

They don't care what I read in here, because, besides Stephen Hawking, I read only poetry and fiction. Poetry can't hurt you because it is not true. They like to see me read; to them, it means that I am getting better. I couldn't read at all when I first came in, or for months before: the words hurt like knives, they were all so sharp, even, especially *love, child, sea*.

My daughter Jenny died on a hot day in August. Jenny never liked August; every August within her child's memory (three of them, in fact) one of the family cats had been killed. I never saw this as synchronistic myself, only coincidental. We've always had too many cats, up to five at one time. The vet said to keep them indoors; I could not keep them indoors, especially the older ones. What would their lives have been? August is the first harvest month. My daughter was harvested in August by the Grim Reaper.

We were at our summer place in Salmon Cove when Jenny drowned. Salmon Cove gets its name from the salmon river that runs through its middle. Jenny used to swim in the part of the river that is by the beach; the water there is only up to her shoulders. Was up to her shoulders. Her little brown shoulders; her little brown face with its blue eyes like two flames. What I want to know is how do you like your blue-eyed girl, Mister Death.

In August, the water in the river is almost like bath water. Jenny was a good swimmer, a natural swimmer, a baby porpoise. Even so, we never let her out of our sight when we were by the water. But she got up early that morning, and went off by herself with old Mickey while her father and I were still sleeping. She had never done that before. And she must have gone to wade in the sea, and she waded out too far, and the undertow got her. The Under Toad. What I want to know is how did you like your blue-eyed girl, Mister Under Toad.

We waited and waited for Jenny to come back. The physicists are right about time; it is relative. I have been here for two months, but it has not been anywhere near as long as the two weeks we waited for Jenny. One of the women here, Cass, told me about a vision she had in which she saw, among other things (for instance, the Face of the Saviour), what a human life is. Cass says it is like an atom in God's body, and each of our lives is less than a second long in God's time. (Cass scares me; but then, poor Cass scares herself.)

They finally found Jenny's body out by the Terrified Rocks. The Terrified Rocks are about ten yards off the beach at Salmon Cove. There are three of them, three megaliths with coarse grass growing on top in which the terns make their nests; they look like Easter Island statues with toupees. Jenny must have been taken way out at first, and then somehow she found her way back to the Cove, like the salmon that swim up its river in the spring. My husband didn't want me to go with him to identify the body, but I went anyway. I had to know. I thought she would be blue and bloated, but this is not the case with bodies that have been in the sea. If she had drowned in fresh water, the pathologist said, she would have swollen up, but salt water has an affinity with our own fluids; there is an osmotic effect. My daughter had suffered a sea change, but her eyes were not coral: she had no eyes. For a long time after, I thought of them lying like twin sapphires on the bottom of the ocean. Later, I learned about the sea lice. (Sometimes, I wish that the Under Toad had kept her.)

Last night I fell asleep in the moonlight. The blinds in my room open even if the windows do not, and the moonlight was right on my pillow at bedtime. The moon was close to full last night; I think they call that a gibbous moon. *Gibbous* is such an ugly word; it has always sounded to me like *gibbet*, and I think of white dead bodies hanging in the moonlight like rotten melons. Or how Jenny might have looked if she had drowned in the river instead of the sea.

I dreamt that Jenny and I were riding bicycles on the dirt road that used to run by my grandmother's house in the country I grew up in. My mother was waving to us from the veranda; she was in her early forties, dark and pretty, around the age she had been when I was Jenny's age. My mother married late because all the healthy young men were away at war when she was young. Jenny and I were going to the little store over the hill from my grandmother's to buy ice cream, but when we got there we decided to get candy hearts for my mother instead. Mine was large and mauve and made of gelatin; Jenny's was smaller, harder, and bright crimson.

When we got back to the place where my grandmother's house should have been, there was a steep hill with a huge bronze lion at the top there instead. "Let's go see," said Jenny, and she and I climbed the hill and sat on the lion's paws. I looked back down; we were high, high up and it had become night all of a sudden, and I was afraid. I have always been terrified of heights, and somewhat afraid of the dark. "What if we fall?" I said to Jenny, and I lay down on my stomach along the length of the cold legs of the great lion, shivering. "We can't," she said, laughing. "Let's go sit on his back." So we climbed up over the lion's face, up over its curly brazen mane and onto its back. We sat down together, and I held on to Jenny from behind, and I buried my face in her child's neck, fragrant as sweet grass.

When I looked up again I saw the biggest church I had ever seen, bigger than the biggest football stadium: its spire touched the moon. It reminded me of our Anglican Cathedral, although it was not neo-Gothic, or any recognizable type of church architecture (it could have been all of them combined, or none of them). The church was made of some kind of iridescent stone, like labradorite. The sight of it filled me with dread and longing at the same time. There was a light around its vast door frame, and I knew that if I were to go in, there would be some sort of celebration going on. And then I heard the sound of galloping hooves, and I looked up. A herd of wild horses was coming toward Jenny and me; they were small but shaggy and fierce-looking; there were hundreds of them, yet they moved as one. Jenny pulled away from me, and got up and ran toward them. They were only yards from us by then, and I saw that they were quite mad—they were rearing up like huge breakers about to dash against rocks; their eyes were rolling, showing the whites, and huge flecks of sweat, like sea foam, flew from their streaming flanks. I screamed at her: "Jenny, come back—they'll kill you!" "No they won't," she said, turning around and looking at me with Yoda's eyes. "They can only hurt you if you *think* they can." And then the lion turned his big, bronze head around, and he was laughing, and I started to laugh, too, and the lion switched his tail gently against my daughter's legs, propelling her into the midst of the horses, and I heard her shriek with pleasure, and then she was gone. And I woke up.

Moonlight was in my eyes and it was all glowing and liquid like moonlight dancing on the sea; it was the whale's path, the swan's road, and in its silver wash phosphorescent sparkles shimmered all blue and gold; it was alive and full of itself. Somehow it seemed to me that I had always known that that was how moonlight really was, not pale and thin and sad, not just the sunlight's ghost, but thick and rich and molten, a live and joyful thing in itself. And I lay there and I let it wash over my face—it felt so good, I felt it go right through my skin, right down into my heart—and I heard voices in the distance, the voices of men and women and children, voices rising and falling in a light, happy cadence, and I thought that perhaps my husband had been unable to sleep, and had gone in to the den to watch television. And then a bright light shone suddenly in my eyes; it was the night nurse's flashlight, and she was asking me why I was awake, and if I needed something to help me sleep. I looked away from her concerned face, and up: the moon was a speck in the top left-hand corner of the window, high and far and tiny; it had gone from my pillow hours ago.

And a line came to me from the Bible, I think, or maybe a hymn, or perhaps the Anglican liturgy: "And the sea shall give up its dead." I started to cry then; satisfied, the nurse went to get me a pill. But I didn't take it, after.

This morning the sun has managed to poke a couple of skinny yellow digits through the slats of the blinds; it is stroking the pewter frame of Jenny's school picture. Mary was by earlier. She is going home next week, home to Francine's house. Apparently, Francine found a bit of space somewhere for her little mother to curl up in. Mary will have to keep taking antidepressants, though, and she's not too thrilled about that, being someone who would rather suffer a headache than take a pill. But that's the way it has to be, says Mary.

On Radio One, Sass Jordan is singing about time and rivers and how all you want to do is hold her, but what you try to grab evades your touch, her voice twining around the sun's fingers like rings of lapis lazuli. In her Grade 2 picture, Jenny is smiling.

I have a feeling I might be going home soon.

# A Piece of Toast

**Kathleen Winter**

Everyone wants Mom to go into a home but she won't go into one. She says, "Joyce, I'm not going into a kennel." I tell her it's either that or Jim builds a basement apartment for her, but she says, "Joyce, I won't go in there either, much as I care about you I just want to live in my own house."

The thing about Mom's own house is that there's a staircase that is way too steep for her, a woodstove in the kitchen, and pipes that freeze in the basement if you get a winter with hard frost. Mom has been on her own there for eighteen years. She's eighty-four years old.

Mom said to me, when I gave her a brochure about the new seniors' complex that's going up on Glendale Boulevard, "Look, you can't get a piece of toast when you want one in one of those places." See, Mom has this friend, Gertrude Halloran, who went in a home eight years ago and she swears she's not the same person ever since she went in. One time Gertrude asked for a piece of spanakopita for her dinner. She knew she wouldn't get one, but she asked anyway, and they gave her some tranquillizers. As if, Mom said, asking for spanakopita was some crazy thing. Gertrude is a cosmopolitan person; she can't live on fish fingers and salisbury steak, which is what they give you in there. So she wants spanakopita, or black olives or some bull's blood wine, and it's a big laugh. The nurses treat her as if she's nuts. Another thing, she's not allowed to have her antique sewing machine in her room: her own antique sewing machine. It's not as if she's asking them to buy anything. There are a lot of things that Gertrude is not allowed to have in that place. Every time Mom goes to visit her she gets depressed or mad. Every time, she says, "You'll never get me in there."

Mom is not even like Gertrude. I mean, she can eat meat and cabbage and she doesn't have an antique sewing machine. Sometimes I think the main thing that's keeping Mom from going in the home and letting us all get a good night's rest is that piece of toast. Ever since I was little I remember Mom getting a loaf of her homemade bread out of the bin, on the counter and slicing off a few thick pieces with her big knife. She had a little rack she'd put over one of the dampers on the woodstove, and she'd toast the bread for her and Dad and whatever kids were still up out of bed and she'd put butter on it, and the butter would run in little golden puddles on the toast, and we'd have that for a mug-up, with hot tea. That's what she keeps on about.

Finally I said, "Mom, for God's sake you know they'd give you a bit of toast if you asked for it in the home," and she looked at me as if I was the most pathetic thing she'd ever seen, someone who didn't know their own way home. "Joyce," she said, "when I was in to see Gertrude one evening before Christmas she asked the nurse if we could get a bit of toast and some tea, and the nurse said no, it wasn't time. Well, when would it be time, Gertrude asked her, and the nurse said Gertrude you know we have lunch at 9:45. Well, it's 8:30 now and my friend's here, Gertrude said. If I could go to the kitchen I'd toast it myself. Where's the kitchen? She doesn't even know where the kitchen is for God's sake. Can you imagine wanting to boil the kettle and there being no kettle until someone else decides for you that there's a kettle and they'll boil it when it's time? So the nurse was a kind nurse anyway and she said I'll get you something, and she came back with two styrofoam cups of tea out of a machine, and two pairs of digestive biscuits wrapped in so much cellophane you couldn't get them unwrapped without crumbling them. That was the best she could do."

I'm not insensitive; I know Mom has a point. She sees Gertrude's situation and she doesn't want it to happen to her. God knows I feel guilty about Mom; no matter what I decide to do about her I will feel guilty. If I leave her in her own house I'm guilty all winter thinking about burst pipes and chimney fires and her breaking her hip on the stairs. If we put her in a home I'll be forever thinking about that toast with the little golden puddles of butter in it. She says it's not only the toast, it's what she calls rules against life. One time she took in some of her garden vegetables for Gertrude. Mom has always had a garden. She took her in some fresh carrots and Gertrude started to cry. It was eight years since Gertmde has seen a raw carrot.

Gertrude had thought she could come and go whenever she wanted, but one day Mom's younger brother took Mom there with the car, to take Gertrude out somewhere. "Where do you want to go?" Mom asked Gertrude, and right away Gertrude said she'd like to go to Cape Blandford Lighthouse, but the home wouldn't let her go. They didn't give a reason but Mom thinks its because if anything happened while Gertrude was off the property they'd be liable because she was still in their care. "So there you go," Mom says to me, "Gertrude is a prisoner. If I want to go to a lighthouse and feel salt wind in my hair," Mom says, "I'm going to feel it, and no one's going to stop me. The only time I'm ever going into a home is when they make one where I can still be the way I was when I was a young woman, because that's the way it is in my own home, only I'm a bit slower, that's all."

Every now and then Mom goes outside in her yard at night and smokes a cigarette while listening to this exquisite Vivaldi piccolo concerto that Gertrude liked, and she picks out the Seven Sisters constellation and looks at her white roses growing in the moonlight. That's not like Mom. She doesn't smoke, and the rose bush is transplanted from the little garden Gertrude used to have. When Mom sits out like that she's doing it for Gertrude. Then she goes in and has her toast.

# The Prisoner

**Irving Fogwill**

Here the calendar of service
Is immeasurable—
Forty years spent at an office desk
Adding columns of figures,
While Summer rolled warmly by,
And Autumn, seen through a grimy window
Pressed his heart with a dark pain.

And the forty summers and the forty autumns
Had curved like arches over him
Four times a day
Back and forth to work:
Back and forth to the prison cell
Of claustral columns of figures,
Mounting and piling;
Smothering and murdering
And burying
The illimitable dream
Of green grass and trees;
And water curling whitely
In faraway streams;
And tall mountains in moonlight
Dark with mystery;
And a woman waiting somewhere
Nameless and beautiful.

But the Springs! The Springs
Were the ultimate agony;
April and May and the warm rain;
And the smell of the earth stirring;
And the young shoots and flowers;
And the everlasting promise of things.
Then the surge would shake him—
This time he would go! This time
He would go headlong through
The grimy window! Yet, he knew
That he would not.
And thus without thunder
There flickered out
The brief candle of wonder.

*Winter Morning,* watercolour, 1974, Reginald Shepherd

*I paint realistically but I am not a true realist because I take poetic license
when painting. I like to feel that I have enabled the viewer to see beyond
a mere likeness of the subject, and understand why I thought the subject
worth expressing. I have been called a poetic realist.*

— Reginald Shepherd

# Preface to *The Labradorians: Voices from the Land of Cain*

## Lynne Fitzhugh

When I began sifting through sixty-odd issues of *Them Days* magazine in 1989 it was with the idea of selecting for a wider readership some of the most colourful stories published in this regional quarterly of oral histories. I found that what I had instead of a simple anthology was the raw material for a social epic, a history of Labrador as it was expected by the people who have lived there—some of them for thousands of years.

They took control of the project early on, these Labradorians, filling my head with stories until my ears rang with voices. A persistent dream image formed in my mind of the darkly silent Labrador landscape spread out below me, a vast and seemingly uninhabited wilderness. People began to emerge, just a few at first, then more, gathering by cabin doors at the edge of the forest, pulling boats above the tide, leaning axes against woodpiles, drying hands on aprons, talking to me. By nature taciturn, by accident of geography estranged from a world most knew little of, the people of Labrador were telling their story with a sense of urgency I had not heard in my original readings of *Them Days*. The task they had assigned to me, it seemed, was to impose some order on the din and see that this story found the place it deserved in the collective record of human experience on this planet.

The material more or less arranged itself according to places where the people gathered on the landscape: Innu (Montagnais-Naskaupi Indians) mainly in the interior; the Anglo-Celtic "liveyers" on the southern coasts, Inuit (Canadian Eskimo) and Moravian Settlers along the north coast, and the great mixed-race trapping clans around Sandwich Bay and Lake Melville. This arrangement became the format for the chapters in the book.

Zooming in closer, it was possible to identify communities on the landscape that shared a section of fishing and trapping grounds, a gene pool, and a common set of memories and yarns. Zooming closer yet, to cove or clearing, the gatherings were of families, generations of them reunited around ancestral homesteads where now only the persistent rhubarb patch on a hummocked bawn signals this was once a place where people lived. Lived by the grace of God in the jaws of a formidable wilderness, and died, most often taking with them to oblivion the stories of the ordeals they survived, the secrets of their own personal courage and pleasure in life, and a piece out of the collective memory of a remarkable race. Were it not for the few voices captured on tape and the memories passed on to grandchildren, there would be nothing but silence, for the modern world has finally reached this country, and the last of her frontiersmen and women are passing away.

My first criteria in selecting narratives for this collection were story, style, and character, especially the narrators'. If it was palpable Labrador talking, it made the cut. Most written articles were omitted, as well as how-to accounts, some excellent but historically superfluous local legends, and stories of the post-Goose Bay generations, since construction of the air base in 1941 and Confederation with Canada in 1949 effectively brought about the end of "them days." Within these omitted categories, and indeed all the narratives excluded from this book, is wonderful material for other books.

The narratives have been arranged in regional and family groups to create a profile of the history, lifeways, beliefs, values, and character of the region. As these accounts were never recorded with any such purpose in mind, they make a patchy mosaic. In time, you will begin to sense its shape and coherence and, ultimately, to feel at home among the people.

Labrador dialects are rich with the soft percussiveness of German-laced Inuktitut, of melodic Innuemun, and the lilting patter of old maritime brogues from the British Isles. The vocabulary reflects these influences, so you may find the glossary of local terms and usage at the back of this book helpful. It is not necessary to understand every word, but names are worth noting because they are often the threads that weave stories together. The population of Labrador has always been small and isolated. With careful research one could conceivably reconstruct the whole woodlot of family trees, Aboriginal and Settler, their roots and branches elaborately entwined. These family trees probably would not exceed three hundred in number.

Genealogical recitations with which many Settler accounts begin are important both because of the significance narrators ascribe to origins and the historical information they contain. Unfortunately, these are usually absent from the narratives of families whose European progenitors came before 1835, perhaps because these men perished too soon, or changed their names, or their children were raised by Inuit mothers who spoke little if any English. Or maybe they did not wish to acknowledge or remember their origins. In these cases the name alone survived, indifferently spelled, providing a single imprecise clue for genealogists to track in merchant logs, shipping manifests, and British church registries. There is almost no written genealogical information about Aboriginal families, although Jose Mailhot has done some excellent research on the Innu, many of whom have retained their traditional histories orally. The Christianization of Aboriginal names during the conversion period effectively eradicated the traces of Aboriginal families in early written records, and the tendency of some Settlers to refer to less Europeanized Inuit by ethnic type rather than personal name has had a corresponding effect in the oral narratives. However, these families have equally rich and venerable histories which, for all their invisibility in the accounts available for this book, remain strong threads in the social fabric of mixed-race Labrador.

Many of the accounts in this book describe life during the first half of the twentieth century. These narrators (most born between 1890 and 1920) had known the early generations of Settlers and historic-period Natives. They also knew one another. Geographic groupings allow you to encounter them as characters moving through each other's stories, since generations that never met in life mingle as freely as neighbours in the multi-dimensional, temporal and spatial environment of isolated communities.

As the pattern of existence in every Labrador community, and indeed, most every family, has the same basic components, a certain redundancy is inevitable in the narratives. I have tried to minimize it by elaborating on different components in each chapter. For example, most Settler families fished in the spring and summer, trapped and hunted in the fall and winter, and experienced the Spanish Influenza of 1918-19, but to degrees varying by community. While there are allusions to these topics in every chapter, the fishery is developed fully in the chapters on the south coast, trapping in that on Lake Melville, and the great Influenza in the Torngat region, where it was most devastating.

With few exceptions, the narratives in this book are transcribed exactly as published in *Them Days*. No alterations have been made in the dialect or wording of sentences, although some adjustments were made in punctuation and spelling of transcriptions. A very few accounts have been shortened, and some by the same narrator excerpted and combined. Occasional citations from the historical record provide what I hope is an interesting counterpoint to the personal stories. Many of these have also appeared in *Them Days Magazine*.

The story of *Them Days* is worth a chapter in itself. Started in 1975 by members of the Labrador Heritage Society concerned that a unique way of life was slipping away undocumented, it has done more than anything else to give the region a sense of pride in its own history and unique character. And it has given us outsiders a more profound

understanding of the inhabitants of this "marvellous terrible place" than we could possibly derive from books or artifacts or even years among the people.

*Them Days* came into being at a time when Labrador's cultural integrity and pride appeared to be disintegrating. Old-timers were disillusioned or bewildered by the changes in their lives. Their children and grandchildren seemed adrift between a culture with no future and a future in which they seemed to have no part. When television reached the country in the late 1970s, the Labradorians could no longer escape the realization that, relative to the world they saw on screen, their beloved country and the lives which they had proudly made with their bare hands, generation by generation, were not only impoverished but irrelevant.

The founding editor of *Them Days*, Doris Saunders, is a Martin from Cartwright whose family belatedly joined the great exodus to Goose Bay in the 1960s. Her mother, Harriet Pardy, was the infant Spanish Flu survivor from Mountaineer Cove of whom you will read in Chapter 4. For nearly twenty-five years, Doris and a handful of dedicated volunteers have collected most of the narratives, manned the office, provided reference services for students of Labrador history, welcomed visiting tourists, transcribed tapes, developed photographs, typeset and laid out issues, serviced subscriptions, raised funds to cover remaining publication and administrative expenses, and created a valuable archive of written and photographic records on Labrador history. Doris's capable daughter Gillian has taken over the administrative and fundraising duties. But the vagaries of public grant funding and below-cost subscription rates have kept the magazine from attaining the kind of financial security a now venerable enterprise should have, especially one which is celebrated across Canada and has contributed so greatly to Labrador's sense of identity.

While the economic dilemma of a people with little control over use of their country's natural resources persists, it can no longer be said that they lack a sense of cultural identity and pride. Much of the credit goes to the resilient spirit of the Labradorians, but some must go to *Them Days*. In recognition of her achievements, Doris Saunders received the prestigious Order of Canada in 1986. She has also earned the affection of her fellow Labradorians from L'Anse au Clair to Nain.

In 1994 Memorial University awarded Doris an honorary doctor of letters for her contributions to the cultural life of the province. In her convocation address she said:

> *Them Days* came into being because Labrador and its people were not often portrayed honestly in books written about Labrador. I was given an article some years ago written by John Moss, a writer and critic teaching at the University of Ottawa. He wrote, 'For people native to the North—native to any place—landscape is the extension of personal being, as intimate and far-reaching as genealogy. Inuit and Northern Indians have lived within the landscape…as an existential fact.' He went on to explain that for writers from outside, the experience of a place—such as the North—becomes a world made of words, and again I quote, 'almost all those words are devoted to the articulation of alien imperatives and dreams.' Moss said, 'Anyone who features himself in his own narrative, whether implicitly like Mowat, explicitly like Peary, or surreptitiously like Stefansson, will inevitably document the landscape and its people as extensions of his own experience.'

> Joe Goudie, Mike Martin and others responsible for setting up the Labrador Heritage Society never read John Moss's article, but they knew that so many books written about Labrador went from being quite good to absolute rubbish. And thus an idea for a Labrador book by Labradorians was born. The idea was to let the rest of the world and, in particular, the island portion of our province understand the real Labrador as experienced by the people of Labrador.

> Labrador's association with Newfoundland goes back a long way. Before Europeans came, aboriginal people lived in Labrador and on the island of Newfoundland. The aboriginal people on the island were wiped out in one way or another, which meant that Newfoundland started over again, as far as human population as concerned, as an extension of the Old World.

> The Natives of Labrador, by that time, were—according to explorers and colonists—Indians and Eskimos. However, their own names for themselves were Innu and Inuit, both meaning "The People."

> The Labrador Natives went from being people in their own eyes to being ignorant savages in the eyes of the newcomers. Many were killed and others were taken as curiosities to the homelands of their tormentors. When the Labrador Natives tried to defend themselves they were called murderers and thieves.

When the first white men came to Labrador they had to marry native women in order to survive. First they gave their wives Christian names because they looked on Native names as "heathen" names. Then they forced them to give up whatever they—the white men—considered heathen customs. They could, however, do whatever was necessary to provide comfort for their husbands, such as chewing skins to make clothing. My own great-great-great-grandmother, renamed Susan, was beaten by her husband when he caught her eating raw meat or doing anything else that he considered heathen acts. The children were raised to think of themselves as white and were encouraged to marry whites.

So you see, people who were secure in their identity and who were self-sufficient, were made to feel inferior by the intruders. Women who married white men lost their names…. They were forced to speak a foreign language, and their children were raised to ignore the heritage of their mothers. As a result, many of the descendants of those mixed marriages grew up being ashamed of their Native roots, some totally denying they even had Native roots. Fortunately some—like my great-great-grandmother Lydia Brooks, then Blake, then Campbell—passed stories on to her children and grandchildren, who passed it on to theirs and so on, until today, and I am now passing those stories on to my grandchildren….

Since the start of Native land claims negotiations, people in Labrador have become very interested in their roots and are accepting the fact that they do indeed have aboriginal roots—and that is good. They are accepting their true identities and will once more become people with pride in their heritage, proud to be The People….

John Moss's indictment of authors whose descriptions of alien cultures are more self-descriptive than perceptive is glaringly, and embarrassingly, evident in the work of virtually all the outsiders who have written about Labrador, however eloquently. I knew from the start that it would be true of any introductions I wrote about these narratives. There is no way around it. Not only did I bring to Labrador a most un-Labradorian optic, I was bringing to this project two decades of my own emotionally charged experiences there. However, my husband and friends convinced me that introductions were necessary to make the narratives in this book accessible to readers from outside the region. Since that was my goal, I agreed to give it a try. Having accepted the responsibility, I have attempted to make the introductions as accurate, concise, and useful as possible and to let my inevitable subjectivity show. I hope these words help set the stage for the real authors of this history, the people of Labrador telling their own story in their own words, just as Doris Saunders and the co-founders of *Them Days* envisioned.

# Some Labrador Narratives

Nat Igloliorite
(Collected and transcribed by Phyllis Artiss)

## Narrative I

I'm going to tell another story
About a famous whale hunter of long ago
In Hopedale, Labrador—
During that time way back
Before guns, before white men came with boats of wood
Inuit people used to hunt in kayaks and also umiaks.
These umiaks were usually referred to as women's boats
However they were used also for transporting whole families from settlement
    to settlement—settlement to settlement—
Or from one hunting ground to the other—
And they used to hunt whales in these boats (*slowly and emphatically*).
What they used to use were harpoons—
Special kind of harpoons made to kill whales
And these harpoons had inflated sealskins
Attached to them on the end
So that when they harpoon an object
Whether it was a seal, or whales or anything of that nature
When they harpoon it they would let go the whole thing
And that inflated sealskin would be, would be the mark to follow or
    pursue to kill the whale.
They also had a special kind of killing thing—
When a whale surfaced
They would follow the inflated sealskin
Because that inflated sealskin cannot go under water.
It always on the surface
And it SHOWS the killer
Or it shows the man
Where the animal is moving, where the animal is moved,
And he knows also how long the harpoon line is
And he kinda also knows exactly
Where that whale is going to come up
According to the distance from the inflated sealskin
And possible (= possibility?) that the whale surfacing
So they would follow that inflated sealskin
And then pursue that whale with another killing instrument
Whole BUNCH of them would be at it
Until they actually KILL it—(*dramatically, with slightly raised pitch*)

The famous whaler, Inuk whaler had told the village, Hopedale village
    people
To be buried on the hill
Northwest of Hopedale, about two miles away from the village on a
    very, very high hill.
And this high hill—on this high hill even when I was a child
I could see a sern (= cairn?).
It was made of wood or rather stones piled upon one another.
And the human being—in that long long time ago
    *(slowly and rhythmically)*
He was buried there
Because he asked the village people to bury him there.
So all—so when the whalers were pursuing whales
Down near Akvituaksuk
This place Akvituaksuk means the place of whales
Even to this day is called Akvituaksuk
Although there is no whales left in Labrador, in Labrador waters,
Because they were all killed out
Way way back I don't know when.
But some people might say that
Hopedale waters was a place of whales,
They might not BELIEVE that
Because there's no whales there now
To prove that there was whales there,
However I remember
When I was a child
We used to play on the beach a lot and
vie and 'nother, other boys
That we used to play on the beach
North of Hopedale village
And there was a lot of whale bones ALL over on the beach
Even and there was even little huts,
Playing with whale bones
That at one time were dwellings of the whalers actually down there—
Among the whale bones
So this shows that
That Hopedale WAS actually a whale hunting area.
Matter of fact before the name Hopedale came along
It was called Akvitok
Which means—a whale hunting place.
When they used to go through a Akvituaksuk area in a motor boat
Going toward the north
Where long time ago people used to catch whales in a kayak
I could see the sern WAY up on the hill

You could, you could hardly see it
But it's there—
It WAS there.
My uncle used to always tell us that
That that sern contained a man
That was a famous whaler of Hopedale
Who, at one time, wanted to be buried up there
Because although dead he would watch the whalers down there at
    Akvituaksuk...
That's the story (*emphatically, with falling pitch*).

## NARRATIVE III

Another very short story
Regarding a woman killing a polar bear with a silapeguk
Silapeguk is a mitten, a sealskin mitten with fur on outside,
And—the story goes that
The woman approached this polar bear
When he—the polar bear stood—
To kill her with her (= his) mouth open.
This woman has a l-o-o-ng stick
And on that long stick was this silapeguk
And when the polar bear—opened its mouth
She just PUSHED that silapeguk right into the polar hear's throat
And she (s)he pulled the stick away
The silapeguk stayed in the, in the polar bear's throat
And the polar bear choked with that silapeguk
By the way, silapeguks when dry are very, very hard to swallow (*laugh*)
And it stands to reason that it could happen
It DID happen, if the story's true it's true.
I can—believe that
Because silapeguks even sealskin when turned inside out or when
    the fur is
YOU try to swallow a sealskin with fur on it
And you'll find out how (*laugh*)
What it means.
That's the story.

## Narrative IV

I have another story—
That has to do with polar bear
That turned into a rock.
This rock—is visible—from Hopedale village—at—certain wantage
 (= vantage) points.
If you go—to a certain hill—in this, in Hopedale village
You could see this white rock
Probably about a mile away,
Or a little over a mile away.
The story goes like—um—
This polar bear was—going to Hopedale
To destroy the whole village
And the angakkuks, the sorcerers, actually turned—this polar bear—
 into a rock.
That's according to the story.
And at some days you could see that white rock
Turning into a shape of a polar bear—on certain days
I think—it's when there's a ship
Or something is come to Hopedale harbour
Or something is coming from the south—southeast of Hopedale—
um—
This rock turns—um—like a polar bear—or the shape of a polar bear.
The story goes like—um—um
When you see the shape of a polar bear
That means somebody is visiting Hopedale from southeast of
Hopedale.

## Narrative V

I gonna talk a little bit about—
Funny incidences when I was growing up.
My uncle as I mentioned earlier
Taught me how to even call living things to me,
To—you know—how to make noises like the animal you pursuing.
Um—my uncle used to tell us that
If we made uh noises like a rat or a mouse
The fox will come—to us.
Uh when I was a child
I was waiting for my uncle—in a rowboat on the beach
And I saw a fox a l-o-o-ng long ways off.
'Twas a beautiful day

And you could hear a pin drop almost.
It was beautiful, beautiful—no wind or nothing.

And I saw fox l-o-o-ng ways, could hardly see it.
And I started making noises like a mouse,
And it heard me.
And it started running toward me.
And uh my uncle had left a 30-30 in the rowboat
But he had taken the 22 along with him
When he, when he went to, to attend to his fox traps on a
    certain island.
And when I started making noises like a mouse that this fox coming
And I was scared of that 30-30, and I was also scared my uncle might,
    might not like it if I used a bullet
You know we didn't have too many bullets on the 30-30
An' I was scared if I missed that fox
My uncle would jaw
You know would give me a hard time,
And the fox was so CLOSE to me
I was aiming at it
And I was thinkin'

"Well if I miss it my uncle's going to give me shit."
And I'm scared of the gun,
I never shoot a 30-30 before,
An' I was scared to death to shoot.
An' I could have shot it because it was so close like
I could see the eyes an' everything right close.
Actually I didn't shoot it
Because I was scared or what my uncle would say to me
When he came back (*laugh*).

## Narrative VII

And uh another time when I was a child
I was probably about seven years old I guess
There was a lot of, lot of ptarmigans, white partridge that year,
And I wanted to go partridge hunting,
And wouldn't, I mean I couldn't use a gun very well then
And I was crying like to my uncle and saying to him
"Uncle I want to go bird hunting,"
And he gives me ten bullets
And said to me—ten 22 bullets and said to me,
"Nat, if you don't come home with ten, ten partridges

I'll never give you—no more bullets to go partridge hunting."
And when I came back I had eleven, eleven partridges.
And I was so PROUD.
I was—I was so proud you know,
To come back with eleven
When, when he only give me,
When he only give me ten bullets.
And I was really, really proud—
You know it's incidents like that
Good times and enjoying life.


## NARRATIVE VIII

'Nother time me and 'nother fellow—
My uncle when he was loaded drunk on a certain day,
It was Saturday afternoon kinda rainy and windy.
We used to wait for birds at a certain point
Where birds used to fly over—
A whole lot of birds would fly right by me an' this child
We only small kids—
He told us to take the shotgun,
An' we was scared of the shotgun
An' every time the birds come by
We would—would try to aim.
I would (be) holdin' the gun,

He would try to hold the other end,
An' we tried to shoot
But both of us were scared to pull the trigger,
Because we never shot, only the uh shotgun before and—
After a while we, we since we were so scared of the gun,
We never even shot
Because, although there was a whole lot of birds goin'
    back an' forth—
When we got back to the house uncle asked us
If we saw any birds,
An' we said "We didn't see no birds" (laugh).
And all the time we were only scared of the gun.
And—we had good times
And bad times also
Now about the end of the tape.
And—I can tell a lot of stories—good stories also
But I hope someone will get something out of this.

*Love*, hooked mat, Kathleen L. Knowling

*I use texture and colour to express the ideas and emotions I have about the time and place in which I live. The hooked mats, achieved in print and yarn, incorporate modern materials and ideas in a traditional form. They link the past, the present and the future.*

*My work is about being a woman, wife and mother living in Newfoundland. I am part of a continuing tradition. I use disregarded "woman's work"—the hooked mats left over from the arduous homemaking of the past—as the basis of my own. I try to remember in my own work the bravery, dignity and humour of the women who preceded me in this barren and delightful place.*

— Kathleen L. Knowling

# Woman of Labrador

### Elizabeth Goudie

October passed by and Jim went setting his traps again. The first evening he was gone I was alone cleaning my floor. I looked around for my children. The girl Marie and the second boy Bruce were sitting by the stove watching the fire burning. I checked them to see if everything was alright and went on about my work. About ten minutes later, the whole house lit up with fire. I jumped to my feet and I was by Bruce's side in a minute. I did not know what to do; I saw a big coat close by and caught it and smothered out the flame. For a few seconds, he didn't move. I picked him up and the minute I moved him he went into a "rock of pain." I was a whole hour trying to keep him on my lap. That was between five and six in the evening; at about six-thirty, he fell asleep. Jim was still not home so I laid Bruce on a big wooden chest I had beside the table. I thought I would have something to eat because I expected to be up all night. I looked over his body as carefully as I could and I saw his right arm was burnt right to his body and one cheek, one ear and both his lips were burned, so I knew I had a terrible task on my hands. I tried to eat but couldn't. I walked the floor and the other children were afraid that their little brother would die and they were crying. Their daddy was not home yet.

About seven o'clock I heard the boat coming and I was there with my little boy all burnt. I did not know how his dad would take it. I thought that he might think that I had been careless and got him burnt so I just sat by my little boy and waited for Jim to come into the house. I told him what had happened. We sat beside our child and when he woke up he again went into a rock of pain. We walked the floor with him the whole night taking turns.

He could not even take a drink during the whole night. In the morning, he seemed to be better and asked for a drink. Then he fell asleep so we had a chance to look over his whole body. There were burns on his legs as well as his arm and face. We sat down and tried to figure out what we could do. The only thing we had in the house was a bottle of castor oil. I said to Jim, "You better get me a juniper stick and I will boil it and use the liquid to bathe the bums." I had no dressing. I had a couple of sheets and I tore them up for dressings. There was a small wound of open flesh on his elbow and I was really afraid that would become infected. I hoped and prayed it would be all right. Jim got the juniper stick. I went to work and boiled it four hours and started to bathe the wounds in the liquid.

On the second day, the spot on his elbow looked a bit red and infected. I took a piece of the stick and peeled the outside bark off and took the inside, the gummy bark of the stick, and beat it to a pulp. I sterilized my dressing by browning it on the stove and I placed a piece of the gummy pulp on his elbow. I greased the poultice with the castor oil and after six days he seemed to be getting a lot better.

There was a doctor at Nain with an explorer, Captain MacMillan from the United States. They were stationed at Nain but traveled all the time. MacMillan's doctor traveled to Hopedale and used to travel north to Okak, so we didn't know if he was in Nain or not. After eight days, my husband thought our little boy was better. Jim went out to Davis Inlet and waited for a day. On the second day, the doctor passed through Davis Inlet on his way to Nain.

Jim brought him up the bay the next morning. He looked at our boy and at what I was using and he said he was over the worst. He told me to carry on with what I was using. He gave me some dressings and I was very happy about what he told me. He said I had done a marvelous job so my mind was at ease then.

I was still sick myself from the infant fever and I had lost a lot of weight. The doctor said to me, "You should be in a hospital yourself." I was so frightened when the baby was burned that I hadn't eaten for four or five days. Jim stayed home with me for a month. It was three weeks before I could dress my little boy. I had three other children and the youngest was only two months old. We both worked night and day for about three weeks. With hard work we helped to save our little boy. We were both upset for a week because we did not know what was going to happen. You can't imagine what we went through that fall but the main thing is that we got through and our little boy got well again. Many, many times after, we both wondered how we had done it. But with God's help, we fought for his life together. For three weeks neither of us had a full night's sleep but the main thing was that he lived and we were both very thankful. When two people work so hard together to try to save a child, it is good to see him recover.

\* \* \* \* \* \* \* \* \* \*

The house I have now I call the house of my prayers because when my children were small and I didn't have enough room for them I used to pray for a bigger house someday. But now they are all gone on their own and I am by myself. I had a bedtime song I used to sing to them when I was putting them to bed. When my husband was away and we were left alone they would be asking for their daddy—when would he come home? I would sing this little song that I made up:

> Hush my dear, lie still and slumber,
> Holy angel guard thy bed;
> Heavenly blessings without number, gently falling on thy head.

# Woman of Labrador

**Andy Vine**

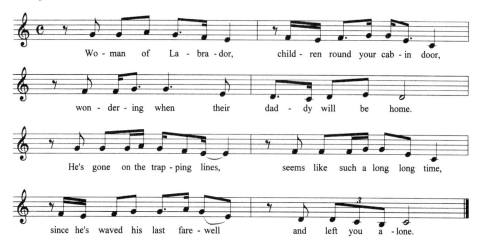

Wo - man of La - bra - dor, child - ren round your cab - in door,

won - der - ing when their dad - dy will be home.

He's gone on the trap - ping lines, seems like such a long long time,

since he's waved his last fare - well and left you a - lone.

Woman of Labrador,
Turn your mind to daily chores,
Hunting and catching fish
To feed your family.
At night when they're all in bed,
You go outside and raise your head,
Watch the northern lights go dancing
High over the sea.

Daughter of Labrador,
Those days are here no more,
You wonder if your baby will ever understand
The hardships that you endured
When everyone you knew was poor,
Sharing everything you had
And living off the land.

Woman of Labrador,
Children round your cabin door,
Wondering when their daddy will be home.
He's gone on the trapping lines,
Seems like such a long long time
Since he's waved his last farewell
And left you alone.

# Dramatic Adaptation of *Woman of Labrador*

## Sherry Smith

Our home was very lonely without our little boy, Bruce. I put his playthings away where we wouldn't see them. His empty place at the table took our appetites away. And when we went to bed at night, I would often hear his little voice callin' out for me. The family chain was broken.

It was time to leave this place.

That's what we did, too…we left Upitik Bay. We weren't able to make a livin' there any more. Each year we got a little more in debt to the Hudson's Bay Company; and they were getting more and more impatient with us. Finally, when Jim went to get our food again for the winter, the Hudson's Bay manager told us that if we could not pay off our debts that year, he would have to cut off our credit. They do that you know. Such power. We decided to move back to my parents' house in Mud Lake. Back home.

I was scared! We had four children now! There was no such thing as a welfare system—you either made do or you didn't.

So we decided, that was that, we were goin' back home. It was about a three hundred mile trip by dogteam. I was sorry to leave our little home. We had worked so hard for seven years, and in some ways it felt like we were givin' up. But change is always good, and we were ready for the challenge of startin' over—a new beginnin'. So off we went! In the dead of winter!

183

\*\*\*\*\*\*\*\*\*\*\*\*\*\*

"Jim! Jim! We got to stop soon! It's gettin' dark and the children are gettin' tired!…Just over that hill?…That's good. Jim! We're not goin' to make it over that! It's too high! Let us get out and walk!…Jim! Jim stop! Please stop!…Oh my goodness. Oh my good…Please let us make it. Please God, please.

Keep my children safe…Oh my goodness, we're slippin'! JIM!! WE'RE GOIN' TO TIP! JIM!! HANG ON!!

Horace! Marie! Jim, catch them! They're rollin' down the bank towards the water! Oh my God! Stop them! Jim! Do something! I can't move. Help us! The baby is trapped under my arm! She can't breathe, Jim! Oh God in Heaven, I can't lose another baby! Oh please God, someone help us! She's goin' to freeze! I can't tell if she's breathin'! Jim! Jim! Where are you?"

Archie managed to catch the children before they got hurt, and Jim got May and me out from under the komatik. The trip took twenty-five days in all—seventeen of those travellin' across some of the most unforgivin' land God ever created.

But, you know, all along the way, complete strangers took us into their homes. They gave us a warm place to sleep and a chance to cook a meal and wash out some clothes and diapers. Sometimes it was very late in the evenin' when we arrived upon them, but not one family ever turned us away.

# Tragedy of CF-BND

Leonard McNeill

My father, my brother Rupert and myself started off from Island Harbour on February 28, 1940. We started off about noon on that day. It was snowing a bit, so my father said we'd camp up the head of the bay, ready to go up across the portage the next day, heading for the country, trapping. That evening, getting in the cove, passing along be the old house I noticed there was a little flag on the corner of the house and there were stove pipes up. We knew the pipes had been rusted out for several years before that. I was very inquisitive about things like that, changes from how things were from past years. That night when we got to where we were going to camp, we unlashed the komatik, took off our load, boiled the kettle and had a fast lunch—we had a couple of hours of daylight left and wanted to teel a few traps up in, what we called, Little Bay Brook about southwest from where we were. We took off with the dogteam with a light komatik and rushed to teel a few traps.

The next morning when we got up it was blowing and drifting but a nice clear day, above the drifting. We could only see the tops of the hills for the drifting. Father said we wouldn't go up across the portage, it was too rough. I said since we weren't going on, I'd go and have a look at the old house, see if I could find out who'd been there. Walking over, all excited sort of, I seen a line that appeared to be a clothesline going across from the house to the old flag pole, which I found out later was an antenna. I went right to the door. At first I didn't notice the writing on the door, I guess I was young and too excited. I pushed open the door and on the wall was hanging a tent, in the kitchen of what used to be the former kitchen of Uncle Samuel Andersen's old dwelling house. This surprised me, I got more excited, I looked on the old-fashioned cupboard on the other side of the doorway, going into the living room, and here was some aluminum plates, a frying pan, some enamel cups and a camp kettle that had been boiled out of doors. Now, I says, whoever was here, they must have the intention of coming back to leave their cooking utensils and tent, those are valuable things and nobody leaves things like that and don't come back to pick it up. I opens the door of the living room and right in front of me was a man on a big bed, which had been built up across from the partition of the little bedroom in the living room, it was built out of a corner sort of affair. Here was this man lying in his sleeping bag with a pillow under his head. There was a cup on the pillow, I guess, where Davidson had been trying to give him a drink of water. It appeared to me his hand was up and he had been trying to reach for this cup at the last. Well, of course, certainly I knew the man was dead. As I looked on the floor, here was another man, Davidson I found out later, lying on his back and his face was all disfigured and eaten right to the bone by mice and weasels…that gave me a shock. I closed the door and made out of that house as fast as I could, and I fainted, the first time in my life I ever fainted. When I came to my senses, I beat it back to tell my father that something bad happened in the house, there were dead men there, however they got there.

Dad got all excited and he said, "You come back with me."

I said, "No, Dad, I can't go back right now, Rupert better go. You know what you're going to see, so you won't get the shock I did."

They went over and were there quite a little while. They found some of the papers, the writings and they found out where the plane was supposed to be, two miles northwest from the house. We talked things over for a while. Father said, "We can't stay here with the dogs because the house isn't in very good shape. We'll try and find out where the plane is."

We talked a bit more, and Dad said it was too rough to go yet, perhaps the wind would drop down later and we'd have it better. Dad got thinking about certain things that he should have found out, and when we found the plane we would have to go to Hopedale so he could send out a report. I was got over the shock by this time, so I suggested we'd all go back and make a good search. When we got back, hanging on the wall inside the door was a bottle, had been a pickle bottle, with a $180.00 in it, the little paper tied on the side of it stated; *This $180.00 is the pocket money of three dying men, Mr. Finder, it belongs to you.* I looked at the other paper on the table on which was written, *Mr. Finder, when you have found our bodies and aeroplane please report at once to the nearest wireless or telegraph office and plane will land here on ice and take our bodies to Montreal.* And the three names were stated; *Gerald Davidson, Joseph Cote and Joseph Fecteau.* There was a box on the table, it reminded me of somebody packed up and ready to leave. This box was done up in a sort of waterproof cloth, similar to these grey looking rain suits now, that sort of cloth. Written on the box was, *This box contains our diaries and our letters to our families.* Also in the house was a twelve gauge shotgun, a box was put upon the little corner shelf and every empty shell was put back in the box. I guess their intention was to kill something to eat. (I was told by the people who came to pick them up that they'd had a month's rations). After looking around and we were satisfied with what we'd looked at, we wouldn't move anything until we notified the Newfoundland Ranger.

Then we started to try and find the plane. We got ready our dogteam, leaving most of our load there because we knew we couldn't carry on in the country seeing this happened. We went light, took our tent and stove and enough food to camp with up to the end of the lake. It was still drifting when we went up over the bank. We had to go over this steep bank and through the woods. We came out on the end of the lake where the plane was supposed to be, but we couldn't see a thing for drift, so we made a place to camp in the woods at the corner of the lake. Rupert stayed to put up the tent and Father and I went to walk up by the north side of the lake. The lake was very narrow at that end, only about a quarter of a mile wide. So we walked a little ways and couldn't see anything. The sun was about to set at that time and the drifting was beginning to go down. While we were looking, we looked across and spotted the plane directly across from us, hauled in tail on. We went over and looked in the plane and that's where they had the date when they made the forced landing, up in the pilot's seat was a notice giving their three names and saying that they made a forced landing there on September 24, 1939. They said they were camped about two miles northeast in what appeared to be an old Hudson Bay Company down post. The plane was perfect, nothing wrong with her, just the floats frozen in the ice.

We went back and camped for the night and the next morning when we got up, 'twas a beautiful morning, the wind had gone down. Rupert, Father and I got ready and went over to Bill Abel's place, which was across the next bay. When you go up across this portage you come out on the bay they call Canairitok Bay and right across there is a place, the Eskimo name for it is Ittibliarsuk, where old William Able and his son Joey lived with their families. Right away when we got there and reported to them what we had found, Joey got ready right fast and took Dad on to Hopedale, so Rupert and I could go south to meet up with the Newfoundland Ranger, because we knew he was on his trip. He, Ranger Bragg, was the Ranger for between Hopedale and Cape Harrison at that time. We went back to Island Harbour and it was time for us to stay for the night. Early next morning Rupert and I started for Makkovik. By this time the dogs were getting tired from being on the go so much.. We stayed there that night and early next morning Bill Andersen took me on south to meet the Ranger. We met the Ranger about noon at Seal Cove, to Uncle Charlie Broomfield's place. The Ranger and Billy Winters, his driver, had just arrived there and were having lunch. I knew Billy Winter's dogteam. I went and told the Ranger about what we had found.

Right away the Ranger got excited and he said, "Is there any report gone out?"

I told him I thought there was 'cause we took Father on to Hopedale. The instructions of the men were to report as soon as possible to the nearest wireless or telegraph office, so we figured that's what we should do.

"Oh," he said, "You shouldn't have done that. My report should have gone out first."

"Well," I said, "We didn't know that. Sorry."

He felt sort of hurt over that.

We went on then, headed back to Makkovik and got there about dark that night. We got a few hours rest and took off for Island Harbour, getting there by breakfast time. When we got there Father was back from Hopedale and he had Harold Stevenson with him. Harold had been working with Adam's from Bishop's Cove in Newfoundland at a lumbering business, the outfit went broke or something, so Harold went to live with his brother Bob, who was the Marconi operator in Hopedale. Bob thought this might be a nice chance for Harold to make a few dollars, he knew that a watchman would be needed, so he sent Harold back with Father. Mr. John Grieve and Rev. Sach came from Makkovik. I think the Ranger called for Rev. Sach because he was sort of a medical man, his assistance was needed in examining these bodies to find out why they just stayed there and died, instead of trying to travel. A whole bunch of us went up in the bay.

Rev. Sach cut the clothing off the bodies to examine them and they started getting them ready to take to Hopedale, where the Ranger felt it would be easier for them to be picked up.

When they cut the pants off of Davidson, the man that was on the floor, the last man alive of the party, they found in his pocket a writing dated September 17th, in it he stated Fecteau was already dead and Cote was in a coma. When he went near Cote he could tell he was still breathing. It appears to me that was the last day he was alive. He stated he was cold and hungry. It appears to me that he was sitting facing the large window at the front of the table, like he was hoping somebody would come before it was too late. When he could last no longer, he fell to the floor, which was where I found him.

After the bodies were taken to Hopedale, the Ranger put Harold Stevenson and me up the lake as watchmen for the plane. We were there fifteen days before the other plane came, a little black plane—CF-AXB—an old model plane, as I can figure out now, there's been so many changes over the years. She was from Dominion Skyways. The pilot had to get out of the cockpit and put a crank down and wind up that plane to get her started, then he'd trip something and send the prop around. It appeared like it was a spring affair. He'd crank counterclockwise and you could hear this whining then all of a sudden, when he'd trip something, the prop would fly around ready to take off.

They brought a pilot and a mechanic for the plane. They brought a drum of aviation gas. They started the motors up right there where she was frozen in the ice, started up perfect, she just ran out of gas. I heard these people weren't supposed to come this far north. They were going to North West River where they planned to start a lumber operation. They left Seven Islands and overran their destination, which was the reason, when the plane was missing, they only searched between Seven Islands and Goose Bay. They never thought to look any further.

So I stayed there then. They took the bodies away and two people stayed there, Smithy and Paul Savarin, a French guy. We shovelled away snow from around the plane and chopped the ice away from the floats. We put jacks under the wings where there was a big snowbank. When the jacks took the weight of the plane they took off the floats and fastened skis on the plane. Billy Winters and the Ranger came out to haul the floats back to Hopedale to be shipped out by boat. So with our dogteam and Billy Winters' team, a total of eighteen or twenty dogs, we pulled the plane to a level spot where they started her up and warmed her up. The pilot said he was going to take her for a test run and if everything was all right he'd make three left turns, that's what he did.

Now, I never seen an aircraft before, not up close, except for this downed plane. My father told us not to ever go in a plane because he said we seen how these people died by getting in a plane and getting lost. The pilot asked me if I'd like to go for a ride in the plane. I said I almost thought I would. I was kind of nervous but anxious. Now, Father was in Hopedale so I thought I would get away with it. The pilot asked which plane I'd rather go in, the one I found? No, I thought I'd rather go in the other plane, the little black one. I thought that plane would be more reliable, the other one had been lying up and only had one little test run, so it might come down again before it reached Hopedale. He said that was fair enough, I could go with him.

After we got in the plane and she started up, I got scared but it was too late then. The drift ridges on the lake was so rough and the plane was jumping so much on the skis, you know. I thought, "What if one of those skis ever hooked into one of these ridges? Where would the plane go? Over and over I suppose and that would be the end of me." I had no choice. After we took off it was all nice and smooth and I enjoyed that trip. I was sitting beside the pilot and he asked me if I knew the land. I told him I did. It looked like a map to me. Then we saw the houses in Hopedale and landed, with the other plane behind us. Bob Stevenson and Father came out to meet the plane. Father got some surprise when he saw me getting out.

"Oh, my, " he said, "You took a chance and come in plane? I told you not to do that."

I said, "It's over now Father. I'm all right. It didn't hurt me. It's all over now and it was good experience."

From there they flew the plane back to where she was from.

This is my story of the finding of the Davidson party.

**ranger** n *OED* ~[1] 1 b (Nfld: 1884 quot), DC 1 Nfld (1771-) for sense 1; DC 2 b (1954-) for sense 2.

1 The common seal (Phoca vitulina), esp in its third year; BAY SEAL, DOTARD, HARBOUR SEAL.

Also attrib.

[1771] 1792 CARTWRIGHT i. 140 [He] gave me a ranger-skin. 1861 DE BOILIEU 97 The next kind [of seal] is a small and beautiful animal, called the Ranger, which remains on the coast all the winter, and is sometimes found about the bays during the summer months. This species is very interesting, as they may be tamed and sent out fishing, which they will do readily. They are beautifully marked, and the skin is much esteemed by the natives. 1873 CARROLL 10 When three years old they are called dotards, and their young rangers, which they have when 3 years old on the different island rocks in the different bays, all round the island, but more particularly in the northern bays. 1906 DUNCAN 281 Archie and Billy came upon a family of four, lying at some distance from their blow-hole—two grown harps, a 'jar,' which is a one year old seal, and a ranger, which is three years old and spotted like a leopard. 1977 *Innu Land Use* 128 In early or mid-June, ranger and grey seals migrate north to shallow areas near rocky shores, where they haul out to bask in the sun or hide from hunters among the rocks. Old rangers (dotters) are especially clever at concealing themselves. Unlike other seals, rangers breed late (mid-June) and moult late (mid-August).

2 Officer of an early twentieth-century force (1935-49) engaged in police and other duties in parts of Newfoundland and Labrador outside jurisdiction of the St. John's constabulary; NEWFOUNDLAND RANGER.

[1933 *Nfld Royal Commission Report* 218-19 We have suggested that the force [of 30-40] should be modelled on the Royal Canadian Mounted Police [and might] eventually take over all public work not only in the interior but in the outports as well, might collect the Customs and other revenue at all but the most important ports, might act as the representatives of the various Departments of Government...and generally might undertake duties, excluding those assigned to the Magistrates and Fishery Inspectors, which are at present distributed among a number of minor officials.] 1939 EWBANK 96 Throughout the greater part of the Island and in Labrador, the Rangers are responsible for maintaining the law and for prosecuting offenders. [1960] 1965 LEACH (ed) 211 "Game Warden Song": And dat was Judge Hodge and a gruff spoken ranger,/ Sure dey was a bringin' a summons for me. M 69-6 He then got angry and said he was going to tell the Ranger on us. That was in 1950, and we still called Mounties Rangers since we had always been told about Rangers up to 1949. 1975 RUSSELL 9 The Ranger (that was before the Mounties) measured the height of Grampa Walcott's fence and even brought the goat into court and measured his yoke. 1977 *Them Days* ii (3), 7 The Ranger...was also the Welfare Officer at that time.

*Christmas Fire*, oil on masonite, 30" x 23", Mary Pratt

*After the Christmas presents had been ripped from their wrappings, and before the turkey, and the gravy, the mince pies, and the flaming pudding were presented, we ceremoniously burned the Christmas papers. Packing boxes sent from distant relatives, the cardboard containers that until minutes before had displayed dolls, or trains, or wind-up motorcycles, the tissues that had hidden lingerie, the foil from chocolates, the cellophane from imported soap—all the casings of Christmas—set alight in the fire-barrel, making, for a few minutes, a blaze that outshone the Christmas tree itself.*

*I love the rituals of daily life. They indicate how important it is for all of us to celebrate the wonder of the mundane.*

*I paint what I love. Perhaps this is why I have come to value especially this painting. It reminds me of so much love, and generosity. Christmas—the warmest of celebrations—set in the coldest time of the year.*

*A blaze to reassure us that even the wrappings of love can light up a dark day.*

— Mary Pratt

# Miracles

## Michael Crummey

or convenience sake, let's say this story begins on a clear night in October. The moon is full, it stands out against the darkness like a single braille dot perforated on a black page. If you could reach your hand up to touch the sky, you would feel it raised beneath your skin like the improbable beginning of a letter, a word, another story. The air is cool, the leaves on all the trees have turned and started falling; they make an ambiguous rustle as you walk through their brittle brilliance, rich and melancholy all at once.

My brother and his wife are celebrating their tenth anniversary. I've been invited to join them for dinner, and after repeated attempts to shirk the obligation, I have relented. I don't enjoy the walk across town. I don't notice the moon, or the cool air except to pull my coat tight at the collar. I have a small package of fresh mussels under my arm—a surprise—my contribution to the evening meal. When I reach their house I stand at the front door for a moment, as if even now I might change my mind. It's been so long since I've visited that I feel compelled to knock and wait for permission to enter.

My younger brother answers the door and takes my coat; his wife, Jade offers me a drink. We make stilted small talk about the weather, the state of things at the mine while Jade steams the mussels and then we sit at the table to eat. My brother stabs a mussel with his fork, eats it, reaches for another.

"Are you sure you should do that Kim?" Jade asks him. That's my brother's name, Kim. A peculiar name for a boy, and even more peculiar at the time he was born, in a small community in Newfoundland. If I want to be honest, I'd have to say that's where our problems began, his name. And now that I think about it, maybe that's where I should have begun.

Mother had always warned us about the danger of putting convenience ahead of other things, like truth for instance, or thoroughness, which in her mind were almost synonymous. She was a strict Salvation Army woman, our Mother, and though Father attended church only for baptisms, weddings and funerals, Mother marched into her uniform every Sunday. Morning and evening she took her black leather Bible and silver trumpet from a shelf in the back porch and headed off to the Salvation Army Hall without him.

She had a no-nonsense approach to her religion that some servants of the obvious would label "military," but might more properly be called rigorous. Practical. She was always raising money for an overseas mission, or an alcohol treatment program, or a Christmas soup kitchen. Mother was also a member of the infamous Salvation Army band that commandeered the busiest corner of Black Rock's Main Street every Saturday in December and honked out metallic renditions of Christmas carols for most of the afternoon.

She loved to sing old hymns as she worked around the house as well, "Onward Christian Soldiers" being her favourite. It was a kind of battle cry against "domestic ungodliness." When she was called upon to break up a wrestling match between myself and Kim, twisting an ear on each head to keep us apart, you could sometimes hear her humming the refrain under her breath. One Sunday afternoon she brought out the trumpet and played it for fifteen minutes in the kitchen because Father had the unmitigated gall to sit down to a game of cards on the Seventh Day. He gave up on it finally, knowing Mother would go on till her lips fell off if he persisted.

But I was speaking about my brother's name. I was only a year old when Kim was born and it was a long time before I realized how strange a name it was and began asking questions. The story goes that in the third month of her second pregnancy my mother had a dream. And in the dream an angel of the Lord appeared unto her and announced she was going to give birth to a girl-child whose name was to be Kimberly. Mother put little stock in dreams and not much more in angels, and the anointed name was so ridiculous that she put the whole episode down to the pickled eggs she'd been eating by the dozen. But such a visitation was so alien to her tradition, so foreign and unexpected, that she was unable to dismiss it completely. Days before she delivered she had the dream a second time and Mother resolved to act in accordance with what she saw as the Will of God.

"But he wasn't a girl," I pointed out.

"Yes, well," Mother said. "There was some kind of mix up I suppose."

Father expressed his misgivings about the name after the birth and even Mother was perplexed by this turn of events. Still, she decided to shorten the name from Kimberly to "Kim" and go ahead with the christening. My father, having voiced his objections, wouldn't stand in the way of what he called her "religious convictions."

As far as I know nothing came of it. No descending doves, no parted waters, no speaking in tongues. I was the one who attended church regularly with Mother, and kept her company outside the Imperial General Store on bitter winter evenings before Christmas with a bell and the Salvation Army donation bubble. I was the one who wanted my own uniform and black leather Bible, who joined the junior band and tried desperately to learn how to play something, descending inexorably from trumpet to tuba to bass drum to the lowly tambourine.

"Mother," I said to her during the walk home from church one Sunday morning, "did you ever have any dreams about me?"

She looked sideways in my direction. It was a hot August morning, there were lines of perspiration trickling from beneath the band of her officer's cap. I felt embarrassed to have asked, but plowed stubbornly ahead. "Before I was born, I mean," I clarified.

"Why yes, of course," she said. Her tone was cheerful but she looked uncertain, as if God was late with a sign she'd been promised. "Haven't I ever told you? Well," she said, "I had this dream three times before you were born. I was asleep in my bed and the angel of the Lord appeared unto me. It was so bright, Stuart, that it hurt my eyes. It was as if the room was on fire. And then the angel spoke without moving its mouth. This voice seemed to come from all around me, from the air. "You are going to have a son! the voice said...."

"Didn't the angel say 'boy-child?'" I interrupted.

"Yes, you're quite right, now that I think about it, that was what the angel said. 'You are going to have a boy-child,' it said, 'and you shall name him Stuart.'"

"But I thought I was named after Poppy Ellsworth," I said suspiciously.

"Why yes," Mother said, hesitating a little. She took a tissue from her purse and mopped her brow. "That too," she said.

Our house on Pine Street was identical to the other Company houses in design, but the details reflected my parents: family pictures, sturdy furniture, basic colours, nothing garish or flashy or outrageous. They even managed to avoid the sparkled stucco craze that gripped the town during the early seventies, sticking resolutely to flat white ceilings. In many ways, Mother and Father were remarkably similar people: serious, stubborn, straightforward.

There was a lot of talk about Saving in that house. Father grew up during the Depression and never fully recovered from the experience. His next meal wasn't something he ever learned to take for granted. He was happiest sitting down with his blue bank book to go through each entry, adding and subtracting meticulously on a piece of scrap paper. The result was never in question, he just enjoyed the confirmation, the sense of security it gave him, however brief.

My mother *tch tched* over this obsession of his. "You can't take it with you Father," she'd tell him. Mother was more concerned with saving souls than money. Though that's too strong a word I think. "Soul" was too airy-fairy for Mother, not concrete enough, not at all practical. She preferred to use "person" or "individual"; to her mind they were more inclusive, they didn't over-simplify.

"Father," she might announce as she came through the front door after a Sunday service, "an individual was saved this morning!"

"Praise be," Father would say over the potatoes and carrots he was peeling for Sunday dinner, and he said it without a trace of irony. He was never fierce in his disbelief, or evangelical about it, he simply hadn't managed to settle anything to his own satisfaction.

Throughout our childhood and adolescence Kim and I fell on either side of that issue like opposite sides of a coin. Our parents never pressured us either way, but being young and being brothers, we weren't as kind to each other. He ridiculed my earnest fundamentalism. I badgered him to come out to church, to the youth group. These encounters usually ended in physical confrontations that Mother was forced to break up with our ears twisted in her fingers and a hymn barely audible on her breath.

By the age of fourteen I had become passionately interested in miracles. Having read through the entire Bible, and the Gospels twice, I was struck by the kinds of stories that were rarely mentioned at the Salvation Army Hall, or were glossed over briefly at best. Sermons and studies tended to focus on the Good Samaritan approach, the Boy Scoutish good-deed-a-day variety of religion. I was fascinated by the inexplicable, by the way Spirit transformed the physical, imbued it with properties it had lost or never possessed: the voice in the burning bush, the feeding of the five thousand, the healing of the blind and the cleansing of lepers. That spark lurked in the cells of all things like a dormant seed, a knot of latent potential.

This passion caused my mother some concern. She'd been brought up to think of miracles as a Catholic thing, a questionable devotion to pictures of the Madonna that wept real tears, and her own ambiguous experience with the "angel of the Lord" made her wary. She *tch tched* over it in the same resigned tone that she used for Father and his bank book.

It was Kim who was most offended by my obsession. His doubts about spiritual matters were confirmed in his Grade Seven science class where they were studying evolution. He began tracing caricatures of apes and tacking them to my door, leaving them on my desk, taping them to the bathroom mirror when I showered. *Stuart*, he scribbled across the top of each drawing, *the one that got left behind*.

I suppose I was an embarrassment to him. He was one of the best players on the local bantam hockey team. He pursued his burgeoning interest in girls with the same adolescent fervour I brought to my faith. He wanted an older brother he could look up to publicly, someone who could fight or smoked cigarettes behind the school. All I offered were lectures on "healing prayer" and "life after death" and inept tambourine lessons. It was Kim's popularity that protected me from the worst of the persecution I might have received from other kids and he probably resented that fact. Even if he had wanted to love me then, I made it impossible.

One Saturday morning the summer I turned sixteen, I was pulled out of sleep by the Company siren. ASAMCo provided fire-fighting services for the community and everyone knew the sector codes-one blast meant fire on Company property; two was the north end, from Main Street across to the post office; three was our side of town, from Main Street to Pine; and four meant the townsite to the north of Company housing. As I scrambled downstairs in my underwear that morning the prospect of disaster set my body vibrating like a struck bell. I'd never heard anything like this before, the siren went on and on in the grey dawn light.

Mother was standing at the window in her housecoat. Father was already dressed and pulling on his work boots, tying the laces with methodical fierceness.

"What is it?" I asked.

Father didn't look up. Mother held her hand to her mouth as if she were about to cry. Kim came into the kitchen behind me, still half aseeep. "What is it?" he said.

We hardly saw Father over the next three days. He'd come home at odd hours, sleep for an hour or two and then head back to the mine. No one in town slept much more than that. The rock had fallen in the Number 7 shaft of the old Lucky Strike mine and seven men were under.

The churches organized a constant prayer vigil, and there was an ecumenical service at the Roman Catholic church, the largest in Black Rock. I spent a lot of time in those three days on my knees. It was the first time I had a concern I felt was worthy of the grand gesture. I don't know what I wanted exactly. Proof I guess, a sign that God was acting in our lives in some tangible, quantifiable way. Something that Kim couldn't refute.

They made it through late on the third day, and six of the men were found alive. The seventh, Clay Keough, had been killed under the fall of stone. He was only a year away from retirement.

"Well," Mother said, "thank God the other six came out alive."

"Not much consolation to old Clay probably," Father said, and that's where they left it.

Kim had dismissed my requests for divine intervention from the start, and he taunted me with the dead man, held up the corpse the way some preachers hold up the Gospel, as if it were ultimate and indisputable truth. There were a thousand things I could have said to him, I could have talked about the unfathomable Will of God, I could have said something about faith and the lack of it. *Where wast thou*, I could have quoted, *when I laid the foundations of the earth*? But Clayton was dead for all that.

"It could've been Father down there," Kim shouted at me.

The slight, almost pretty features of his face had the ruthless focus of a predator on the scent of blood. "They could both die tomorrow," he said.

Things seem completely inevitable in retrospect. Even though it took place two years later after countless ordinary events, after thousands of inconsequential moments, it seemed to me that the next piece of this story—the hardest part—was set in motion and followed inexorably from that time, from those arguments.

It was a clear night in October. I was supervising a youth group sleep-over at the Army hall, Kim was away at a weekend hockey tournament in Corner Brook. I'd managed to settle everyone into their sleeping bags with the usual combination of empty threats and pleading, and had just begun drifting off when the siren began wailing. One. Two. Three. "Stuart," one of the kids whispered in the darkness, "that's your side of town."

They tell me my parents died in their beds, of smoke inhalation, before the flames touched them. An investigation placed the blame on faulty wiring and speculated that the fire may have smouldered behind the wall for days before erupting into the living room. By the time I reached the house that night the entire quad was burning. A helpless audience of neighbours stood about in nightgowns and undershirts. The light of the fire gave the street an intense, subterranean glow that made it seem as if the event was taking place underground. As if the entire town had been swallowed by grief.

The next September Kim left for university in St. John's. I was hired on as a clerk at the Company office and eventually worked my way up to accountant, taking night courses at the public school. I lived alone in a Company apartment and kept to myself. I stopped attending church, and as much as possible in a town the size of Black Rock, I avoided the people I'd grown up with at the Salvation Army Hall. My days were devoted to the artless certainties of arithmetic, my evenings to the television's bland menu of black and white movies and hokey Hollywood biblical epics.

In St. John's, Kim fell in love with Jade, a fine arts student who had come to Newfoundland from New York to study after she'd read *Death on the Ice*. She thought it would bring her closer to a world where nature still reigned, like Job's God, both provident and pitiless. She was disappointed to find herself in a real city, a small one granted, but a city nonetheless, with cinemas, theatres, public transit. Her only real consolation, she claims, was meeting Kim.

At their wedding Kim wore a traditional tuxedo, while Jade was adorned in a paper gown hand-sewn from the love letters she and Kim had written one another in the previous two years. "I know he doesn't seem like my type," I overheard her explaining to a friend from New York. "If it hadn't been for his name, I wouldn't have looked at him twice."

After he completed his engineering degree, Kim moved back to Black Rock where he worked with a team of prospectors, searching for a new mineral strike that would save the local industry from collapse. He made periodic attempts to establish a relationship with me but I kept him at a distance. Kim had never meant his ape caricatures as prophecy, I'm sure, but there I sat in the grey television light night after night: sullen, hopeless, deficient in some significant way. The One That Got Left Behind.

"Are you sure you should do that Kim?" Jade asked my brother.

I looked at her quickly, then turned to Kim. "Is there something wrong with the mussels?"

"No no," Kim said. "It's me."

"The last time he ate mussels," Jade explained, "he had an allergic reaction."

"Don't make it sound so dramatic. I got a tickle in my throat, that's all. And it's worth it. These are great Stuart." He stabbed another one with his fork, knowing I would have been uncomfortable if he didn't touch them at all.

"I don't think it would be a good idea to eat any more," Jade said. There was an abrasive note of warning in her voice, like grains of broken glass in the fibres of a carpet, and Kim held up his hands in mock-surrender. "All right," he managed as he chewed.

After the meal, we moved into the living room and sat with liqueurs. The conversation lurched uncomfortably as it had for most of the evening. Jade began presenting some of her latest sculptures and paintings and I tried to humour them both by paying attention.

"I'm trying to connect with something here," she said, holding a canvas upright on the floor. "Something at the core of things. I don't know if I've got it yet." There was a gnarled leafless tree against a background that might have been the barrens around Black Rock. The tree was in the approximate form of a cross. The piece was called "Salvation Landscape III."

Kim cleared his throat loudly and sipped his liqueur. "That's one of my favourites," he said to Jade. "I think you've really hit something there."

I stared at him in surprise. "That sounds a bit too flakey to come from you," I said, a little unkindly.

Kim shrugged, as if the abuse wasn't out of order. "Who knows, maybe she'll make a religious man out of me yet." He cleared his throat again. "There's that tickle," he said.

Jade scowled at him. "You know better," she said and got up to start clearing dishes from the table. Both Kim and I moved to help her but she waved us back into our chairs. Kim smiled at me through his obvious discomfort. "She's as stubborn as Mother," he said.

We sat in almost complete silence then, except for the clatter of Jade stacking dishes and the frequent sound of Kim clearing his throat. And as I stared at his reddening face, at his helplessly watering eyes, my grey, abysmal life unexpectedly erupted. It came to me like a vision, I saw it happening this way: the muscles at the back of Kim's throat swelling so severely that his windpipe was blocked, his body going into shock, convulsions. My brother, who had been right about the world all along, dead on the floor of his living room, a glass of *Creme de Menthe* spilled on the carpet.

It was as if a fire smouldering in the walls of a home had finally surfaced. "Jade," I shouted, my voice constricted to an octave above its natural range. "Jade, come in here."

Kim waved at me in annoyance, as if he was trying to quiet a child. "I'm all right," he said. "I'll be fine."

This story ends with the dream I had the night my brother and his wife celebrated their tenth anniversary, the night my brother said he would be fine and it was so, a clear night in October. There was a full moon, it stood out against the darkness like a single braille dot perforated on a black page. The leaves on all the trees had turned a brilliant red and were falling. All the way home 1 was shaking, pricked by this revelation, aware for the first time that what I wanted more than anything in the world was my brother to go on living. And to be there with him. Living.

I woke up in the old house on Pine Street. The rooms were full of light, luminous, as if the sun was out on all sides of the house at once. Downstairs I found Father in the kitchen, peeling a sinkful of potatoes and carrots for dinner. Sunday morning. I could hear the knife shearing the wet brown skins from the potatoes, and the serene tick of the stove clock. I don't think I was there as myself, in this body. Father took no notice of me and I didn't try to speak. I felt transparent and dispersed, like the air. There was a loud tramping on the step, and Mother marched in through the front door in her uniform, holding the gleam of her silver trumpet.

"Father," she said triumphantly, "an individual was saved today!"

And my father looked up from the vegetables with a smile.

"Praise be," he said.

# The Home

Raymond Hillier

…In my parents' bedroom, behind the door, underneath the slant of the roof, there was a large round-covered trunk with leather straps and brass buckles. A coloured picture of a steeple chase decorated the inside of the lid. A tray, approximately six inches deep, fitted into the mouth of this treasure chest. There were two sections to the tray, each covered with a leather-hinged fabric-covered top, held in a closed position by leather tabs buttoned over brass rivets. One section was my father's treasury department, which contained his money. As scarce as cash was in those days, it was quite understandable that he was so miserly about it.

The trunk was kept securely locked and the straps buckled, until one day he became desperate for a leather strap. Somebody else must have had a string of jingles around their horse's belly, and he was not to be outdone. Nobody would have guessed that when old Harry trotted along the icy paths on a frosty morning that the string of jingles which throbbed so melodiously were strung on a belt from the trunk in the bedroom.

Father carried the key in an empty money belt which he wore. The trunk held the secrets of special items such as clothing, books and oddities he had brought home from time to time on working trips, generally in carpentry around Boston, Massachusetts. He was noticeably conceited because of his adventures there, and often spoke of them with pride, and considered this experience an object of envy by of the local people. Few traveled far from Newfoundland in those days, so deep down in the trunk were secreted many mementos of personal pride. One such item was a white silk vest; known then as a waistcoat. It was stitched in padded fashion, no doubt a formal garment of the day.

There was also a pair of white satin-and-fur booties, intended, I believe, for me as an infant. I do not recall that I had ever worn them. Years later they were presented as a gift to the mother of a first-born in New Harbour. The value my father placed on them, I felt, could not possibly have been appreciated by the new mother. In this manner, piece by piece, throughout the years, his collection of mementos vanished.

*The Trunk of Tir-na-n-og*, distressed wood, copper, leather, hemp rope, 24"H x 30"W x 21.5"D, Eamonn Rosato

*Tir-na-n-og is Gaelic for Avalon, which means Land of Eternal Youth or the Land of Destiny. The ancient Celts believed in reincarnation and their spiritual resting place was known as the Land of Tir-na-n-og.*

*I have chosen to create a wooden trunk which would have been used by immigrants from Ireland and seamen in their long journey across the Atlantic to their new home in Newfoundland and Canada, fifty years ago or more. The wood is from a St. John's house that was built with red cedar from British Columbia. It represents the strong link Newfoundland has maintained with Canada. Each provides one another with invaluable assets. Newfoundland provides a unique culture and famous workforce, ready to take on all adversities, and Canada offers in return the protection and sustenance of a powerful nation held in high esteem throughout the world.*

*The traveller's trunk refers to our immigration trunk from Ireland, in a philosophical sense, to the Avalon Peninsula, Newfoundland in 1974. When Lily and I arrived in Newfoundland, the trunk was all we had and was almost empty, but between us we had known skills and unknown skills to offer Newfoundland and her wonderful people. Since then the trunk has been filled many times by their generosity and kindness and our new skills.*

— Eamonn Rosato

*Seaman's Chest*, Eamonn Rosato

The design is based on drawings and long hours of research with my friend
Frank Breen. He is an 85 year old Newfoundland seaman and I thank him
for his help and advice.

This centuries-old chest design was used by seamen for their main personal
storage while on the high seas. These were constructed to withstand the
rigours of life at sea and passed on from generation to generation. The chest
is designed with a number of drawers and even a concealed bottom section
for the sake-keeping of special papers, maps and valuables.

In the construction of the chest I have used traditional methods where possible.
It is mainly constructed of 120 year old pine boards rescued from the old
bond store and Newman's Port warehouse from lower Water Street, St. John's.
The knotted hemp-rope handles are called a "Carrick Bend" and was used
frequently on the old sailing ships. The metal spikes are from the old
Newfoundland Railway while the brass screws and washers are from the
old steeple of St. Patrick's Church.
The copper originated from the roof of the St. John's Anglican cathedral. Strap
hinges and hand-cut nails are found as well in the construction. To enhance the
nautical patina of the wood I have finished the chest with my own formula of
beeswax polish.

— Eamonn Rosato

# Help Me, Hepplewhite

**Anne Hart**

hen I first saw that chair it was all piled up with coke cans in the corner of Lauraleen's bedroom.

"Help me!" it seemed to cry, holding out gentle, graceful arms. Poor blind chair, were you hoping to clutch at skirts as I went by? How could you know, when I came to save you, I would be wearing jeans?

I am wearing jeans. I am clearing off a corner of Lauraleen's kitchen table to make room for soap and dusters. Good God, I am thinking, it is all worse, far worse, even, than Miss Minnow had described. Crusty dishes, broken cereal toys, worn out saucepans, chip wrappers, mouse droppings, broken glass, dirty ceilings, dirty walls, dirty floors, mould, smells, flies…Good God. Already, in my imagination, I am leaping forward in time to a bridge table at which I am sitting and at which I am saying: "'Mould, smells, flies …dirt all over the place. Who would say that I'm a great housekeeper? But when I saw all that, I can tell you I was shaken. It was another world.…"

You see? Already I am at the bridge table, feeling good. In point of time, however, I am actually leaping towards Lauraleen's Hepplewhite chair. I don't know it yet but I must sense something because I am crossing the kitchen without a second glance, however horrified, and I am heading straight for Lauraleen's bedroom door. There I am, opening it, and there before me, piled with coke cans, is the chair:

> George Hepplewhite, cabinetmaker of Cripplegate Ward in the City of London, died 1786 (date of birth uncertain). The simplicity grace and disciplined elegance of his designs brought the art of furniture making in England to its highest point. So far-reaching was his influence that it is strange to record that little is known of his life except that he was born in Lancashire and his wife's name was Alice…

Good God, Lauraleen, whoever you are, where did you get that chair?

The shock is so great that I close the door and I'm shaking so much that I have to sit down at the kitchen table to recover. I put my head in my hands and try to recall everything I've ever learned about chairs, which is a lot. When I finally decide that it's not possible for that chair to be there, in Lauraleen's bedroom, I feel so much better that I get up to have another look.

"Poor Lauraleen," I say, the door knob in my hand, "so poor she doesn't even have a chair in her bedroom to pile her coke cans on." There I am, opening the door, and there before me, Holy Jesus, God, is the chair:

> Hepplewhite obviously derived inspiration from many sources. In his designs can be traced the survival of such graceful rococo forms as the serpentine front and the cabriole leg. In the gildings and marquetries of his inlays can be studied the influence of the Italianate painters. The elegance of Chippendale he retained while replacing its massiveness with

a lightness and delicacy of a distinctly new style. To the rationality of his contemporary, Sheraton, he added the grace and fantasy which has become synonymous with his name…

Was it just yesterday that Miss Minnow, social worker, told me about Lauraleen?

But first let us not be deceived by Miss Minnow's name. Miss Minnow is actually a very with-it kind of person with long, straight hair and an uncluttered face. She is reading out loud from Lauraleen's file:

Lauraleen Delany: age 32 yrs., Grade IX educ., four children: ages 12 yrs. (girl), 10 yrs. (boy), 7 yrs. (boy), 3 yrs. (girl). Deserted by husband when youngest child 6 wks. old. Until recently managed fairly capably on social assistance although often depressed and anxious about future. Four months ago became very depressed and apathetic. Children discovered to be without proper care or food. Voluntarily relinquished them to foster care and agreed to admittance to mental hospital. At time of report is making average progress towards recovery…

Miss Minnow sighs and so do I. We both feel very, very badly about Lauraleen.

"What can I do?" I say. (Spontaneous concern is my thing, actually.)

Miss Minnow clasps her calm hands together and looks at me intently,

"Since that report Lauraleen has come along quite nicely, Mrs. Ealson, although she still resists the idea of returning to her former life…."

"And who can blame her?" I exclaim and Miss Minnow nods her sleek head in agreement.

"Who indeed?" she echoes.

We understand each other, Miss Minnow and I.

"Which is unfortunate," Miss Minnow continues, "since her children are not adjusting at all well to their foster homes. The youngest boy, especially, is becoming quite disturbed."

In our minds we regard the youngest boy, age 7. In mine he is thin and angry. "Where is my mother?" he is shouting, in his foster home.

"What can I do?" I ask again.

Miss Minnow shuffles her files.

"Ordinarily," she replies, "we wouldn't think of asking this of our newest Auxiliary members, Mrs. Ealson, but I've been told your volunteer work with the disadvantaged in other areas has been really quite outstanding."

(Right on, Miss Minnow. That's me. Outstanding. Show me a senior citizen or a head start and I'm out of my house like a shot.)

"And so," continues Miss Minnow, "I'm going to ask you to do something very special for Lauraleen." She leans forward. "I'm going to ask you, Mrs. Ealson, to clean her apartment."

"Her apartment?" I say. I just let the idea lie for a moment on the top of my mind. Clean? Her apartment? Miss Minnow, are you trying to con me?

It takes a moment for all the implications of this good work to sink in and then I am suddenly seized with enthusiasm for the whole idea of cleaning Lauraleen's apartment. Right there, in Miss Minnow's office, my hands itch to get at it…by the time I get through with it, it will be the cleanest, most attractive disadvantaged apartment in town…

I am already potting geraniums for the windowsills as Miss Minnow is saying things I know she is going to say even before she says them…

"At first thought this may seem a strange request to make of you, Mrs. Ealson, but we're convinced it may make all the difference in bringing Lauraleen and her children together again. I must tell you that the apartment is a mess. There's a lot of dirt. There's a lot of garbage. To return to it the way it is, and the hospital may be sending her home any day, would be very depressing for Lauraleen. Before her breakdown you see, she tried very hard, under difficult circumstances, to keep her apartment clean. It's far too small and lacks many things but she always managed, somehow, to keep it liveable and in order until one day, about six months ago, she just seemed to give up. Everything—the dishes, the dirty clothes, all the housework—began to accumulate. She started neglecting the children. She shut herself in her room. In the end she simply stayed in bed all day, drinking coke."

Coke? That coke thing at the end really surprises me. Up to then I'd been with Lauraleen all the way. I start substituting Canada's Food Guide for the geraniums.

"We can't let Lauraleen return to that apartment the way it is, Mrs. Ealson. She must make a new beginning."

Enough, Miss Minnow, enough. I hear your clarion call. Already I am in the soap aisle, arming myself. Soap, rubber gloves, disinfectant, ammonia…

"Psychiatry is not enough!" I cry, gaily, at the supper table. Tomorrow, with my little bucket and a key, I'm going over to play house at Lauraleen's.

Lauraleen's apartment is on the top floor of a thin green house which overlooks the harbour. The house itself presents no expression to the street: above its sloping piebald roof the winter rain falls.

I know all about these thin green houses which overlook the harbour. I've been in ones like this several times before: "My dear, how ever did you find it?…that view! Will you put new windows here, do you think? And a balcony?"

Now I, Mrs. Ealson—adventuresome volunteer with adventuresome friends—climb three flights of worn, wet stairs and at the top, in the silent half-dark outside Lauraleen's locked door, I surprise a child. He slithers by me, head down, overshoes clattering, and in a moment I hear the street door bang closed behind him.

Ah, Lauraleen, is that your child? Ah, Lauraleen, is that your kitchen? Ah, Lauraleen—darling, lost, shut-away mother—is that really your chair?

> Hepplewhite furniture was generally executed in mahogany, occasionally in satinwood, sycamore and chestnut, with finely proportioned inlays applied in a variety of rare woods: rosewood, tulip-wood, ebony and holly. Many items were exquisitely carved, others were painted or gilded but, however elaborate the decoration, every detail was rendered subordinate to the harmony of the final design…

Lauraleen, my pet, you must listen carefully to what I say. Design. Let us talk about it. In most lives there appears to be none. Take you and me—what are we? Ordinary women. I may clean your kitchen, you may clean mine. Who cares? When our grandchildren are grown up, who will remember us? But don't cry, Lauraleen, I have something important to tell you. You may not know it but we are very special after all, you and I. Into our lives—first into yours and now into mine—has somehow come this wonderful chair. You must believe me when I tell you that this may be the most important thing that has ever happened to either of us. Long, long after that child at the top of the stairs has forgotten his tears, Lauraleen, long, long after Miss Minnow's files have all been thrown away, there will be this perfect chair. And what do we know of the man who created it? Where he was born? That his wife's name was Alice? Practically nothing! Yet his work was so perfect that palaces are honoured to have it, Lauraleen, and when people hear his name…

"Mrs. Ealson? I'm just checking to see that they've reconnected the phone. I didn't recognize your voice for a moment. Is everything all right?"

"Quite alright, Miss Minnow. The phone just took me by surprise, that's all. I'm surveying the scene, you know, and planning what to do with everything here. The kitchen first, I think, and then the bathroom."

"Splendid, Mrs. Ealson! Lauraleen's in for a great surprise, I know."

Would you be surprised to know, Lauraleen, that once the garbage is removed your cupboards are bare?…Would you be surprised to know, Lauraleen, that your oil stove is in a dangerous condition?…Would you be surprised to know, Lauraleen, that little black bugs live under your sink?…Would you be surprised to know, Lauraleen, that behind that door there is an eighteenth-century chair?

203

> Hepplewhite's mastery of neo-classicism may be clearly seen in the designs of his tables, commodes and sideboards. His use of the curved front and the inlaid drawer has rarely been surpassed. His sofas should be studied for the delicacy of their tuned mahogany frames and the graceful concaves of their arms…

Let us sit down, you and I, Lauraleen, on the edge of this cracked bathtub and calmly discuss this whole situation right from the beginning. Let us first accept the incredible fact that you—by some unimaginable series of events—happen to be in possession of an exceptionally fine Hepplewhite chair. And let us move on—without further question—to the next important point: the future of this chair. Now after all I've been telling you, Lauraleen, you must realize that this can no longer be left simply to chance. What would happen to it, for example, if your stove caught on fire? What would happen if someone offered you ten dollars for it and your cupboards were bare?

Ten dollars, Lauraleen! What a sacrilege that would be. And, while we're on the subject of money, can you imagine what a chair like this might be worth? A thousand dollars, perhaps? Ten thousand dollars? Who knows? But just let us say, for the purposes of discussion, that this chair is worth at least three thousand dollars. And just suppose that I was to offer you three thousand dollars for this chair? What would you do, Lauraleen? What would you say? Do you really think you could prevent yourself from saying to someone, sometime—to Miss Minnow, perhaps, or to one of your children— "That crazy woman has given me three thousand dollars for a chair"? And then do you know what would happen, Lauraleen? I'll tell you what would happen—those people with the forms and files would hear of it and they would take it all away. Yes, bit by bit off every welfare cheque, so much at a time, year after year, they would take it all away. And, what's more, those people with the forms and files would never trust you again. So you can see, from what I've been telling you, how utterly wrong it would be of me to offer you three thousand dollars for this chair. And when it comes to that, Lauraleen, where would I get the three thousand dollars? Because—just between you and me—I may look rich but I really have no money of my own at all. Why you, with your welfare cheques, are really far better off than me. Do you know that I have to ask my husband for every penny I want, Lauraleen? And you, of all people should know what husbands can be like. I mean it was you, wasn't it, who wrote all those nasty things about them all over these bathroom walls? So what if mine said "Christ, three thousand dollars for a chair? and what about the kids' scholarship cruise? Look—I know you're crazy about old furniture but this is something else." My God, Lauraleen, what if he wouldn't give me the three thousand dollars?

> Some of the best examples of Hepplewhite's carving designs are to be found on the fluted posts and straight cornices of his four poster beds. An especially handsome specimen, hung with crimson silk, is to be seen in the Victoria and Albert Museum…

204

And speaking of beds, Lauraleen, we've got to do something about your children's. Two beds, three blankets and one pillow are hardly enough for four. And where do they hang their clothes, Lauraleen? And where do they keep their toys? And have they a junior microscope to more closely observe this mildew on their walls?…

"Hello, Mrs. Ealson? I have exciting news."

"News, Miss Minnow?"

"In two more days they'll be sending Lauraleen home. Will that give you enough time?"

"Time?"

"To finish, Mrs. Ealson. To finish Lauraleen's apartment." "The apartment? Of course. Why it's almost done, Miss Minnow. I'll return the key tomorrow. I've left Lauraleen's bedroom to the last, you know, and I was just about to open her bedroom door when you called."

"I hope we haven't imposed on you too much these last few days."

"Imposed? Not at all, Miss Minnow. On the contrary, I regard all this as a great opportunity."

"An opportunity? I knew we could depend on you, Mrs. Ealson."

And on you, chair, are depending exactly thirty-seven coke cans. Look, I'm taking them off your beautiful lap right now, one by one, and I'll never leave you again. I promise you. The last few days have been very hard for both of us, haven't they? Did you think I had forgotten you? Ah, as if I could.

> Above all, he is remembered for his lovely chairs. It is with them, undoubtedly, that English furniture-work reaches its peak. The shield, the oval, the heart-shaped back, the turned, the tapered, the cabriole leg, the

use of the wheat-ear and the bluebell as decorative motifs: probably no cabinetmaker better understood or expressed his art than did Hepplewhite with his famous chairs…

Ah, Lauraleen, have I hands to work? Look—your apartment is clean. Have I curtains for your windows? Look—they are hung. Have I food for your cupboards? Look—they are full. Have I clothes? Toys? Blankets? Look around you, Lauraleen—they are all yours. The sun is shining in your windows and your children will soon come running up the stairs.

Have you a Hepplewhite chair, Lauraleen? Look—it is mine.

Let us describe such a chair. Imagine that it is made of the finest of satinwood. Its back is an oval, a shape Hepplewhite handled more delicately, perhaps, than even the shield or the inter-laced heart. Four curved balusters, inlaid with designs of flower petals and acanthus leaves, are contained within…

Now, Lauraleen, please, don't cry. Don't you see that I can't leave it here? Don't you see that you won't even miss it? What do you know, after all, of acanthus leaves and bluebells made of holly? What can they say to you over the crying of children and the scuttle of black bugs?

Its slender arms and supports are fashioned into Grecian scrolls. Its legs, reeded and fluted, taper into graceful feet. When this lovely chair was young it was upholstered in rose-coloured silk, perhaps, fastened by polished brass nails…

Oh dear, Miss Minnow, was I so anxious to make things tidy that I threw away something I shouldn't have? With all the other junk and garbage? A chair was it? An old chair? Perhaps I can compensate Mrs. Delaney for it in some way? Now, Lauraleen, I can appreciate your feelings about that chair. It may have belonged to your mother. Perhaps to your grandmother as well. All of us become attached to childhood things and for a little while we may feel lost without them. But you must remember that there are other chairs. As it happens, I have collected a number of old ones myself. I'm thinking particularly of a very pretty Victorian armchair I have at home. If it would make you feel any better, Lauraleen, I would like you to have it…

You see, chair, how easy it all is? How carefully down the stairs and through the door? Look my darling, the street is empty. There is my car and not so much as a child to see us go.

What was the function, you may ask, of this enchanting chair? Briefly, it was this: to look beautiful…

Come, George, help me. Come, Alice, be with me now. Do you see this satinwood? Against the winter snow?

Ah, Hepplewhite, help me, help me.

*Hepplewhite Chair*, Gerald Squires

Excerpts from

# Wind in My Pocket

**Ellen Bryan Obed and Shawn Steffler**

### WIND SONG

"When one is in love with the Wind, Mother,
When one cannot sleep for its blow,
When all one can feel are its arms, Mother;
When one loves the Wind does it know?

Yes, I am in love with the Wind, Mother,
And all I can hear or can see
Or feel or want is the Wind, Mother;
Do you think the Wind also loves me?"

## ARCTIC FOX

White as the white of snow on snow,
He curls in the whirls of the arctic blow;
We can't see him sleep and can't see him go—
White as the white of snow on snow.

## WIND IN MY POCKET

With wind in my pocket up from the Sea
    and a cloud from the sky to wear,
With a bundle of sun tucked under my arm
    and ribbons of rain in my hair,
I walked to a bend in the afternoon
    for a friend who was waiting there.

# Borrowed Black

## Ellen Bryan Obed and Jan Mogensen

No one who belongs to the Labrador
Knows where Borrowed Black lived before
He came to stay on the tall, dark shore
On the wildest tickle of Labrador.

Some say he came like a wolf through the snow;
Some say he came like a seal on a floe;
Some say he came like a jaeger in flight;
Some say he came like fog in the night.

\*\*\*\*\*\*\*\*\*\*\*\*\*\*

He stayed there, yet no one would visit his shack,
For Borrowed Black borrowed—but never gave back.
He borrowed his hands from the paws of a bear.
A patch of brown seaweed he borrowed for hair.
His eyes were a wolf's, and he borrowed to hear
Two empty seashells—one for each ear.
He borrowed the beak of a gull for a nose.
He cut off the sails of a schooner for clothes.
Thin shells of goose eggs he had for his face.
His bones were dried driftwood shivered in place.
He walked on seal flippers; they were his feet.
He borrowed some whale's teeth so he could eat.
A borrowing wind he had for a heart
(It held him together, each small borrowed part).

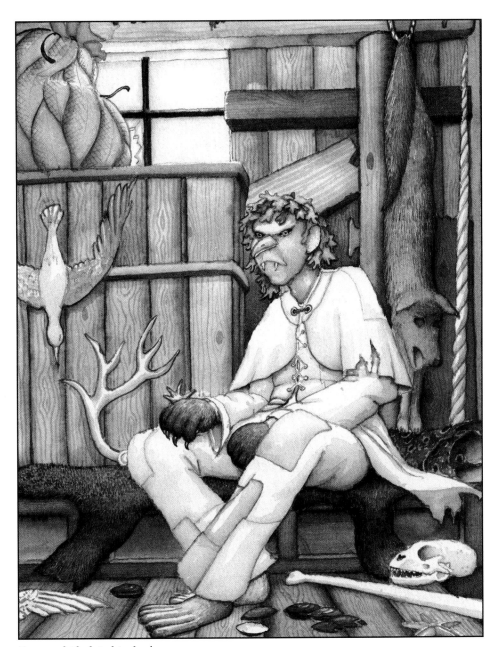

Borrowed Black in his shack

Excerpt from

# Down by Jim Long's Stage

## Al Pittman and Pam Hall

A sculpin named Sam
thought as he swam
how wonderful ugly
was he.

He said with a grin,
"I'm as ugly as sin."

"I'm the ugliest fish
in the sea."

**Excerpt from**

# On a Wing and a Wish: Saltwater Bird Rhymes

## Al Pittman and Veselina Tomova

Have you ever sailed in the salt sea sky,
Or ever wished you could?

Oh, wouldn't it be wonderful.
Oh, wouldn't it be good
To whirl and swirl and swing about
Without a care or sorrow,
Without a care about today
Much less about tomorrow.

And wouldn't it be heavenly
Not to be confined
As fish and other creatures are—
People and their kind.

Oh, you might think so,
And be quite right
To wish yourself as free
As any bird who ever sailed
The sky above the sea.

But do be careful with your dreams
(With what you wish for and desire)
For no matter how high you are able to fly,
Up will always be higher.

213

*Polar Bear on the Labrador Coast*, Ray Fennelly

*In 1973 I went to St. John's to buy a stereo. On the way to The Great Eastern Oil I passed by Tootons and saw a camera in the window. I bought that instead!*

*My father was shocked at the price of the camera and asked me what in the name of God I was going to do with it.*

*"I'm goin' to be a photographer," I said.*

*I was sixteen.*

— Ray Fennelly

*Cotton Grass*, Dennis Minty

*I photograph what I love—the expanses and the details of this land that is my home. Their texture, colour, moods, and interconnectedness are my inspiration. The wondrous light that bathes them shapes what I see. With camera in hand, I slow down, stop, and become absorbed by my surroundings. This process gives me peace of mind like nothing else. In fact that's what these pictures are—my peace of mind.*

*I owe this place, Newfoundland and Labrador, a great debt. It has given me a quality of life that I suspect is unattainable, for me, anywhere else on earth.*

215

*Cotton Grass*, Dennis Minty

*On the side of Saglek Fjord, with the Torngat Mountains of northern Labrador stretching to the north, I found what looked like the root-source of all the world's cotton grass—a veritable breeding colony. Like a frosted, floating meadowland, they swayed with each waft of mountain air across the inlet. This sedge is also know as Hare's Tales and "puffs out" in late May or early June on many peatlands throughout the province. I wonder if they all started from here on Saglek Fjord?*

— Dennis Minty

# The White Fleet

Richard Greene

## I

Barefoot, they played football beside their ships,
The fishermen of Portugal's White Fleet:
Hard tackles on the planking and concrete,
And always foreign tongues shouting pleasure
In tones unmistakable to a boy
Who watched their old leather fly to makeshift
Goals among the nets and ropes and barrows.
The ships, docked three abreast, filled the harbour
With a swaying thicket of masts and yards
And the white blaze of their clustered hulls.
I cannot imagine how it must have seemed
At night on the Banks, their city of lights
Over a sea that teemed with endless catch,
But in port they were magical enough
To paint the town with rough benevolence,
A giving of half their lives, year by year,
To the fishing grounds and this Irish place.

## II

I am five or six, holding my father's hand,
Looking onto the deck of a square-rigger,
One of the last that could have laboured
On the open sea, this fleet's centuries
Salted and stacked in its shadowy hold,
A few men on deck, olive faces burned
Dark by sealight: they stand for thousands.

## III

Two lives, divided by sea and season,
Some fathering casually in St. John's
Children they might not speak of in Lisbon
When Autumn sailed them to their legal loves.
As for the rest, they were faithful or cheap,
Fished abroad and bred quietly at home.

In a city of rum-drinkers, they drank
The wine that travelled with them, sold brandy
On the dock to the bootlegger women.
Public order bore with their offences,
And the constabulary made nothing
Of loud drunkenness and small affrays,
Because their charities stood in balance:
At any late hour, a Portuguese crew
Would genially pour out its twenty pints
To save some stranger bleeding at St. Clare's.


## IV

They rowed out, single men in their dories,
As the ship stood to seaward like a wall
Built hard against the ocean's farther death.
They paid our trawls, hooks baited with caplin
Or squid, and hauled in the twisting cod
Until their boats brimmed with silver thrashing.
Then, pulling the oars back and back, they brought
The dories to the ship, loaded their catch
In lowered tubs, and climbed out of the sea.
But sudden mists came on the Banks, white ships
Vanished, and there was nothing to row for
But the fog-horn sounding on a muffled deck.
Easy enough to pass all safety by,
Go in circles or row far past the ship
Towards a swamping on the open sea.

## V

Fishermen in procession from their ships
Carry Our Lady of Fatima
Up through the city's winding old-world streets
To the Basilica of the Baptist—
This to honour Mary in their other home
And to make a tighter kinship in her prayers
With those who got the gist of an Ave.
That was years before I was even born.
Their virgin stands now in a shrine beside
The altar, kindly and bland and southern
In the midst of a severe architecture
Out of place among terrible stone saints.

I look for the fishermen in their gift
And find that they are barely knowable:
Their hands hardened by rope and oars and salt,
Hers a little pale plaster outstretched;
Their sailors' eyes narrowed by the sun,
Hers widened toward the light's clemency.
And yet she, Stella Maris, was the prayer
They uttered when they left port in blessed ships,
The prayer for plenty, the prayer for passage.
Fish and fishers gone, she prays for them still,
Their dangers passed and all petitions moot.

## VI

Something ended: thirty years of dragnets
Harrowed the seabed to a kind of hell.
I cannot remember when the last white ships
Went through the Narrows, old friendship extinct,
And the ocean breeding only grievance.
At the far end of the harbour I watch
A container ship swallowing cargo,
And, before me, three or four fishing boats
Roped to the wharf waiting for a good year.
So many lifetimes of the Portuguese
Are berthed in the silence of this afternoon,
As their voices ring to a quietness
In memory, just at the moment's edge,
Where sunlight reflects on moving water
A bounty beyond our best intentions.

# A Seaman of the White Fleet

## Wayne Ralph

It was a standard Woolworth's in shades of tan and red, located in the Stewart Building on Water Street. For a school-boy with little money, it was a welcome oasis, the place to buy your mother a gift—the usual pack of bobby pins and set of bright plastic combs, or an oval hand mirror. The uniformed women behind the lunch counter would let you loiter a long time with a soft drink poured over ice cream, or a banana split.

I had run pell-mell down the steep hills from Bond Street after school, making a wide detour around the policeman directing traffic on Duckworth at Prescott, heading for the harbour. I wanted to see what ships were at the docks, and spend my allowance at Woolworth's.

You could not see the harbour from the lunch counter, but you knew it was there. It was spring, one of the rarest of St. John's days with light winds and eye-squinting sunlight, with the oil-slicked waters almost, but not quite, post-card blue. My Uncle Fred always said there was nothing so fine as a fine day in Newfoundland. It was one of those days.

School was out, and the White Fleet was in, anchored in line-astern, squeezed between the harbour craft, motorized fishing dories, British destroyers, and Greek tankers. They were three- or four-masted 19th century sailing vessels, converted to diesel power. Their crews, men and boys of Portugal, had been crossing the Atlantic to fish the Grand Banks, and had been sheltering in this harbour for centuries. The furled sails and tall masts brought fiction to life, right in my front yard, right there in the St. John's harbour. With the possible exception of a Royal Navy submarine, no vessel had greater romance for a boy than a White Fleet schooner.

I could see aboard, count the little dories, pat the ship's dog, and nod to the sailors as they fried caplin on deck. They always smiled back, and posed for photographs. I had never been to the banks—that fog-bank-creeping, gray-sea-heaving world. No rope-burned, fish-blood hands for me. I was a *hangashore*—only a school-capped kid with a romantic heart. The total of my seafaring experience was Spencer Tracy drowning, and Freddy Bartholomew crying at the climax of *Captains Courageous*, the B-movie of a little-known Kipling story or, *Treasure Island*, with me, not Jack Hawkins, scuttling up the mast of the *Hispaniola* to escape Israel Hands.

I had never had a one-on-one exchange with a White Fleet fisherman until that afternoon at Woolworth's. I was eating my way through the strawberry section of my banana split, savouring as only a 14-year-old can that subtle mixture of chocolate ice cream covered with squashed, pectin-soaked strawberries out of a tin, washed down with Orange Crush. He sat down on the stool to my right, and asked, with a word and gesture, what was I eating? When I turned to answer I saw first his callused hands with red knuckles, then brown eyes and black hair.

The younger waitress, the good-looking one, moved down the counter towards us. Without removing the cigarette from her mouth, she asked him what he wanted, and he said: "A beer." Glancing towards me, she winked (near stopping my adolescent heart), and replied: "We don't serve beer here."

The seaman pointed towards my drink, while reaching into the left pocket of his worn, shapeless canvas pants. As he drew out a folded $1.00 bill, a green one with George Washington's face on it, something about the downward tilt of his head signalled to me that this was not a man, but a boy like me. I was certain of it when he smiled, and lifted his glass in a friendly toast, saying nothing, but eyeing the waitress as she strolled back to the far end of the counter, back to her interrupted conversation. It was quiet, the store soon to close, with only he and I sitting on the chrome stools.

I continued dissecting my banana split, making it last. I wanted to ask him about life at sea, what it was like on the banks, and in his village in Portugal. But that was not possible, so we drank Orange Crush, staring ahead into the gold-flecked mirror on the back wall.

His fingernails were dirty and his hands were rough, while mine were girl-smooth, stained with the ink of Latin verbs—"Amo, Amas, Amat." He had spent his afternoon repairing a torn net on a wooden deck, while I gazed longingly at the sunlit South Side Hills. Our Latin instructor had been teaching us blue-blazered, gray-flannelled snots how to conjugate verbs in a dead language. Not half as dead as we were, but dead none the less.

I knew I was going to remember this Portuguese seaman, and I watched from the corner of my eye as the waitress counted out his change, coins with the young Queen Elizabeth on them. As he stood up, he slid a coin towards the back edge of the counter, grinned at me, and walked away.

He had left behind a tip, a dime for a quarter drink, something I had never done because my weekly allowance did not permit such generosity. But his was not the act of a boy, but the casual gesture of a man, one who earned a dangerous living by the sweat of his brow. There was no striped school tie for him, just hand-lining in a tiny dory on a heaving, greasy sea, with his eyes rivetted on the fog bank moving in.

*The White Fleet*, Ben Hansen

*Creoula*, a Portuguese Training Ship

Excerpts from

# Terras de Bacalhau (Land of Cod)

## Resource Centre for the Arts (RCA) Theatre Company

**Collectively written by Kay Anonsen, Rick Boland, José E. Silva, John Koop, Jim Payne, Janis Spence, Greg Thomey, and Mary Walsh**

**Music created and/or arranged by Jim Payne**

CAST OF CHARACTERS (In order of appearance)

**JOÃO:** Young Portuguese fisherman on his first visit to Newfoundland, Kay's lover.

**ROSA:** João's mother in Portugal.

**JOAQUIM:** João's father, who fishes off Newfoundland, Doreen's lover.

**TONINIO:** João's younger brother in Portugal.

**ROS:** Rosalynn Dunn, Newfoundland woman, friend of Doreen.

**DOREEN:** Newfoundland woman, friend of Ros.

**RICKEY:** Rickey Dunn, Ros's son.

**MR. FORD:** Social worker.

**CAPTAIN:** Captain of the *Manuelá*.

**CARLOS:** Radio operator on the *Manuelá*.

**PILOT:** St. John's harbour pilot.

**COCCYX:** Friend of Doreen and Ros.

**PEDRO:** Portuguese fisherman.

**MANUEL:** Portuguese fisherman.

**RITA:** Employee at the Arcade Store.

**KAY:** Kay Halloran, young woman who falls in love with João.

**AGNES:** Agnes Halloran, Kay's mother.

**CECIL:** Cecil Halloran, Kay's father.

**RONNY:** Ronny Halloran, Kay's younger brother.

**UNCLE VANYA:** Kay's uncle.

**AMBROSE:** Ambrose Lewis, friend of Cecil Halloran.

**ALBERTINO:** Portuguese fisherman.

**MARGE:** Cocktail waitress at Mike's Bar.

**RICKIE:** Rickie Ricketts, piano player and singer at Mike's Bar.

**CYRIL:** Kay's former boyfriend.

**FRANK:** Patron at Mike's Bar.

**MIKE:** Bar owner, friend of Cyril.

**LACKEY:** Bar patron, a flunky friend of Doreen.


## ACT I, SCENE 1

*A mandolin plays two Portuguese waltzes in the dark, over which a taxi horn is heard. Music fades. Lights up. The play opens in a kitchen in Portugal, as Joaquim and his son João are leaving for the Newfoundland Grand Banks. Rosa's wearing a black wig and a black shapeless dress.*

**JOÃO:** O taxi deve estar a chegar.

**ROSA:** Credo homem nem me fales, nisso, que me aperta coração.

**JOAQUIM:** Mulher, a vida é assim.

**ROSA:** Why don't you get a job inland?

**JOAQUIM:** The earnings are small here. The way of living is always going up. It is starving us to death.

**ROSA:** There are many people here. They take care of themselves.

**JOAQUIM:** Yes, I know, but I don't think it is this time that I stay.

**ROSA:** No, I think not now or ever, and this time you take the boy.

**JOAQUIM:** He has to learn to make a man out of himself, and even though his makings will be small, it will be good for all of us. *(To João)* Where were you earlier, João? I was worried about you.

**JOÃO:** I said good-bye to Maria. She was sad.

**JOAQUIM:** No time to think aboout that now. You have everything packed? Gillette, blades, soap. There is no store out there where you can buy those things; and you pack a tie. I want you to look good in St. John's. And Antonio, what you want me to bring you back this time?

**TONINIO:** Uma tenda.

**JOAQUIM:** Well, I'll see what we can do. It's between your brother and I what we can do. You be good, eh! Get good marks in school, then when you come out maybe you'll be an officer, eh.

**ROSA:** No, no, no, Joaquim, the sea will not have this boy.

(*Taxi horn sounds.*)

**JOÃO**: The taxi is here.

**ROSA**: You take care, you take care of the boy.

**JOAQUIM**: Be good. You, boy, take care of Momma, eh!

**ROSA**: You write. Okay.

**TONINIO**: Boa pesca.

(*They leave and walk across stage to the ship.*)

**JOAQUIM**: Ah, como está, Capitaõ.

**CAPTAIN**: Ah, Joaquim. Como estás.

**JOAQUIM**: Estou bem. Este é o meu filho, João.

**CAPTAIN**: You'll be bunking together in cabin thirteen.

**MANUEL**: (*Singing*) "Only a Fisherman."

> I'm only a fisherman, and I do whatever I can,
> I don't like to take from my brothers and sisters,
> Who are just as poor as I am.
> When Mother Portugal was a great power,
> We left our homeland to die by the hour,
> In some foreign land, we'd take what we can,
> And leave nothing for the people.
> We incurred the wrath of Jah,
> When we plundered Ethiopia,
> Bullets flew against the wall,
> We marched in and took it all,
> But Jah said colonialism must fall.
> I'm only a fisherman, and I do whatever I can,
> I don't like to take from my brothers and sisters,
> Who are just as poor as I am.
> Yes, I'm only a fisherman I take my living from the sea,
> We catch the fish, one man chop the head off,
> Then it's out with the guts, split the backbone,
> Salt'em down in the hold.
> In India, in Guinea and Cabo Verde,
> We were masters there and we were feared,
> Everywhere the war plan was tried,
> But like Mozambique, the people's spirit never died,
> 'Cause they cried out,
> "No, no, no, no, to your prisons.
> No, no, no, no, to exploitation.

No more I'll be your slave,
No more go to early grave.
No, no, no to oppression."
We finally left Angola alone.
Now they are masters of their own home.
Much to the dictator's dismay,
The people's revolution had its day.
There's still bad blood in Brazil.
People there have had their fill.
Still many tears, still much pain,
People there are still in chains.
Workin', workin', workin' for the rich man.
People shed their tears for freedom,
For a better way, they had their say,
Like Mozambique, like Angola, they cried out.
They said, "No, no, no, no, to your prisons."
They said, "No, no, no, no, to exploitation."
They said, "No more I'll be your black slave.
No more go to early grave."
They said, "No, no, no, to oppression."
Yes, I'm only a fisherman, and I do whatever I can,
I don't like to take from my brothers and sisters,
Who are just as poor as I am.

## ACT I, SCENE 6

(*Ladies department in the Arcade. Rita pushes in a large bin on wheels, it is full of ladies' lingerie.*)

**VOICE OVER**: In our Arcade shoe department, downstairs, brand name sneakers. Out they go, while they last, at the incredibly low price of three for a dollar. That's right, shoppers, brand-name sneakers, out they go, while they last, at the low, low price of three for a dollar. (*Muzak plays.*)

**RITA**: My God, girl, I don't know why we stays open on Thursday night. We're never busy. All we got to do is tidy up the bins.

**KAY**: I know, girl. Just as ya tidy 'em up someone comes along and messes 'em up again, right, Rita?

**RITA**: (*Folding clothing busily as she speaks.*) I know, Kay, I'm bet out from tidying up these bins.

**KAY**: Oh well, it's nine o'clock. We'll be off in half an hour.

**RITA**: I know, Kay, but half an hour here is like two days any place else. And then, all I got to do is go home. I got nothing to do at home. I might as well be here tidying up the bins. Oh no, here come the gees.

**KAY**: What's the gees?

**RITA**: The Portuguese. There's a whole flock of 'em on their way in. (*Carlos, Pedro, Joaquim and João enter. Rita rushes to prevent the men from messing up the bins.*) No, no, no, no, no! I'll get it for you. What size do you want?

**CARLOS**: Size?

**RITA**: What size do you want? 34,36,38,40? What size?

**CARLOS**: Wife size.

**RITA**: Is your wife a big woman or is she small like you?

**CARLOS**: Sim, sim, 93-56-93!

**RITA**: She must be deformed. You're gonna have to go into yardgoods to get something to fit her.

**CARLOS**: Não, não, não, 93-56-93, like you, smaller. Like you.

**RITA**: Like me! Smaller! I don't have to take that from you. (*Calling out to the manager*) Mr. Baird, Mr. Baird! And me after starving meself all day. Do you know what I had to eat all day? A piece of dry toast and a cup of weak tea, that's all.

**KAY**: Rita, I think he's talkin' in kilometres or something! (*Kay mimes using cash register. Pedro is buying a bra. She asks Rita.*) Is this a dollar-sixty-nine or sixty-nine cents?

**RITA**: No, it's marked down, Kay honey. It's got no hooks on it.

**PEDRO**: (*Turning to Rita*) What is the name for you?

**RITA**: My name?

**PEDRO**: Sim.

**RITA**: Rita.

**PEDRO**: Rita? They call me Pedro. Pedro.

**RITA**: Good, very good…

**KAY**. That's sixty-nine cents plus tax is a dollar-forty-three.

**JOAQUIM**: No, no, no—no tax.

**KAY**. Rita, do the Portuguese pay tax?

**RITA**: No girl, the Portuguese don't pay tax.

**KAY**. Now, what am I gonna do? I've already got it rung in.

227

**RITA**: Well, I'll fix it after. I've only got one pair of hands.

**KAY**: Okay. (*She puts the bra into a bag for Pedro.*)

**JOAQUIM**: Obrigado. Até logo.

**RITA**: (*To Carlos who has found a bra*) Did you find one in kilometres? Take it to the cash.

**CARLOS**: (*Puzzled*) The cash?

**KAY**: (*To Carlos*) I can't ring anything in 'til I get this straightened out.

**RITA**: Look, I'll straighten that out and you come and serve him, okay?

> (*Rita gestures to João. She comes over to the "cash register" and Kay moves to help João who is holding a pair of trousers.*)

**KAY**: Do you wanna try them on? (*She points. He doesn't understand.*) You have to go in the dressing room. I'll take you to the dressing room. (*She uses hand gestures.*). Me—you—dressing room. Okay, you can take those off to try these on. (*João puts an arm around her, suggestively.*) No, no, no, no! Rita! Rita, he thinks I'm gonna go in the dressing room with him.

**RITA**: My God, girl, ya gotta be careful. They're out to sea for eighty days. Men got needs, Kay.

**KAY**: (*Laughing, unafraid. To João*) Just you in the dressing room.

**RITA**: (*To Carlos*) What do you want now? It's twenty-five after nine. You're not gonna have time to buy anything else. You already got a bra.

(*Carlos demonstrates slip by moving his hands voluptuously down his body. Shaking his hands he cries "Woo, woo!"*)

**RITA**: Oh, you want a slip? Here. Now this is the same size as the bra.

**CARLOS**: Wife size. Like you.

**RITA**: Yeah, wife size.

**CARLOS**: Like you.

**KAY**: (*To João*) Oh, no, no, no, you want…you want this? Oh yeah, they're nice. You might have to shorten them a little bit. Are you goin' to take them?

(*Kay moves to the cash register.*)

**JOÃO**: Sim. You finish?

**KAY**: What?

**JOÃO**: You finish?

**KAY**: Oh yes, we're closing, soon. That will be twelve dollars and eighty- seven cents.

> (*João pays.*)

**PEDRO**: Rita. (*Trying to give her a note*) For you.

**RITA**: (*Speaking slowly and distinctly*) Take it to the cash.

**PEDRO**: (*To Kay, pointing at Rita*) You give this Rita? Goodbye, cash.

(*Pedro exits.*)

**KAY**: Yes. Okay. (*To Rita about João*) He was kind of cute.

**RITA**: My God, Kay, you wouldn't go out with a Portuguese, would ya?

**KAY**: I never said anything about goin' out with him.

**RITA**: Sure, Kay, you're goin' to university in the fall, you don't have to go out with Portuguese.

**KAY**: (*She mimes trying to enter tax at cash register.*) Rita, I don't know how to fix this.

**RITA**: Oh, don't worry about that, Kay girl. You go on home now, I'll fix that later.

**KAY**: Gee, thanks, Rita. I'll see you tomorrow. Oh, someone left a note for you, it's on the cash. (*Site exits.*)

**RITA**: (*Finds note.*) Oh, no. "You—me——movies—'Herbie Goes Bananas.' Love Pedro." What am I goin' to do now? He's probably on the street waiting for me. I'm gonna have to spend the whole night in the store. I'm gonna have to sleep in me bins.

(*On sidewalk outside store*)

**KAY**: (*Surprised to see João there*) Oh! I kinda thought you'd be here. (*He smiles charmingly, but he looks forlorn.*) You don't understand, do you? Well, I have to go now.

**JOÃO**: A onde está Basilica?

**KAY**: The what?

**JOÃO**: The Basilica? Where is Basilica?

**KAY**: Oh, the Basilica; oh yeah, it's up, just up there on top of the block to the right. (*João looks confused.*) Oh right, I'm sorry, look. (*She gestures.*) Well, you go down this street and when you get to the courthouse then you go up the steps and it's to the right.

**JOÃO**: This my first viagem a St. John's.

**KAY**: What?

**JOÃO**: First voyage to St. John's.

**KAY**: Oh, your first voyage to St. John's. Oh, I see. Well, that's nice. Listen, I have to go to my house. My house.

**JOÃO**: Your casa. You—me—your casa?

**KAY**: No, no, I'll take you to the Basilica, okay?

**JOÃO**: Me—you—Basilica.

**KAY**: Yeah. (*They exit.*)

## Act II, Scene 3

**MANUEL**: (*Singing*) "Salt Water Charly"

> She was only a Salt Water Charly,
> In a dress of chiffon and a glass of John Barley,
> She dreamt of a life of ease.
> In the warmth of her bed, in the dark of night,
> She'd hold them, and kiss them, and cry,
> "Carlos, Manuel, Francisco, Miguel,
> I love you, don't leave me, I'll die."
> I'll marry Miguel, oh, the lies he would tell,
> As he held me and called me his own,
> He kissed my soft cheek, sweet words he would speak,
> "Mi amore, mi amore," he'd moan.
> She was only a finger pier girl,
> But a lady to the boys at the bar,
> With a twirl and a turn, she'd dance and she'd yearn,
> For her sailor to take her afar.
> I'll marry Luis, oh, the sweet dreams of peace,
> As he gently caressed my brown hair,
> My gown is all ready, is your arm steady?
> His answer dispelled my despair.
> When the piers of the harbour are empty,
> No velvet-eyed boys at the Dust,
> She'd squat down to Cross's, forgetting her losses
> With men who knew nothing but lust.
> I'll marry Jose', he'll take me away,
> To Coimbra, Lisboa, Oporto,
> And the scent of red roses, sand warm 'neath my feet,
> We'll drift 'til the red sun sinks low.
> She was only a Salt Water Charly,
> But a queen to the Portuguese,
> In a dress of chiffon and a glass of John Barley,
> She dreamt of a life of ease.

> (*The ship, crew's quarters*)

**JOÃO**: Albertino, como está?

**ALBERTINO**: Ah, como está, João? Uma cerveija?

**JOÃO**: Manuel told me you write in English? Do you write English?

**ALBERTINO**: Yes, sure I do.

230

**JOÃO**: I was wondering if you could write a letter for me?

**ALBERTINO**: Yeah yeah, I can write a letter for you, yeah.

**JOÃO**: Ah, well, it's to a girl.

**ALBERTINO**: A girl, eh?

**JOÃO**: From St. John's.

**ALBERTINO**: Las mulheres de St. John's são muito bonitas.

**JOÃO**: She's a good girl though, I know.

**ALBERTINO**: Ah, yes, they're all good girls, João.

**JOÃO**: She's going to be a nurse.

**ALBERTINO**: Yeah, well what do you want to say to her?

**JOÃO**: I don't know. Make it good, make it good.

**ALBERTINO**: Well, I don't know what to say. Did you say good-bye to her when you left St. John's?

**JOÃO**: Yes, we stayed up all night, we talked.

**ALBERTINO**: Oh, you talked, eh. All night?

231

**JOÃO**: I met her family. It reminded me of home. I miss home.

**ALBERTINO**: Well, don't get too serious.

**JOÃO**: Yeah, well, I know what I'm doing.

**ALBERTINO**: Hey, what about your girl in Portugal.

**JOÃO**: Ela é muito nova e inocente.

**ALBERTINO**: Ah, leave the girls for the boys, eh. Men want women. So, ah, tell me about your—what's her name?

**JOÃO**: Kay. Querida Kay.

**ALBERTINO**: Kay, querida Kay, that's a good start. Now tell me about your Kay.

**JOÃO**: Ela tem cabelo da cor de areia so pôr do sol e olhos como o mar de Aveiro.

**ALBERTINO**: Sounds like you know what you want to say. Let's go write your letter.

(*They exit. João speaking in Portuguese to Albertino telling him what to write while Kay, at home, reads the letter.*)

**JOÃO**: Querida Kay, Desejo que so receberes está carta, te encontras bem de saude em companhia dos teus pais…

**KAY**. Querida Kay, I wish you happiness and good health in the company of your family. I am fine. We just stopped in Greenland for half a day which gave me some time to quickly write a letter to my favorite girl. The days out here at sea pass extremely slowly, and I long for the day when I will see you again standing by my side. My father thinks you are very pretty and is anxious to meet you the next time we are in St. John's. How are you doing in your studies? Are you still working at the Arcade? I hope you are enjoying yourself. I am not very happy. For one, you are very far from me and also I do not like this life. I have been thinking that maybe in the future, I can get a job in St. John's and migrate there, like some of my friends who work at E. F. Barnes. Then we can be together making a life for ourselves. I'll have to go now, my love. Say hello to your parents for me, your uncle and your little brother. Hopefully we'll go to St. John's in exactly three weeks. (*She looks up and exclaims.*) Oh, that's tomorrow! I miss you very much. Goodbye, my love. João.

232

**poor john**: dried and salted cod-fish; DRY.

[1585] 1905 HAKLUYT x, 100 In this ship was great store of dry New land fish, commonly called with us Poore John. [1612] 1958 SHAKESPEARE *The Tempest* II, ii, 23-6 A fish: he smells like a fish: a very ancient and fishlike smell; a kind of not-of-the-newest Poor John. 1628 HAYMAN[1] 37 Yet let me tell you, Sir, what I love best / Its a *Poore John* thats cleane, and neatly drest: / There's not a meat found in the Land, or Seas, / Can Stomacks better please, or lesse displease. 1672 [BLOME] 189-90 But the whole *Coast* of the *Island*, affords infinite plenty of Codd, and *Poor John*, which is the chief *Commodity* of the *Isle*. 1720 FISHER 62 And besides this Fishing upon the Coasts for dry Fish, or *Poor-John*, as they call them, there is a most lucrative Fishing for Green Fish. 1940 INNIS 11 Cod taken in winter in Iceland and dried in the frost were known as 'stockfish'; when taken in summer and dried they became the 'poor john' of Newfoundland.

# The Incubus

## Carmelita McGrath

 IT was during the summer after I turned twelve, the summer that we arrived later than usual at the cabin at Mingling Pond to find the giant maple spilt in two and lying at the porch steps, it was that summer that my mother was visited by the incubus.

In the beginning, his presence was almost imperceptible. Black ash in milky white ashtrays. The brown stubs of unusual cigarettes. A rustling of fabric in the night. The screen door's bang! bursting into my sleep. Then silence followed by disturbed dreams in which laughter caromed around the walls and set them echoing. Then dawn but no rest.

My father had left in April. Every time I heard the screen door I would wake, leap up, heart pounding, thinking he had returned. Even now I hear his footsteps cross the rooms of my sleep. But I had heard his footsteps leave the house, and I never heard them return. The sound of an entrance is different from the sound of an exit. And often in sleep I still hear a woman's wild laughter.

This woman, the entertainer of the incubus, the beauteous Helen, survived to tell the tale of footsteps and laughter, but never did. She still lives, on that other coast across the continent. She has had three more children.

I do not see her. I have turned my back on the fog-wrapped east, its cold that lies in bones waiting for winter to wake it, and I look to the Pacific, the blue-eyed sea, to save me from confusion. I will never go east again.

*Never say never*, Helen would say, if she still likes adages, one-liners, quips that say it all. Helen carried greeting cards in her head, one for every occasion.

I heard the creature on the stairs once. I was up with a towel under the door to block the light, since I didn't want Helen to come in and lunge on my bed and talk the way she liked to talk, a hand running through her wavy black hair, or a finger keeping time to invisible music against her knee.

I was reading about the witch trials in Salem, Massachusetts. Young girls like me turned to accusing horrors. Women with no explanations for dying cows and blighted crops, turned to dust. I was fascinated. Death was all around me, pulling me into odd books, movies about the occult, stories of macabre dealings between worlds, drawing me to tales of witches and to the possibility that the house, the garden, the street harboured secret dark dimensions.

April. It was just after Easter. I remember when because the house was still scented with the twin pungencies of chocolate and oranges, the leftover breaths of pastel mints and expiring lilies. I couldn't eat lamb that year, having gone off meat, not understanding two things: how anyone could slaughter lambs in the first place, and why no one objected to calling Christ the lamb of God, and then devouring his symbol in mint sauce. We should have adorned the lamb with ribbons and bells, paraded them through meadows braceleted with daffodils to the sound of pan pipes. I was queasy all year; even the animals moulded in chocolate stirred deep disgust in me, even as their scent encouraged me to eat.

The beauteous Helen and the morose Patrick. Her with her skeins of wavy hair and him with the shuffle, the hands in pants pockets, the cuffs dragged down to sweep the floor. All winter they walked around each other, taking turns making patterns of concentric circles, dizzying arcs, moving in, close, then out. I would draw their movements with my spirograph set. Obsessive patterns piled up in the study, maps to the house and ourselves and where we were in relation to each other.

Eventually, some time in spring, Helen and Patrick sat down, holding parts of their faces in their hands, the unknowable epicentre of something. The radio was playing country music, something about divorce and how this broken heart would not be healed by time. "Time wounds all heels," Helen said, and laughed.

"Turn off that crap, will you, Helen," said Patrick.

"You're closer to it. You turn it off. Don't worry. Good Catholics don't get divorced."

Even I knew he wanted her to change the station to show she was on his side. But, after a time, it was him who spun the black plastic-knot in search of one of the three things he listened to—obscure news from far away, hockey games, string quartets.

One of these nights right after Easter when the air was soft with rain they were sitting there at the table when the tumblers in the cupboard exploded. We didn't know what was happening at first. A sudden profusion of bangs, glass popcorn, and a shivering of cupboard doors, a sparkly substance leaking out underneath. Small shards, tiny crystals stirring and settling like sugar, arrangement for glass and glass; the pieces were too small to whisk up, too lethal to vacuum. Helen mopped them up with cloths coated in Vaseline to make them stick. She said that she'd heard on the radio about a certain kind of glasses, imported from France, that were known to spontaneously explode on occasion. "And I heard on TV," she said, "that things have been known to explode or break in houses where there is a lot of tension. So I guess we'd better lighten up, folks."

The next morning Helen announced that my father was gone. She said it flatly, pouring orange juice into mugs and never meeting my eyes. And it was only later that I remembered hearing his footsteps, a sound filled with the eagerness and fear of escape.

During the summer, after I'd had my first period, Helen said I was old enough to know a few things. We'd just had THE TALK. She was sitting on my bed with a book in her hands. On the cover above a girl with an unblemished face, dressed in white right to her hairbow like a vision of an angel, were the words "Isn't It Wonderful to Be a Woman!" It wasn't even punctuated properly.

"Your father," Helen said, "has had some problems, dear. With depression. He told me about it after we were married, but he needn't have worried. I would have married him anyway. Things were pretty good back then. But, you know, it always took a lot out of him to keep up a face for the world." She hesitated. "You know those nights he's sit out on the porch with a beer in his hand, just sit there for hours?"

"Yeah."

"And your Nan used to say, 'Look at Patrick, Helen. One beer takes him all night. You could have done a lot worse. There should be more sensible fellows like him around.' Well, what she didn't know was often by that time he'd have been at it all day. In some bar on the waterfront. Would have left for work but not gone to work. Would have been looking at the gulls and the boats and yakking with the alkies. They'd call me from the office."

"How can you say those things? He's not even here to stand up for himself."

"Look girl," she said sharply, "This is not the schoolyard and I'm not spreading gossip. What reason have I got to lie to you? And I'm not blaming him. I'm just saying that it was this depression thing. Everything bothered him, everything got him down, nothing could raise his spirits up and keep them there. And the beer seemed to take away some of the sadness. It's like there was always something…missing…in him. We can't blame ourselves that he's gone, Diane."

"He might come back."

"He might." She smiled, "How are the cramps? Did the aspirin help?"

"No," I lied, "I think I'll lie down." Just to make her go. She put the book on the night table, and the beribboned angel smiled through her period. Something missing in him. And in me. Missing him. Wanting him to come home so that he could sit in his favourite chair and sigh with the comfort of it and, after a while, he'd see me and say, "You're still my little girl." And I'd go to him and he'd hug me to the birds-eye check of his shirt until the pattern disappeared. "Always will be," he'd say.

But Helen didn't tell me what she knew about him until long after he was gone. When I was old enough. Early that summer, when the demon spread his black wings inside our house, I was not old enough to know.

Sometimes the incubus was hardly there at all. In my mother's room, I heard the pulling of chintz curtains, the wheeze of the wicker settee, whispers. A muffled conversation followed by a long groan. A sigh sometimes. But as the summer grew on, Helen's eyes bloomed inside dark rings, circling outward in search of something, darkening her whole face. Inside these smoky caves, opalescent gleams flickered and retreated, appraised and retired to secrecy. In her eyes you might find pirates' treasure. And then, in the evenings, she'd start to sparkle. She'd clean the house to an immaculate state. She'd wash the dishes and hold the new glasses up to the sun to check for spots. All the while, she'd be swinging her bum to the music on the radio and singing along. And as soon as it got dark, she'd send me to bed. Said a girl my age needed her rest. She had been lackadaisical in the past, but that was over. She had full responsibility for me now. I was not allowed to stay up and watch TV.

And so I could not talk to her about the demon, even as his visits became more frequent. I knew him though, by sound and by a name I'd found in a book last borrowed in 1947, by his throaty laugh and the sense of foreboding he left behind.

Although I had not seen him, I had read about him. I had read about incubi and succubi, the demons of the night, male and female, knew how they could infect dreams and inhabit houses, lie upon the bodies of sleepers, leaving behind a little of hell when they left. In my borrowed books, I traced the lines of old woodcuts and shivered at the description, extracted from a woman by the Inquisition, of what an incubus did when he visited her. I held my breath and read of how the unclean spirit had been cast out. But I could not talk to Helen about any of this. Even as I saw her standing on the porch one night wearing only a peignoir. Stretching her arms toward the sky. A glass of dark red wine in her hand. I could sense him there in the shadows, outside my field of vision, watching her too. I could not talk to her. Even after he started bringing the things into the house.

The things, like whatever power had shattered the glasses, were capable of moving objects through the air, were able to shatter, cause disintegration. Invisible and winged, they were at my command, as if he put them there to tempt me, to take my mind off whatever else was going on in the house. I had only to lie in bed and let my thoughts wander, and things would move of their own accord. The air changed its dimensions, became a sky where things could move around and above me, where things could fly.

A book would shut, open, shut, open again on the same page. The cigarettes I'd begun to smoke would arrive on the night table, matches and ashtray following close behind. All this with nothing to set it going except the drawing of curtains at dusk and me banished to my room nursing queer pains in my stomach.

And the music-box, given to me by the beauteous Helen and the shuffling Patrick, shattered to pieces against the wall behind the dresser. This smashed with so much violence that I was half afraid to pick it up. But I did after watching for while to see if it would move on its own. I bagged the broken china clowns with their pieces of smiles and put them aside. I would glue them, put them back together. The mechanism that had moved the music sat exposed, a metallic jumble, wires glinting in the scattered shards of moonlight that fell between the curtains and the wall.

It was natural for the incubus to get braver. What, after all, did he have to fear? The mother started to transform toward evening, became dreamy, perhaps influenced by some telepathic messages he was sending her. The daughter was in her room with a towel under her door to shield discovery of light and smoke, nursing a strange set of shooting pains centred in her lower abdomen, willing the objects in the room to stay still. I could sense that he knew I was in hiding. It was a captive house.

So he got braver. His footsteps grew more reckless on the stairs, and glasses clinked and jazz was turned up loud. I heard him laugh, a deep rumbling. He was enticing my mother, perhaps torturing her. Such sounds! Smothered laughter that was cut off suddenly. An abrupt intake of breath stirring the house with its urgency. A sigh like the end of a rain storm. Once, a frightening moan, sobbing, hoarse pleading, the words strangled, "Oh no, please." Only her voice usually; from him a deep silence, as if he didn't need to speak. Occasionally, a volcanic rumble you'd think was laughter if you didn't know better. I listened, let all my anger rise in me, and a doll rose off the dresser and came, arms outstretched, eyes locked to mine, into my arms.

The pigeons nesting in the eaves moved out. A heat, unseasonal in that city of foghorns and visiting silver tides of capelin that left the air rank, set in and occupied the rooms with a dusty fatigue. Strange insects appeared in the garden and feasted on nasturtium leaves. Dust motes lay unmoving in the glaring light. There were rumoured visits by ruby-throated hummingbirds. I kept pestering my mother to go to the cabin.

"We can't go yet," she said.

"Why?"

"Remember, I don't have a car anymore. Your father took the car when he left. Besides…."

"Besides what?"

"Well, Diane, we're running a little low on money. I'm going to have to try to get a job before the fall. Don't know doing what. But I promise. I'll get us up to the cabin sometime soon. Just give me a little time. I'll work something out."

And then one day when I'd just about given up, she asked me to be good and mind the house while she went out. About an hour later she came back and blew the horn of a bile-green station wagon. I was on the porch eating a tuna sandwich and reading about the habits of the undead when she showed up grinning from ear to ear.

"We got a car!" she announced. "We're going to Mingling Pond."

"Where d'you get it? I thought we had no money."

"We had enough for this," Helen said, tossing her black hair, "I drove a hard bargain."

A fury of packing. Helen said I wasn't packing enough shorts, and where was Maggie Jane, my favourite doll?

I said my legs were too fat for shorts and I was too old for dolls. I left out the news that Maggie Jane had flown through the night into my arms, her lapis eyes full of understanding. "Since when?" Helen said to both statements, but she sat wearily on the bed. "Diane, honey," she said, "This is a hard age you're going through, a hard age for a girl. But it'll pass. Believe me, it will pass."

"Any news from dad?"

"No, I told you I'd tell you right away if there was. I would, you know."

It was funny on the highway that evening. My hope all summer had been that we'd get away from the city, from the house, and whatever had invaded us would let us go. I knew that demons and spirits can follow you wherever you go, but Mingling Pond had always seemed a charmed place, and I felt the bad things wouldn't follow us there. In the car, I could feel a change coming, could sense the absence of any kind of *thing* that might come between Helen and myself, could sense some lightness stirring in the air. We had the radio on and Helen was singing, even as the sky went black, and fat drops came and sat on the windshield, heavy as oil, even as the wind picked up and carried sheets of water toward us like tidal waves coming out of the sky. The worse the weather became the harder Helen drove, her hands taut on the steering wheel, eyes focussed directly ahead. By this time, the wipers did little but clear one onslaught to make way for another, and there were moments when I thought that we must have gone into a river and were slowly sinking. But Helen said, "Sinking isn't a slow thing, honey, have a nap and I'll wake you when we get there," and there was something about her sheer determination, how she never even glanced at me when she spoke, that inspired confidence. Eventually, I did go to sleep, although I was quick to deny it later.

We arrived at the cabin at sunset, but the storm had gotten there before us, and it must have been far worse than anything we'd experienced on the highway. In a yard littered with flattened meadowsweet and blown roof shingles, the old maple that had been there long before Patrick bought the place (for a song, he said) lay prostrate at the cabin door. It had split and fallen, uprooting itself completely from the soaked earth. Its roots filled the driveway, its matted leafy head lay almost on the doorstep of piled, cemented stones. It looked sadder than almost anything I'd ever seen.

I was crying, for the tree, for the mess of the place, for everything being spoiled. "What are we going to do?" I wailed.

Helen opened the trunk of the car and lifted out a picnic basket. "It's not blocking the door," she said. "We'll walk around it. We'll deal with it in the morning. We'll have help later."

"What help?"

"We're going to have a visitor. If he hasn't gone off the road in the rain. It's a surprise. I'm not saying another word until he gets here. Come help me unpack."

Her eyes were full of dark lights.

We didn't have to wait long. He came in a late-model beige car, and he wore clothes so new I could tell that he didn't spend a lot of time around woods or ponds. Creased chinos and low leather boots. A shirt of birds-eye check that sent shock waves through my heart. He had dark hair like Helen's, only carefully cut, and he laughed almost all the time when he spoke.

"This," Helen said, "is Mark Philbin. Mark, this is my daughter, Diane."

Helen put an arm around each of us and marched us inside. She filled their glasses with dark red wine, and even put some in a glass and brought it over to me where I was sitting on the loveseat, unable to take my eyes off the curly black hair emerging from the open neck of Mark Philbin's shirt.

I learned a lot that night, and the wine helped. I learned that Mark Philbin had his own car dealership, and that it was doing really well. I learned that he liked wine and kissing my mother every time she came within kissing distance. I learned that Helen had already told him a lot about me, although, where she'd met him, and when they'd been together, I couldn't get straight in my head. I learned that Helen liked smoked salmon, which Mark had brought on ice just for her. I learned, as the three of us smoked, and Helen never batted an eye when I lit up, that she wasn't going to get a job in the fall after all. It would be better for me if she didn't. And I learned that my mother was going to marry Mark Philbin.

*This is the way the world ends,* I used to sing to myself, watching the sky for signs of catastrophe. Or at least the way it changes forever. Three months after THE TALK, when the unstated thing was that Patrick might return to make claims on me but never on her, Helen and Mark got married in an office during the Friday evening rush-hour. I never did find out how she'd found Patrick; how she'd got a divorce, and I'd never ask, and Helen was never one to volunteer information.

Mark insisted we move to a larger house, and when we did, I cleared out all my toys and gave them to the children's hospital. Even Maggie Jane, whom I'd loved, but couldn't bear to look at now after she'd come to me, her arms outstretched, sailing on nothing but air.

I had to give Mark credit for one thing. It was his presence that banished the incubus, or at least I thought it did. In the new house it was hard to know. Mark and Helen chose the largest room at the end of the long upstairs hallway, and they suggested I take the one at the other end, which had its own bathroom. But whatever happened, whether the spirits had stayed in the old house or whether Mark's presence kept them off, they never returned. Things in my room stayed where I put them. I slept long, dreamless sleeps. I heard no tortured moans, no long sighs, no breaths that occupied all the air until there was none left to breathe. And the period had already come, like long-awaited rain, banishing the pain and the deep heaviness in my gut, washing me out, leaving me lightened.

I suffered them. There was something wrong with it all, all that going out to dinner and exchanging secret glances. Helen and Mark quit smoking and said I had to too. And the beauteous Helen getting pregnant one time after another, three babies whom I loved, although I could not love their parents. Her still nursing and pregnant again. Always, it seemed, larger and more beautiful, building in size and force like a storm cloud. She who used to say to young couples, friends of ours, "If you want to have a baby, have ONE." I stuck it out, babysat and got good grades and ate *coq au vin* with them by candlelight, until I was seventeen.

Patrick committed suicide. Patrick found a medication that allowed him to function. Patrick still watched gulls from bar windows and was in danger of losing his job. There were the stories possible for Patrick, and I wanted desperately to know how he was. I had received four cards, three gifts, and one long, rambling letter asking for forgiveness since the night the glasses shattered.

Eventually I found him. I was on my way west then, and I found him in Calgary. It's funny about telephone directories, the secret lives they give up so readily. There he was. The fourth P. Donnell I tried. The others had all been women.

It was strange finding him in a city driven by oil and male bravado. Among so many large and loud young men seeking a fortune, my small, quiet father seemed like some shore-bird blown in by a storm, what the birding books call "occasional visitors." He was working in accounting, as he always had, and he had found help for his depression, but he said that drugs were one thing, life was another. The best thing was that he was on an even keel most of the time.

We were walking toward the rusty block of brick buildings that housed his apartment. I'd been surprised that it was a two-bedroom, as if he were always waiting for a guest. And I realized when I entered the room that I was the first person who had slept there since he rented it,

"Look," he said. "I did want to get in touch many times. I don't know what stopped me. I suppose I didn't know what to say. There were those scattered cards. I realized after a while that it was probably worse for you. A card, a gift: you expect something else. Some kind of follow-up. I didn't know I could deliver it. So I stopped."

"He stopped short of telling me I was still his little girl, but he did ask me if I would stay for a while. But I'd become unused to Patrick's drooping moroseness. Now I discovered it dragged me down even more than I was already. I'd had some uncomfortable dark periods for quite a while. When we walked, our shadows were twins. Heads hung low, shoulders hunched, hands destroying the seams of our pockets. We were almost the same size. We both had a habit of saying, "Well, then, that's that.""

"I'm on my way west," I told him, when he asked about my plans. "I'm going to find a job, a place by the sea. I'm going to grow things in a garden and listen to the sea all night."

"It's really rainy out there now," he said.

"I know," I said. "I don't mind rain."

"Well, then," he said, "that's that."

I suppose I have a lot of Patrick in me. It's what my friend Beth used to call my "grey raincoat." She said that usually I was wearing it but it was always a pleasant surprise when I wasn't.

One time when we'd talked ourselves back through adolescence, I told Beth about that weird summer when I was twelve. It was difficult to talk about, but Beth drew me out. She'd told me so much about herself, and she said that she was dying to know why I always referred to my mother, father and stepfather as The Beauteous Helen, The Morose Patrick, and The Dashing Mark.

We'd just treated ourselves to champagne and oysters because it had been raining for six days in a row, and I had been thinking that I might like to try and make love to Beth, since I had failed with as many men as there'd been rainy days, although I used to be good with men. Besides, I could talk to Beth like no one else.

So I told her about how the glasses exploded, my father left, and an incubus came to visit my mother and sent spirits to my room, and how at the end of it all, a handsome stranger had shown up and I'd lost both my father and mother.

Beth was quiet for a long time. "You know what really happened, though. Right?"

I was silent.

"Right?" she repeated.

I had nothing to say.

"Look, Diane, you were pretty suggestible at that time. There must have been all kinds of confusion in you. The things in your room—these things happen—puberty is a weird time, and some kids—"

"Beth, you asked me if I know what really happened. Of course I do. What happens is what you experience. And you can only experience a thing once."

The end of the day by the sea is a fine thing. Waves wash blue to grey, and there is no diminishing of beauty, only a soft change. The sound of the water stills me. Sometimes I make fires and light the sky with red.

They have written to ask me to please come to their twentieth anniversary. The card has a picture of them, now after the last child has left home, awaiting some kind of grand reunion. In the picture, they are in their garden, surrounded by the lacework of leaves, their heads together, black wavy hair melting into strands of its own kind, until it is impossible to tell where one head leaves off and another begins. I touch their faces. They do not seem to age, grow lines, go grey. But I do. I think of what Patrick said about giving a little, and then having someone expect more. I could put "I can't deliver" on the response card and mail it back.

This is a good night to light a beach fire. Rain threatens, and will put it out later. I fold the card inside an empty wine bottle, watch it stain red, insert the cork. I toss the bottle into the western sea. Such things have been known to travel great distances, arrive in the hands of strangers.

# The Rain Hammers

Michael Wade

The rain hammers at my window
    with fists abandoned by the wind
    my curtains billow with delight
    at the curious black waters bludgeoning

inside
    a semi-precious bumblebee
    mysteriously hums above
    a plastic flower

eternity becomes
    the sound of the sea in the night
    the pound of the tide in the black
    the flood of the shore in the dark
    the cry of the gull in the dawn

the sun comes out of the sea
    covered with weed
    surrounded with sound
    cornered by clouds
    and breathes on the world.

# Empty Nets

**Jim Payne**

Get up in the morn-ing at a quart-er to four, try
not to make much noise as you go out the door, jump in the
boat, you can hear the gulls roar, at the start of a bra-nd new
day. Fire up the eng-ine, your read-y to go,
head out the har-bour you don't want to be slow, What's out there today, well you nev-er kn-ow, just hope that it turns out ok - ay.

> But it's empty nets, that's what he gets,
> When you're out on the water, no time for regrets,
> Those empty nets, that's what he gets,
> How's a poor fisherman to pay off his debts,
> When he goes out each morning to haul empty nets?

You can blame it on the foreigners, blame it on the feds, cast all the blame on
  each other instead,
But when it's all said and done, it's something I dread to see, Newfoundland
  give up the fishery.
What of our communities, will they just die? Pack up your duds, give the
  mainland a try?
But I'm staying here till someone tells me why I should put up with this misery.

> Of those empty nets, 'cause that's what he gets,
> When you're out on the water, no time for regrets,
> Those empty nets, that's what he gets,
> How's a poor fisherman to pay off his debts,
> When he goes out each morning to haul empty nets?

And here's to the plant worker toils on the shore, waits for the fisherman to
    catch a few more,
And then pack it up for the grocery store, till it ends up on somebody's table.
How can they feed multitudes on fishes so small? How can they feed families on
    no fish at all?
Get down on your knees for a miracle call, we'll stick it for as long as we're able.

> Those empty nets, 'cause that's what he gets,
> When you're out on the water, no time for regrets,
> Those empty nets, that's what he gets,
> How's a poor fisherman to pay off his debts,
> When he goes out each morning to haul empty nets?

Here's luck to the fisherman, he'll need it I know, as he bobs on the ocean, God
    bless his poor soul.
May good fortune follow wherever he goes, and keep him from debt load and
    danger.
And wherever you live, no matter which bay, may bankers and loan boards not
    stand in your way,
May you bring home a boatload each single day, and to poverty be ever a
    stranger.

> No more empty nets, 'cause that's what he gets,
> When you're out on the water, no time for regrets,
> Those empty nets, that's what he gets,
> How's a poor fisherman to pay off his debts,
> When he goes out each morning to haul empty nets?

> Repeat chorus

# If Sonnets Were in Fashion

Tom Dawe

If sonnets were in fashion,
I think I would try one
about a dog I heard
barking one time
in a taped poetry reading
by Robert Frost.
The imagery would be geological
and the old man of fire and ice,
plain diction, the gravel voice
could have the octave
all to himself,
free to be crafty
yet seeming so undesigning
within the confines
of iambic walls,
his presentation glacial, powerful,
moving on the slow import
of its melting…
And then, intruding into line eight,
in a tree-at-my-window pause,
that audible fossil,
just for a couple of seconds,
a dog barking faintly somewhere.

The creature would have the sestet
all to itself,
so perfectly autonomous out there
in pussy-willow swamp
and prime New England sunshine,
casually scanning its territory,
cocking its leg
against the world perhaps,
its primitive spondee
lingering and wonderful.
Oblivious to any
iamb or anapest,
it would just be
its own wild poetry,
a summons
from the wordless places
once again.

*City Homes*, Paul Parsons

*Your creativity comes from your soul, your spirit—not your mind. If I feel a painting, I can paint. I see things that are lost as more precious than the things you have. And then you bring them back, through music, painting, poetry. Painting is only one of the forms of art. Painting is like poetry—words to the poet are like paints to the painter. With music, you can be alone and not lonely. You can go into the world of music. Even when the person who wrote it is dead, he's alive whenever that piece of music is played. Music is everlasting—a living thing. And you look at paintings too. You don't think of Michaelangelo as dead. They leave behind something beautiful.*

*Perhaps tomorrow if the world disappeared—and you could do something just today—it would make all the difference in the world. If you could only create something beautiful. That's the meaning of life.*

— Paul Parsons (recorded by Jane Burns, 1982)

# Message

## Adrian Fowler

They say
loneliness
creates a
kind of
madness
even in
those who
survive

People
meeting
these
survivors
are first
impressed
with the
fact of their
survival

see them
as self-
reliant
even perhaps
as mystics

Gradually
they come to
realise the
destructive
ferocity
of the beast

within

Reporting this
they are
often told
by those who
know: That's
loneliness
That's what it
does to you

I am
afraid
to call
you up

afraid
that the
sound of
your voice
will release
the madness
I can feel
within me

afraid
of all
your voices
my friends

# waking from a dream

Nick Avis

```
m
   i
      g
         r
            a
               t
                  i
                     n
                        g
                       e
                     e
                   s
                 e
```

without a word we get up
and walk toward home

in the pattern of frost
on the old attic window
                    a dead fly

                              coming to the end
                              of my grandmother's diary
                                    cold november wind

                              november nightfall
                              the shadow of the headstone
                              longer than the grave

stepping from stone to stone
across the stream
        the autumn moon

waking from a dream…
        only the sound of snowflakes
              on the windowpane

the morning star
        above the snow     the tip
of an alder bush

sunrise
                poking at the
embers of last night's fire


                                a fresh pot of tea
                                frost steaming off the window
                                the new year's sun

                                freshly fallen snow
                                        opening a new package
                                        of typing paper

# springsmistory

**Nick Avis**

a light spring rainfall…
tapping against the window
the fly that survived

spring is here
        the cat's muddy paw prints
        on the windowsill

pothole puddle
a robin          bathes
        in the blue sky

        a young girl
sneaks through the broken fence
                crocus tips in the garden

spring rain
        her scent
        in the bath towel

liptoliptulips

# Old Flame

**Gildas Roberts**

Sentimental
    I warmed both hands
    In an old flame's glow.
    No harm, I thought, full control—
Oh, like hell!
    The old flame hissed into a
    Blow-torch jet
    In three seconds flat
    And the firm metal
        of my resolve,
    Quick-melted, crumpled sideways
    And sent sprawling
    All other structures
    Standing near.

Not good
    To think of this
    Sleepless at three a.m.
    Throbbing darkness all around.
Oh, that I could wrench time
    Five years back
    Or had never been born
A fool.

*Satin Wrap*, Barbara Pratt Wangersky

*Painting, for me, is about capturing beauty. Sometimes this beauty can be found in the luxurious depths of plum-coloured satin. Often, in my work, it is found in a hand on a hip or a flower glowing with fragile life. Most important to me is the beauty in a woman's soul; her strength, her struggle, her potential.*

— Barbara Pratt Wangersky

# To Be a Bee

Nellie Strowbridge

Like a floating black spot she came
before my eyes.
Circled my head—
droning on,
then settled quietly
on my window sill.

Afraid of her
I backed away—
wrapped my hand around
an aerosol can
and pressed the button.

Angrily
she multiplied Zs.

And then she grew and grew
and became me,
And I became the bee,
lying on my back
on the window sill,
kicking the air
and buzzing for help.

My husband, passing by,
thought I was only an insect.
He picked me up with tissue,
and flushed me away,
while the bee chatted to him
in her dress
of black and yellow stripes:
colours I never wore—
nor liked.

# Purgatory's Wild Kingdom

Lisa Moore

ulian is thinking about the woman and child he left in Newfoundland when he moved to Toronto. He's remembering Olivia preparing him a sardine sandwich, the way she pressed the extra oil out of each sardine on a piece of paper towel. Then she cut the head and tail off each sardine, until they were laid carefully on the bread. Her head was bent over the cutting board. Her blond hair slid from behind her ear. He could see the sun sawing on her gold necklace. The chain stuck on her skin in a twisty path that made him realize how hot it was in the apartment. She was wearing a flannel pajama top and nothing else, a coffee-colour red birthmark on her thigh, shaped like the boot of Italy. Eight years ago.

Julian is sitting at the kitchen table with a pot of coffee. His bare feet are drawn up on the chair, his knees pressed into the edge of the table. It's a wooden table top that has been rubbed with linseed oil. There are scars from the burning cigarettes his wife occasionally leaves lying around. Small black ovals. There are thousands of knife cuts that cross over each other like the lines on a palm. He runs his finger over the table, tracing the grain of the wood. He pours another cup of coffee, and glances at the phone. Sometimes the university calls for Marika before nine, although they have been told not to. Marika requires only seven hours sleep, but if she's disturbed she's tired all day. She wakes up at exactly nine every morning. She's proud of the precision of her inner clock. Julian likes to pick up the phone before it rings twice. Lately, when the phone rings and Julian answers, nobody speaks.

Marika is fifteen years older than Julian. The people on this street are very rich. The brick houses are massive. Some of them have been broken into apartments and rented. There's almost no traffic. The trees block most of the noise. He and Marika don't know their neighbours. Once, while out taking photographs, Julian met a man three houses up who was riding a sparkling black bike in circles. The man said he was Joe Murphy. Joe Murphy's Chips sold a large percentage of their product in Newfoundland. He gave the silver bicycle bell two sharp rings.

"The bike's a birthday present from my wife. It's a real beauty, isn't it?"

The trees shivered suddenly with wind and sloshed the bike with rippling shadows. Joe Murphy was wearing a suit and tie. The balls of his feet pressed against the pavement and there were sharp little crevices in his shined leather shoes. A crow left a tree and flew straight down the centre of the street. Julian lifted his camera and took a picture of Joe Murphy. In the far distant corner of the frame is the crow. Joe Murphy is out of focus, a blur in the centre of the picture, his face full of slack features. The crow is sharp and black.

"That makes me very uncomfortable," said Joe Murphy. "I think you have a nerve." He gave the bell another sharp ring, and pushed off the curb. His suit jacket flapping.

For two years, Julian has been sleeping a lot. It's taken him two years to fall away from any kind of sleeping pattern. This way he's always awake at different hours. This seems exotic to him, but the cost is that he can't will himself to sleep. He sleeps in the afternoon and then finds himself awake at four in the morning. At dawn he sometimes wanders around the neighbourhood. The light at dawn allows him to see straight into the front windows of the massive houses of their street, all the way to the back windows and into the backyards. It makes the houses seem like skeletons, with nothing hanging on the bones.

Sometimes Julian is asleep when Marika gets home from work. If there's no supper cooked for her she'll eat white bread and butter with spoonfuls of granulated sugar. Julian likes to cook for her and she likes what he cooks. But she's also happy to eat bread and sugar. She makes coffee and folds the bread and sinks it into her coffee. The soaked bread topples and she catches it in her mouth. The cats slink in from all the different rooms of the apartment and curl around her feet, or on her lap. She lifts the kitten and puts it inside her jacket. Julian stumbles down the stairs, half awake, and he sees Marika bathed in the light of a fashion show on TV with her sugared bread, he feels that he has failed her. The failure makes him even sleepier. He can't keep his eyes open.

Marika is not one for dwelling on the past. Julian knows very little about her past. Not that she's secretive. It's the kind of conversation that bores her. Marika has a powerful charm. She's a chemistry professor, but most of her friends are artists or writers. At parties, for conversation, she offers crystallized stories about nature or the stars. If someone interrupts her to ask about her parents, or something back in France, she answers in short sentences, faltering.

She thinks of memory only as a muscle that must be exercised to keep the whole mind sharp. She is interested in sharpness. If asked, she can recall exactly what she did on any date two years before. She will remember what she wore, what Julian wore, what they ate, the content of any conversation that occurred on that day. But this is just a game.

Marika thinks about infinite tracts of time, about meteorology, about humming-birds, about measuring the erosion of coastlines, and whether the continents could still lock together like a jigsaw puzzle, or a jaw grinding in sleep. She thinks about the Tower of Babel, or about fish that swim up the walls of fjords as if the walls were the lake bottom. What such swimming against the stream does to their skeletons. When she isn't thinking things like this, she watches soap operas, or drives in her car, or she and Julian make love.

Julian has watched Marika simulate theoretical galaxies on the computer. She has found this program mostly to amuse him. He has seen two galaxies blinking together, dragging their sluggish amorphous bodies toward each other across the black screen. Each blink represents a million years, until they pass through each other. The gravitational pull of each galaxy affects the shape of the other until some stars are clotted in the centre, and the rest spread on either side of the screen like giant butterfly wings. Marika has shown him thousands of things like this. She has described the path of the plague in the middle ages, drawing a map on a paper napkin at a donut shop.

She told him that in Egypt they have found the preserved body of a louse, on the comb of Nefertiti. A drop of human blood, perhaps Nefertiti's blood, was contained in the abdomen of the louse. They have discovered many things about ancient disease from that drop of blood.

Julian collects the stories Marika tells him, although they often lose their scientific edges. He can't remember how old the louse was. For some reason the only thing he remembers about the plague is a medical costume, a long robe with the head of a bird. The doctor looked out through two holes cut in the black feathered hood, over a protruding beak.

When he is awake, Julian pursues the morals of these stories, something other than what lies on the surface. Just as he can't imagine how much time it took to create the universe from a black hole, he can't get at that hidden meaning.

Recently Marika contracted a virus that caused a nervous disorder. If not diagnosed, this disease can spread quickly through the body and destroy the tips of all nerve endings irreparably. It started with a numbness in Marika's left cheek. She had it checked immediately. Of course, she had access to the best medical care in Toronto. The disease was arrested before any serious damage was done, but the nerves in Marika's saliva ducts grew back connected to one of her tear ducts. Now when she eats her left eye waters.

Julian has begun to suspect that Marika doesn't talk about her past because she is afraid she will seem like an old woman. It was her eye, filling of its own accord, that started him thinking this way. The eye is the first sign of Marika's age. When her eye waters he's filled with fright. That fright causes its own involuntary response in him. He's remembering things he hasn't thought about in years. He has noticed that the skin on Marika's face looks older than before. The pores are larger. There are more wrinkles. The soft white pouches beneath her eyes are larger. That skin seems as vulnerable to him as the flesh of a pear he is about to bite.

He was going through their wedding photographs. Julian took them himself, so most of the pictures are of Marika. She is wearing a white silk jacket, cut like a lab coat, and the apartment is full of white blossoms. Her face looks so much younger that for a moment he has the feeling the photographs have been doctored.

They're eating a dinner of lamb and fresh mint. Marika's knife is whining back and forth on the dinner plate.

"Could you stop that noise?"

Marika's body jerks, as if she didn't realize he was sitting beside her.

"I was lost in thought. Thinking of crabs."

A tear is running down her cheek.

"In Guatemala," she says, "there's a species of crab that burrows into the ground and brings up in its claws shards of ancient pottery."

She lays down her knife and wipes a tear off her cheek with the back of her hand.

"The crabs descend beneath layer after layer to different cities that have been piled on top of each other, over time. Each city is hundreds of years younger than the one below it. The crabs mix the pottery shards together, all these ancient layers mixed together in the light of day. You really know very little about me. You know nothing about science."

Julian notices that both Marika's eyes are watering now and realizes she's crying.

In his dreams the stories Marika tells him are fables. He dreams about a crab that presents him with a jacket of glass shards that came from a wine bottle he once threw at Olivia. Olivia wears a cloak of stars. She opens her arms and the cloak is wrenched away from her, leaving her naked. She becomes two women, a blurred image, Marika and Olivia both.

That night Julian leaves the house at midnight and walks for hours. Outside the Royal Ontario Museum the moonlit gargoyles are covered with burlap bags, and look like robbers with nylon stockings over their faces. A group of five people dressed in cartoon costumes emerges from a church basement. They skip across the empty street and get into an idling mini-van. A man in a Pink Panther costume trails behind. He has removed the head of the costume and carries it under his arm. The man's own head looks abnormally small against the giant pink neck of the costume. Julian takes a picture of him.

Lately, Julian thinks about a memory lit with a big number one candle, a wax monkey wrapped around it. Julian carried the cake. He could feel the yellow of the flame under his chin, like the shadow of a buttercup. He could see his daughter's face buried in Olivia's blouse, both their party hats sticking off the sides of their heads. There was a blizzard outside and Julian felt like they were wrapped in white tissue paper. He left a few days after that. He hasn't spoken to either of them since.

Julian remembers things he didn't notice when they happened. He remembers a party in the country. Someone had shoved a hotdog wiener through a hole in a screen door, and every time the door slammed the hotdog wagged obscenely. It was the night he met Olivia. At midnight everyone went skinny dipping, the sound of diving bodies swallowed by the dark water. He was drunk and naked. When it came time to get out of the water he suddenly felt embarrassed. He asked Olivia to give him a hand, so he could hold a towel in front of himself. When she did haul him out he managed to drop the towel and got caught in the skittering path of a flashlight.

When Julian gets home from his walk he finds Marika asleep on the couch, a bowl of chips resting on her knee. She has fallen asleep in the middle of the night with her wrist hanging over the rim of the chrome chip bowl. The phone is ringing. Julian nearly trips over one of the cats in his rush to get it. It's ringing near Marika's ear. She doesn't stir.

Olivia's heels click down the hall through the loose pools of fluorescent light. It's Monday and the Topsail Cinemas mall is mostly deserted, except for the games arcade which shoots out synchronized pings and buzzes. Most of the stores have been in various stages of renovation all winter. Someone has been going at a cement wall with a jack hammer. Chunks of cement have fallen away and rusted bars stick out.

When Olivia turns the corner she sees the exhibit by a taxidermist from British Columbia named Harold. He's standing next to a chair, one hand on his hip, his index fingers looped through his change apron. When he sees Olivia he becomes animated.

"Step this way beautiful, beautiful lady. Let me take you on a whirlwind tour of purgatory's wild kingdom. Here you will see beasts miraculously wrested from the claws of decay. They have looked death in the eye. They have been consumed by death, but they are not dust. Thanks to the strange alchemy of embalming fluid and my own artistic wizardry, they live. They live."

He does this with a little flourish of his hands and a slight bow. Then he sighs as if he has used up all his energy. Pinching his nose, he says, "Two-fifty if you want to see it."

Olivia is twenty minutes early for the movie, so she says, "Sure, I'll treat myself, why not, it's my birthday."

Harold has a thick mop of black hair with silver at the sides; his body is very tall and thin. One of his eyes is lazy, straying off to the side.

The display takes the shape of a mini-labyrinth made of ordinary office dividers. At each turn the viewer comes upon another stuffed animal.

257

"Most of them are from endangered species. But the truly unique thing about this exhibit is that these animals have all been hit by trucks. Trucks or cars. Every one of them. Please don't think I would ever hurt these animals for the sake of the collection. I collect them only after they have been killed.

"I'm different from those taxidermists you see on the side of the road during the summer, of course. I've seen them in this province, in Quebec and Alberta as well, lined up in roadside flea markets next to tables that display dolls with skirts that cover toilet paper rolls. Those guys have a few birds, maybe, a couple of squirrels mounted on sticks, a few moose heads in the back of the station wagon. I take my work seriously. I'm always trying to get a lively posture."

Olivia has stopped in front of a moose. The moose is making an ungainly leap over a convincingly weathered fence, one end of which had been neatly sawed off for the purposes of the exhibit. The moose is raised on its hind legs. Its head and neck are hunched into its shoulders, as if it were being reprimanded.

"This moose looks funny."

Harold points to the neck, saying, "A less experienced man might have stretched the neck forward, and if I wished to be true to a moose in this position, that's what I would have done. I took this artistic license with the moose because it died on the hood of a station wagon. The antenna of the car, unfortunately, entered its rectum and pierced the bowel twice, like a knitting needle. After that I felt this moose should be preserved in an attitude of shame."

"Are you serious?"

"I travel the continent with these animals, setting up in strip malls all over the United States and Canada. I have a license. It's educational. Ottawa pays me. I am very serious. People have to know what we are doing to our wild kingdom. I try to respect the animals as individual creatures. Every sentient being deserves respect. Some of these species may never roam the earth again. They're dead, of course, but I have preserved them. My part is small, I guess. I'm like a red traffic light. That's how I see myself. I do my thing, I make them pause for a minute, before they march off into extinction. It's a chance to say goodbye. We can't forget what we've destroyed."

The last animal is a polar bear. The office dividers are set up so that you come upon it suddenly. Its head and forepaws tower over the divider, but Olivia has been looking at a stuffed mother skunk and suckling skunks on the floor. When she walks around the corner she almost bangs into the bear. The animal's coat is yellowed, its jaw wide.

"She scared you," chuckles Harold and he pats the bear's coat twice, as if it's the bear that needs reassurance.

"This polar bear is my drawing card. The only animal not hit by a truck. This bear was shot. It wandered into a small town here in Newfoundland. It had been trapped on an ice flow. Starved. Dangerous. A mother bear separated from her cub. At seven in the morning a woman was putting out her garbage. The bear chased her back into the house. There was only an aluminum screen door between them. She got her husband's shotgun and when the bear crumpled the aluminum door, just like a chip bag, she shot it in the throat."

Harold parts the fur of the bear's throat. He has to stand on tippy toes to do so. Olivia can see the black sizzled hole, the fur singed pink.

At the end of the hall Olivia can see the woman in the ticket booth for the movie theatres. There's just one woman on tonight, although the twin booth is also lit with flashing lights that circle the outline of the booths. The ticket woman has taken a Q-tip from her purse and is cleaning her ear.

"You have a truck outside?"

"Yes, an eighteen-wheeler."

"Would you consider joining me for a beer? I can give you my address and you can pick me up later. I have a daughter but I have a babysitter lined tip for the evening. I was going out anyway."

Olivia has asked the taxidermist out for a beer because she suddenly feels sad about being alone on her birthday. She has an image of this man driving across an empty Saskatchewan highway with these wild beasts frozen in attitudes of attack, stretched in frozen gallops in the back of his truck. He is the first person she has met in months who seems lonelier than she is. There's the chance he won't show up.

At the bar Olivia gets drunk very fast. Harold drinks the same bottle of beer most of the evening. At last call he buys himself another. He feels jumpy, excited. He's been on the road for six months and almost always finds himself eating in empty hotel restaurants where the waitress watches a miniature TV with an earphone so as not to disturb him.

Olivia is beautiful, Harold thinks. She's wearing a man's shirt of moss-coloured material, and grey leggings. When she walks to the bar he can see all the muscles in her long legs. She reminds him of a giraffe, graceful despite her drunkenness and the fact that her legs are too long for her. Harold is adept at recognizing different kinds of drunkenness. In some people it twists free something bitter, but Olivia is blossoming. Her cheeks are flushed, her "S's" are lisping against her large front teeth. She has been telling him about the father of her child.

"My memories are like those animals in the back of your truck. I can take them out and look at them, all but touch them. Today is my birthday. I'm thirty, but time hasn't moved at all since he left. I don't look any older. I'm just waiting, that's all. Do you know what I think? I think he'll be back. I know he will. I know how to get in touch with him if there's an emergency with Rose, our daughter. I've got the number in my bedside table. But I haven't called him since he left. I'm waiting until he comes to his senses. You know what I think? I think he's been enchanted by an ice queen. You know, a splinter of glass in his eye, but one of these days an unexpected tear is going get it out. He'll be back, don't you worry, Harold."

Suddenly Harold is seized with worry. He removes his glasses. He puts his hand over hers on the table.

"Be honest with me, now. Does it bother you that I have a wandering eye?"

Olivia lays down her beer glass and draws one knee up to her chest.

"At first it was strange. I didn't know which eye to look into."

"In some cultures it is thought to be auspicious. In some cultures it's a sign. I'd like very much to go home with you this evening."

Olivia looks into his eyes, first one, then the other. Without his glasses they look even stranger. They are flecked with gold, the lashes, long and black, like a girl's.

They are lying side by side in bed. Harold is already asleep, his cheek nuzzled into her armpit, her arm over her head. He insisted on bringing the polar bear into the bedroom. He said it was worth thousands of dollars. He couldn't afford to leave it in the truck. A gang of men in a Montreal parking lot had broken into the truck, which was empty at the time, but he hadn't yet gotten the lock replaced.

The steps to Olivia's apartment were icy and when they got to the top, both of them straining with the bear, it slipped and its head thunked down the fifteen steps, denting its cheek. This almost made Harold cry with frustration.

He said, "What an indecency for that poor creature, the most noble creature in the wild kingdom."

The thumping woke the babysitter, who had fallen asleep on the couch. She pulled on her coat and boots and helped them with the bear.

The cold sobered Olivia considerably. They are lying in bed talking, with all their clothes on except for their shoes. She says, "Harold, do you mind if we don't make love?" and he says, "Not at all," but he is very disappointed.

She talks more about the father of her child. She has glow-in-the-dark stars pasted onto the bedroom ceiling. When Harold removes his glasses, the galaxy blurs and it looks as though they are really sleeping under the milky way. While she talks he puts his hand under her shirt onto her belly. The warmth of it, the small movement as she breathes is so charged with unexpected pleasure that Harold becomes almost tearful. He can't trust his voice to speak, so he lies beside her silently. They both fall asleep.

Olivia's eight-year-old daughter, Rose, is awake in her bed, terrified. She heard the thumping of something large and dangerous on the stairs outside, and drunken laughter. She heard whispers from her mother's room. She makes herself small against the headstand of the bed. She sits there watching the door of her room, waiting for something terrible to bash it open. She watches the clock radio with the red digital numerals change, change, change. Then she gets out of bed. She creeps along the hall to her mother's room. The hall light is on. She squeezes the glass doorknob with her sweaty hand and slowly, so the hinges won't creak, pushes the door open. The light falls on the raging polar bear, frozen in the act of attacking her sleeping mother. Rose doesn't move. The bear doesn't move. Everything stays as it is for a long time until the man next to her mother raises himself up on his elbow and says, "Little girl?"

Rose slams the door and runs to the phone. She dials the number and it rings several times. She can hear her mother calling her. Then a man answers the phone. She says, "Daddy, is that you?"

Julian has been awake, although it is four in the morning. He has been sitting on the couch holding Marika's hand. He hasn't moved her or disturbed her in any way since he took the chip bowl from her, except to hold her hand. He says, "Yes, this is daddy."

He has been awake but it feels as if the child's voice has awoken him. He knows who she is but for a moment her name slips his mind. For a moment, he can not for the life of him remember it.

# Ballad of Captain Bob Bartlett, Arctic Explorer

A. C. Wornell

Bob Bartlett, born in Brigus, of a bold sea-faring breed,
Became a master-mariner as destiny decreed:
He won renown by practicing the brave explorer's role
When Peary used his services to reach the Northern Pole.

The briny spray of Tumavik he faced in early youth;
While fishing with his kin-folk there, he learnt the ocean's truth:
Where wrestling with the ropes and lines, the windlass, oars and sails,
His strong physique developed to withstand the Arctic gales.

In early manhood days he showed great promise of that fame
Which history in later years accorded Bartlett's name.
He furnished for museums countless specimens worthwhile,
And scientific data for the Hydrographic file.

His little ship the *Morrisey* possessed his heart and mind,
As gracefully she sailed along, close-hauled against the wind;
He cheered her on with ev'ry wave which broke across her bow,
As, through the hissing foam, he watched his vessel swiftly plough.

The gulls which hovered over him in whistling Autumn gales,
The bull-birds, turrs, and kittiwakes—the porpoises and whales;
The bosun, hawk and curlew—the phalarope and plover
Were frolicsome companions of this North Atlantic rover.

The off-shore squalls, the rain and fog, the drizzle, sleet and snow
The frothy-lipped North-easter, the close-packed Arctic floe:
The rocks and shoals, the treacherous tides, the rough forbidding shore
Present their dangerous challenges to Bartlett nevermore.

The sealing ships whose bloody decks betokened paying trips,
As ev'ry Spring they wriggled through the Ice-field's crushing grips:
The *Nimrod*, *Neptune*, *Algerine*,—the *Bonaventure*, *Kite*
No more, with Bartlett on the bridge, shall pass the harbour light.

Makkovik, Ailik, Kiglaipait, Cape Harrison and Nain
Shall never see our Newfoundland adventurer again;
For now beneath his native sod there lies, in sacred trust,
A legacy immortal—Bob Bartlett's honoured dust.

*Bartlett's World*, Janice Udell, 1995

# Print: Captain Robert A. Bartlett

*In what is now known as "The Golden Age of Discovery"
Captain Robert Abraham Bartlett stands out as a stellar
example of vision and leadership. He came to age in an
era poised on the brink of a new century, filled with
hope and promise. There were worlds to discover and
knowledge to be gained. The time was ripe for "Iron men
in wooden ships" to push the boundaries of our existence
toward the ultimate quest, to enter the unknown.*

*The print illustrates the life and times of such a man.
I chose to frame the interior panels with a border taken
from an old Italian map printed in 1482. It represents a
thread to the past, linking the discoveries of the first great
explorers with those of Captain Robert Bartlett. The
three squares inside the frame represent the three most
important elements in his life: The left panel shows his
beloved boat, The Effie Morrissey, the middle panel
shows him in front of a map of his expedition with
Peary to the North Pole, and the third panel shows his
birthplace, Brigus, with a drawing of the home where he
grew up, Hawthorne Cottage. On the steps is his mother
reading a letter which is enlarged below her on the panel.
It is a copy of an actual letter sent to her in 1927.
He cared deeply for his mother and wrote her almost
everyday. The bottom part of the print bears his name
in a typeface style I chose because it resembled that
of letters chiselled in stone. I think it is fitting as a
symbol of a man whose memory is now and forever
carved in history.*

— Janice Udell

263

# In Memoriam: Captain Arthur Jackman. Died 31 January 1907

Daniel J. Carroll

Silence and stars and the night dreamed on,
In the realm where the North Gods reign,
And lo! the soul of a Viking passed
Majestically in.
Radiant Aurora, rising from her throne,
Flung all her brilliant banners to the sky
In welcome to the brave, and Thor—the hero
Of that hero-land took Arthur's hand, and
Then, the harps by Sagas grew in Northland fame,
Burst forth anew.

I heard the heart of a man bemoan
The strong man's death.
The blood that won the sea's domain was his;
The winds of the North and the white floe's brood
Know of his bravery.
In danger's hour when dark shores loomed alee,
Where coward hearts would wither in white Fear's fell grip,
With foam-anointed forehead he stood forth a Leader true,
And wrought high deeds while maddened Ocean raged,
By manhood and the courage of his Soul.
Yes—full many a year shall pass ere he's
Forgot, and many a captain brave shall
Quote his name, as towards the North, proud prowed
The fleets advance, manned by the brawn and blood
Of Newfoundland—Captains brave. From headland
And from hamlet as they pass, a people's heart
Shall give them this good wish, *"May Arthur's luck
Be with them on the Sea."*

# Tribute to James (Jimmy) Butler, Blacksmith

**Anonymous**

On Saturday, March 30, drivers along the shore may have been surprised by an uncommon sight.

It was only fitting that a man who laboured most of his life with horses ought to be carried the last mile in this way.

For the greater part of his eighty-three years, James Butler of Peacheytown provided invaluable service to many in our community in his capacity as a blacksmith. Many a horse was to kick its heels in sureness and pride upon receiving a new set of shoes or freshly trimmed hooves.

A simple living man, and not rich by earthly standards, Jimmy was abundantly rich in ways that counted for greater value than material things.

He was blessed with a keen wisdom and common sense which characterized so many of his day. These qualities were always evident, whether making a new set of shoes or talking about life.

But his greatest riches and strength were witnessed in his love for his family and their love for him. This love was shown in his loyalty to his wife Winnie after sixty-eight years together. If anyone doubted his love they must not have seen his great sadness over the loss of his son, Edgar.

Mere words do not do justice in describing one's human existence and many of these same words can be used to describe so many of our people.

In closing, let us not only pay tribute to and celebrate the life of Jimmy, but also the lives of so many of his era. Let us celebrate the triumph of the human spirit and especially the Newfoundland spirit from a time and an age almost lost.

Let us celebrate ourselves, and most of all encourage and support each other along that often rugged road of and to life.

God bless you, Jimmy. It's been our privilege to have known and shared with you awhile.

# This Is My Home

**Harry Martin**

*A tribute to Henry John Williams, a well-known fisherman, trapper and dog team driver.*
*It was sung at his funeral.*

I have no sil - ver no dia - monds or go - ld,

but I am far rich - er by the vis - ions I hold.

'Cause I've seen the mount - ains, and I've seen the se - a,,

I've seen all that beau - ty and lived a life that was

free. When the cool aut - umn moon - light shines

When the cold autumn moonlight shines down through the trees,
No place under heaven would I rather be.
Where the wild birds are flying and the caribou roam,
Many places I've rambled, but this is my home.

When I am weary and it's time to rest,
Just take this old body to the place I love best.
Somewhere on that mountain, turn my face to the sea,
And let the wind in the treetops just sing me to sleep.

'Cause I've seen those mountains, I've been to the sea.
And all of that beauty is like heaven to me.
Where the wild birds are flying and the caribou roam
Many places I've rambled, but this is my home.

Where the wild birds are flying and the caribou roam
Many places I've rambled, but this is my home.

# A Statement

## Samuel Bloomfield

*I was born in Gros Water Bay in 1852. My father was an Englishman from Dartmouth, England. I came to Jack Lane's Bay 34 years ago [1875]. I have been fishing and trapping ever since. I have gone into the interior trapping every winter, a distance of about 50 miles. I have paid revenue to the Government of Newfoundland ever since revenue was collected on the Labrador, and have been obeying its laws and recognized myself as a citizen of Newfoundland and under jurisdiction of its Government. I have never had anything to do with any Canadian officers and have traded with Newfoundland traders and the Mission traders and no one else, and nobody ever interfered with me in my rights as a resident of Labrador. I have never heard that Canada had any claim or made any claim to the interior of Labrador.*

(Sgd) SAMUEL JAMES BROOMFIELD

*Sworn before me at Jack Lane's Bay aforesaid this 25th day of August A.D. 1909.*

(Sgd.) F. J. MORRIS Judge of the Court of Labrador

Privy Council Records
Vol. III, No. 609, Pg. 1557
[3.3:37]

# A Tribute to Samuel Broomfield

**Author Unknown**

Tucked away somewhere between Hopedale and Davis Inlet lies Jack Lane's Bay—the home of the late Samuel Broomfield. Uncle Sam, as he was known from one end of the Labrador coast to the other, died last year at the good old age of 88 years, and with his passing went a gallant gentleman, a true friend and a most hospitable host. There remains, however, a memory as long lasting as the rocky coast on which he lived.

Short of stature, and rather thick-set, his piercing blue eyes peeping out from beneath heavy white brows, and with long, flowing white whiskers, he presented a most picturesque and somewhat patriarchal appearance.

Uncle Sam hailed from Groswater Bay originally, but lived most of his life much farther north in the vicinity of Hopedale, where he made his living at trapping and fishing. He was also game warden for the Newfoundland government, which position he held until the day of his death.

In latter years, after he retired from active work, he was to be seen in a long-tailed black coat and stove-pipe hat. One thing he always wore, day in and day out (and there are some who say he also wore it at night) and that was the Gold Medal commemorating the 250th anniversary of the Hudson's Bay Company, which was presented to a few of the oldest and most loyal of their customers. This medal was presented to Uncle Sam by Mr. Ralph Parsons, fur trade commissioner, on behalf of the Hudson's Bay Company.

He was a musician of no mean talent, and played the violin exceptionally well, providing entertainment to the many wayfarers who habitually frequented his house. He was the first Labrador man to ever speak over the radio, which he did on one occasion from the good ship *Bowdoin*, owned by Commander Donald MacMillan, famous explorer and close friend of Uncle Sam's. At one time Uncle Sam made and sent to His Majesty, King George V, a fine sealskin pouch and a letter expressing his loyalty to his sovereign. In return he received a letter of thanks from the King. Needless to say, this letter was kept among his prized possessions.

# A Tribute to Samuel Broomfield

**Mabel Manak**

Old Samuel James Broomfield was my grandfather. He was a game warden. I remember he used to have a great big bag with S. J. B. marked on it, that it was to keep all his papers and stuff in. He'd carry that bag when he went around seein' people....

I hardly know the way he come to be in Big Bay. I think he used to live at Island Harbour Bay with old grandfather McNeill and them when he was a little boy. He used to tell me the story about how he went to look for his woman, my grandmother Eliza (Learning), up around Rigolet, or Cartwright. He had to travel away up there to look for a wife. He used to laugh about how he had just a small komatik, just long enough for his komatik box and this young man he had in company with him, Uncle George Lane....

I used to hear grandfather talk about Hunt & Henley days, that was before I can remember. I think that was the place grandfather built up his place from—the houses that was there and what he built up on his own. He had a good lot of houses, like for puttin' stuff in, and he had stages and all that. He had young boys makin' paths between the houses and the stages. He had a lot of little stores for puttin' his nets in and things in and net racks for hanging the nets on.

Grandfather was only a short kind of man with a long whisker. He'd always have the radio on and when he'd hear a good tune he'd grab his fiddle and play along wit' the radio tune. He was a man that used to ke'p services, like when he was home there wouldn't a Sunday pass but he'd ke'p service. He could preach as good as a minister yet he liked his dances between that.

269

# Dr. Agnes C. O'Dea, 1911-1993

**Anne Hart**

Agnes O'Dea, a librarian both distinguished and much loved, died in St. John's on January 26, 1993. In 1987, in an address to the Bibliographical Society of Canada, she said:

> When Newfoundland joined Canada in 1949, a sense of identity emerged as never before. Newfoundlanders became rabid Newfoundlanders—"I'm a Newfoundlander, not a Canadian," some would cry—and we began to take pride in our heritage, in our long and continual struggle for survival, and in the literature which tells our long and interesting story.

Hunting and gathering the literature of Newfoundland was at the heart of her remarkable career. Some people are blessed with a life-work they truly enjoy. Agnes was one of these.

Agnes graduated from the University of Toronto in 1932 with a diploma in library science and returned home, Newfoundland's first professional librarian, to become Assistant Head of the infant St. John's Gosling Public Library. In addition to actually building its collection of Newfoundlandia, she began as well to work on something she called "the Bib," the record, in her memorable words, "of everything ever published in Newfoundland, about Newfoundland, and written by Newfoundlanders." In 1939 she obtained a Bachelor of Library Science degree from the University of Toronto and stayed on to work first with the Toronto Public Libraries system and then the Ontario Research Foundation.

Being part of Canada was still a novelty when Agnes returned to Newfoundland in 1952 to take up a position as a reference librarian at Memorial University. Memorial, a college since 1925, had recently become degree granting. What would its new role be? In the words of historian Dr. Peter Neary:

> The answer given by a gifted generation of scholars who appeared on the scene at Memorial in the 1950s was that regional work characterized by the highest standards of scholarship would *ipso facto* be of transcending interest and importance. Thus, in the interest both of the province and of learning in general, a number of major and long-term scholarly projects were started at Memorial in the 1950s.

One of these, with the aid of a Carnegie grant, was to identify the printed records of Newfoundland. In 1955 Agnes was appointed to the task. It would be 1985 before the *Bibliography of Newfoundland* would be published in two large volumes by the University of Toronto Press, but in the thirty-year interval Agnes, seemingly always with time to talk about other things, performed a major feat of detection and compilation. In its published form "the Bib," whittled down to monographs published to 1975, lists over 6,000 publications on Newfoundland and Labrador and provides detailed indexes by author, title and subject.

In 1965, with the bibliography well underway, Agnes was given a second mandate: the establishment of a Newfoundland collection at Memorial University Library. Beginning with forty volumes, by the time of her retirement she had built the Centre for Newfoundland Studies to a collection of some 20,000 volumes. It must have been like seeing her bibliography come to life. In return, the Centre, with the people who work there, has become an ongoing support system for Newfoundland bibliography. After Agnes's retirement in 1976, the editing and preparation of the monographs portion for publication became the work of her colleague, Anne Alexander. Today Joan Ritcey of the Centre is readying for publication a bibliography, already at 41,000 citations, from the Centre's data base of Newfoundland periodical articles. All this continues to be part of Agnes's legacy.

Many honours came to her. In 1976 she was awarded the Canadian Historical Association's Certificate of Merit in local history, in 1977 she was presented with the Newfoundland Historical Society's Annual Heritage Award, in 1980 she was awarded the Atlantic Provinces Library Association's Merit Award and a lifetime membership in recognition of her outstanding contribution to librarianship, and in 1987 she received the degree of Doctor of Laws, *honoris causa*, from Memorial University.

In the course of receiving these awards, she was often called a pioneer. Sometimes this word conjures up a person in a sun-bonnet and forever at toil, the antithesis of Agnes, whose hats—when she wore them—were very elegant, and whose time was a wonderful mix of significant scholarship, numerous close friendships, and many pleasures, travels and interests. For her beloved family, for her many friends and colleagues, and for the province of Newfoundland, her death came as a great loss.

271

# A Tribute to Michael Cook

## Clyde Rose

Newfoundland and the people of this place were the sources of inspiration for many of Michael's dramatic works. Although not born here this place became his home.

"Some men are born at home." he wrote:

> Others spend all their lives in search of it. I spent thirty-four years looking for one. When I came to Newfoundland I found it. Instinct again. I know I shall have to leave it (periodically) but I'll always come back. It is the source of my imagination and the seat of any joy I have ever found.

With Newfoundland as his home, his inspiration, his creative catalyst, Michael Cook rocketed to fame and became this country's most magnificent voice in the world of play writing. His vision of a Newfoundland with no fish in the sea shocked us twenty years ago. His images like a wild Nord Easter. His language even stronger. His metaphors pitched-forked to our minds—one prong piercing the heart, the other the soul. His prophetic vision raging. The lund of our lives battered by a terrifying wind. The tormented voice of Skipper Pete speaking to John in *The Head, Guts and Soundbone Dance*:

> The sun is on the water. Just like it always was. Days like this when we've given her every stitch of canvas and foamed down the sound—the water alive with boats about us all rushing to git to the grounds first. Good men, John b'y. Good men. But they's gone. And their boats gone wid'n. And the land gone wid'n too. The fences broken. The trees marching back over the hayfields.

No one today—no fisherman—or fisherwoman—in our bays, harbours or coves—no one on any island of islands—Joe Batts, Fogo, Random, or Petley doubts the veracity of this vision now. Oh that we had listened more closely to this man and placed more faith in his poetic vision.

His plays as one European put it were like cathedrals—big enough to move around in and inspiring. His words like thunder and lightning filling the stage. Moments of brilliance and insights in the theatre that he loved with a passion. Always the chronicler of this place. An intuitive sense that he as the outsider in love with Newfoundland could see us with fresh eyes in a way that we could not. Like the devoted lover of this place that he was he lamented the course on which we were bound. Michael recognized the tightly knit family and social structures—almost like blueberries in bunches on the barrens—and he recognized the survival instincts of our culture but he was fundamentally concerned with the impending dissolution of the spirit, language and culture of our people:

> I'm very much an outsider in Newfoundland. I guess I always have been. It's not that I'm not accepted as a person, but my work is still viewed

with suspicion, because as an outsider I have not followed the current trend—the Irish trend, actually—of romanticizing and mythologizing the glories of the past. It was a very dark and soul-destroying past in many ways, a survival culture with incredibly tight-knit family and social structures. I've addressed those issues because they fascinate me. I was excited about an island sitting on the edge of time, very beautiful on certain occasions, but for eight months of the year, very violent. As I fell in love with all of those things that are immediately obvious to the outsider who goes there, I became aware that it was a culture that was not only threatened, but doomed. I became a chronicler of that—what I consider to be the destruction of a spirit, language, culture and people.

Michael Cook is no outsider here today. The ashes of this man—a brilliant teacher and playwright—will be swept by the wind over Random Island and Fogo. Over the places he loved. His legacy of literary works will be long remembered. No young actor in Newfoundland will mount the stage and not feel the power of these words from the radio play *This Damned Inheritance*—words from the ghost of Jack Kelly, speaking to the character Aiden who is sitting on his headstone in the graveyard. (This might well be Michael's own epitaph):

> ...it don't matter to me if the old church spire that used to call us home disappears, and the foundations sink back into the cold earth. It don't matter that there's no record o' me other than what yer arse is sitting on, and it won't matter when that gets split be the frost and crumbles either, for I belongs now to the wind and the water, and the silence of a January night, when ye can hear nothing save the crack of a tree split be the frost, or a loon mourning far off fer all the wrongs of this wasteful world. And I won't be gone after all...I'll be in the mist and the cold ruin dripping down for eternity.

This is what he wrote. And this is why we shall remember him—always.

# In Memoriam: Cassie Brown—A Tribute

Helen Fogwill Porter

I admired Cassie Brown for a long time before I actually met her. As a writer half a generation older than myself, she was an inspiration to me and a number of other Newfoundland writers my age and younger. Long before Cassie published *Death on the Ice* in 1974 she was writing plays, short stories and newspaper columns. For a period before the Newfoundland literary renaissance she and Harold Horwood were the only people from our province who were doing what we wanted to do.

Cassie and I really got to know each other about ten years ago when we were staying at the Holiday Inn in Clarenville. We were both touring schools in the Trinity-Bonavista-Placentia area, talking to the students about our writing and Newfoundland writing in general. I envied Cassie's marvellous rapport with the young people: her flair for drama had them hanging on to every word. It was over meals at the hotel that I saw a different side of Cassie, the mystical, intuitive side.

Cassie was reluctant to talk about that part of her character. She was no early-day Shirley MacLaine, talking glibly about previous lives. It was clear, however, that to Cassie the material world was not everything. Her three books, especially *Death on the Ice*, were the result of meticulous and loving research but there was another important element operating as well. Cassie Brown made her readers feel that they were there with the 120 sealers who spent two days and two nights on ice-pans in the cold North Atlantic, most of the time in a raging blizzard. Seventy-eight men died; many others were crippled for life. Cassie captured the scene the way she did because, in a way, she herself was there on the ice with them.

Before Cassie died she had finished a draft of her autobiography. In *Death on the Ice*, *A Winter's Tale* and *Standing Into Danger*, Cassie concentrated on the lives, and deaths, of other people. With the publication of her autobiography readers will learn something about her own life.

Cassie Brown died late in December after a brief illness following a heart attack. Her body was cremated and her ashes were scattered over the waters of Conception Bay near Topsail where she spent some of her happiest hours in solitude and meditation.

# Noel Dinn

**Harold Paddock**

You made me cry before I knew
your name back in the slowing seventies
when your latest widow took me
to your haunted house and watched
in wonder the trickling of my tears
onto your kitchen table as I strained
to decrypt her grief engraved on empty sheets
and I shall never forget her resonance
for lost rites in Noel and in Dinn
her fluffing up with pride
at *Figgy* and at *Duff*

You made me wary before I'd even
met you because you had enthralled
our middle-friend Neil Murray but I too
fell softly to your spell and the three
of us spent hours very high on ethno-
cultural sweeps across the face of earth
we felt the oomph of drums that urged
ancestral feet we heard hypnotic pipes
that pumped triumphant blood and
we recited syllables that raised elusive grails
you were a genius with dark Guinness
you were a Messiah with mixed hormones
you were John the Baptist with his horn still on
you were a private saint of asceticism
you were a public demon of indulgence
you were a bewitcher of women
you were a wizard of renewal

You made me tremble before I knew
your trouble wading crabwise at Bridgett's
on a crowded Wednesday night I swung open
a door to find you swaying depleted to a depth
I'd never seen before and we embraced that night
shouting our solace through beating decibels
trying to salvage something from ephemeral lives
of a few mutual friends next day at dinner
spread out for two in sober shyness you unfolded
in front of me a poem you'd made for Neil
and in shared silence of its reading

our faces twitched over the unswallowed sorrows
of talents thwarted careers curtailed
of pregnancies postponed of marriages not made

You made me buoyant as I stared
at your coffin in strong sunlight stained
by the bright glass of St. Patrick's you were
our unpaid envoy to some larger world
with the unbending of your will and the sinuous
woven beat of your bodhran you made us
the envy of many another nation
your hands have unsettled
the way we hear ourselves
your soul has resettled
the way we see ourselves.

**figgy duff**: a boiled pudding containing raisins. [1900] 1975 WHITELEY 57 Dinner—salt meat, turnip and potatoes, figged duff (boiled in a cloth). [1911] GRENFELL 65 'Figgy duff,' a big boiling of family-mess pork, some crackers, a tin of condensed milk, a poy of real jam (not Labrador berries), and some apples. [1894-1929] 1960 BURKE (ed White) 35 "The Terra Nova Regatta": Where the figgy duffs are seen, / That would sink a brigatine. T 181/2-65 You'd have figgy duff, boy; all the figs go down to the bottom o' your bag; when they cut the duff he'd cut off [the bottom] —the other fellers'd get none o' the figs. 1977 BURSEY 24 Tuesday was 'duff day' and we must buy the necessaries. The duff was made of water and flour and a generous addition of raisins and all saturated with molasses. We called it a figged duff and it was indeed a luxury.

# Pamela Morgan: A Voice for Newfoundland's Roots

Ken Roseman

Vocalist, songwriter and arranger Pamela Morgan occupies a seminal position in Newfoundland's musical history. With the folk-rock band Figgy Duff and several special, one-off projects, Pamela has helped create a modern music inspired by the region's distinctive heritage: a unique blending of traditions from England, Scotland, France and Wales.

Figgy Duff is a North American parallel to the pioneering British groups Fairport Convention, Steeleye Span and The Albion Country Band. Like them, Figgy Duff combined electric guitars, electric bass, keyboards and drum kits with the more tradition-drawn instrumental choices of fiddle, mandolin, accordion and dulcimer to create a new setting of centuries-old ballads and tunes. And hailing from Newfoundland gave Figgy Duff a unique sound. The Irish influence on their instrumentals, more so than the dryer English approach to tune, is unmistakable, but it was a stripped-down sound minus the ornaments and decorations commonly associated with Irish players. There was a subtle difference in Figgy Duff's handling of ballads as well. At times, it sounded as if an Irish singer were performing an English ballad, or the other way around—a delicate contrast that set the group apart from, yet equal to, its peers across the pond.

The group members' approach to finding material also differed from their British counterparts, who discovered songs primarily from printed sources or learned them from recordings. Figgy Duff's quest to fill its repertoire began with book research, but the members soon found, as Pamela explains, that "the people the songs were collected from were still living" and they sought them out through repeated trips into the countryside.

"We did our own informal research, not as scholars did it—we befriended the people," Pamela explains. And that process led to two-way exchanges. She remembers how a group member would "jolt someone's memory" with one song on one visit, and by the next visit "they'd remember more." Figgy Duff made repeated visits to sources in areas like Bonavista Bay, Fogo Island, Placentia Bay, Bonne Bay and Port-Au-Port Peninsula. "We got to know more of the people and their lives that way," Pamela says.

One of the most important sources they met in those early days was fiddler Emile Benoit, a native of the French-speaking Port-Au-Port Peninsula on Newfoundland's West Coast. Not only did the group record several of his tunes, but Pamela and Figgy Duff founder Noel Dinn co-produced Benoit's *Vive La Rose* recording. Mose Harris, a native of the Bonavista Bay area, was another key figure in the musical development of Figgy Duff and Pamela's primary source of traditional songs.

It's noteworthy that Pamela didn't come to Figgy Duff and traditional music as a complete novice. Her interest was first sparked in high school where, she recalls, she "had a a teacher who taught language arts and drama. He was a staunch Newfoundland nationalist and taught us to take pride in our culture. Because I was musical, I naturally gravitated towards the music of Newfoundland. I was absolutely fascinated." Just two short years later, Pamela first met Noel Dinn, who, she says, was "also investigating traditional material." Dinn's vision was already in motion, and he had started a band before meeting Pamela. But their mutual interests soon evolved into a collaboration. The result was Figgy Diff's self-titled debut recording, a set of traditional ballads and tunes recorded by the basic quartet of Dinn (drums, piano and harmony vocals), Morgan (vocals, guitar, tin whistle and piano), Dave Panting (mandolin, bass, guitar and harmony vocals) and Geoff Butler (button accordion). One of the group's main challenges at the time, recalls Pamela, "was to arrange the ballads. All the songs we found were sung without accompaniment." The arrangements they created for the ballads—such as "Matt Eiley" and "Rosy Banks of Green"—maintained an understated beauty, backing Morgan's clear, smooth vocals simply with acoustic guitar or mandolin and piano along with underlying accordion fills.

Figgy Duff's second outing, *After the Tempest*, released two years later, was a more ambitious undertaking. The band had expanded to a quintet, adding bassist Derek Pelley, which enabled Panting to concentrate on mandolin and guitar. The keyboard and synthesizer were moved forward on several tracks, providing a more orchestral feel. It was here that the first original material joined the recorded repertoire, as well: an

instrumental piece by Panting, and "Honour, Riches," Dinn's musical setting of Shakespeare's words written for a theatrical production of *The Tempest*.

With Morgan and Dinn at the core, accompanied by a revolving cast of supporting musicians, the band kept busy for the next half-decade—plus playing small concerts and festivals. With state-of-the-art recording equipment unavailable in Newfoundland, the costs involved in transporting musicians and instruments slowed Figgy Duff's recording output. But it was during this period that Dinn and Morgan began thinking seriously about writing original material.

The fruits of that labor were revealed on *Weather Out the Storm*, which was evenly divided between originals and arrangements of traditional material. The title song and "Heart of a Gypsy" were co-written by Dinn and Morgan and are well-described as "folk ballads gone pop." While their elegant lyric phrasing recalls that of ancient balladry, these new songs borrowed moderate rock tempos and revolved around catchy, repetitive choruses. The band's sound had also altered, as Dinn opted for a more complex, radio-friendly sound for the arrangements. Guests were brought in to supplement the core quintet, adding saxophone, extra guitars, organ and more synth, giving the entire proceeding a richer texture. The fiddle and accordion were moved from lead position to more of a "color" role in the sound, as well. Interestingly, Dinn and Morgan next moved to two projects that demonstrated their continued commitment to Newfoundland's roots.

*Vive La Rose* featured the great traditional fiddler Emile Benoit, who supplied Figgy Duff with much of the band's early material.

Dinn, Morgan and Gary Furniss co-produced the recording and Noel and Pamela arranged the music and accompanied Benoit on bodhran, acoustic guitar, synthesizer and backup vocals. They were joined by other Newfoundland artists on bass guitar, piano accordion, electric and acoustic guitars, dobro, bouzouki, mandolin, dulcimer and "supporting" fiddle. Benoit sounded at ease sawing away within the semi-electric setting and melded by the Figgy Duff principals and their companions. *Vive La Rose* became, in truth, more of a collaboration than a solo outing for Benoit, and certainly stands as one of the most successful bridgings of an older traditional artist with his younger counterparts.

Benoit was, undoubtedly, a major influence on Figgy Duff, both as a source of tunes and as a spiritual colleague. They met him on one of their music-seeking trips to Port-Au-Port Peninsula, when the band stopped at a local bar and found Benoit playing in an informal session. For Dinn and Morgan, getting to record with Benoit was the realization of a longtime goal and a dream come true.

"Emile Benoit was the most joyous person I've ever met," Pamela recalls. "He was a visionary, and he wrote a lot of his own tunes, you know. Noel and Emile had a great rapport, and Emile was a bit of a renegade"—a quality with which young musicians interested in blending folk with rock 'n' roll could well identify.

The next tradition-based project for Morgan and Dinn was *The Colour of Amber*, a collection of Newfoundland love songs sung and performed by Morgan and Anita Best and produced by Dinn. The English, French and Gaelic language songs sported largely acoustic instrumental settings, nicely framing the singers' voices. "Anita was a perfect partner for the recording," says Pamela. "She had traditional music in her life since birth, coming from a community where the music was very much alive. I love working with Anita. We have a similar feel for the ballads."

Figgy Duff's next—and as it turns out, its final—outing was *Downstream*. Dinn had been suffering from throat cancer for several years and, as Pamela recalls, "knew he was in trouble. He had some things to say, and he needed to do that before he died." *Downstream* included four Dinn compositions, as well as five by Morgan and one collaboration between the two: "Pirates of Pleasure." This time the recording was clearly folk-influenced pop rather than the other way around. Acoustic instruments were definitely in the background, with electric guitars, keyboards, bass and drums in the front. But while Dinn's lyrics tended to speak of leavings and departures, *Downstream* was not a downbeat affair. Pamaela's singing was more confident than ever, and songs like "Freedom" and "Pirates of Pleasure" had a restrained exuberance.

On July 26, 1993, at the age of 45, Dinn died, effectively marking the end of Figgy Duff. But the band's career was capped last July with the release of the Morgan-produced *Figgy Duff: A Retrospective, 1974-1993*, which included selections from all four recordings as well as two previously unreleased songs from a 1978 session. The thick accompanying booklet contains an essay on the band written by Pamela, an interesting photo gallery and quotes from many of the musicians who passed through Figgy Duff's ranks over the years.

Earlier this year, Pamela finished her first solo recording, *On a Wing and a Prayer* (Sleeping Giant/A&M), and found the experience, in her words, "a whole different ballgame" after all the time she spent with Figgy Duff and in collaboration with Dinn. "My whole world changed after Noel died," she says.

Two of Dinn's last songs appear on the new recording. Particularly striking is "Something Calling" with its unforgettable melody and vivid imagery of uncertainty, disappointment and longing: "A genius on a tightrope tastes the bitter fruits of life / While a beggar lives in the cloak upon his back /A dreamer sleepwalks through the pain of day / All are searching, searching for the quiet life." Pamela's vocal performance on this song is outstanding, clearly coming right from the heart. "There were some of Noel's songs that I wanted to record before they became dim memories," she says.

The recording also includes two Dinn and Morgan co-writes as well as six penned by Morgan alone and one traditional ballad, "Blackwater Side," the last song Pamela learned from mentor Mose Harris.

Pamela developed the songs for the recording with her current live touring unit (George Morgan on keyboards and percussion and Serguei Tchepournov on violin) before entering the studio. For the recording, Pamela, George and Serguei were joined by others, including some Figgy Duff alumni: Sandy Morris (acoustic and slide guitars), Rob Laidlaw (bass) and Kelly Russell (fiddle). Overall, the sound is fairly acoustic, and even has a slight multi-cultural flavor, thanks to Tchepournov's Russian heritage and George Morgan's use of hand percussion. "I was after a melding sound in terms of influences from other cultures," Pamela explains. "That was deliberate."

With this, another album of primarily original songs, the question arises whether Pamela is moving away from the source material. "When you've sung traditional material for a long, long time, it's as though you're always telling someone else's story," Pamela explains. "There came a point in my life that I felt the need to express my own thoughts." Still, Pamela has set lofty goals for her songs. "The lyrics in folk songs are polished and perfected over the hundreds of years the songs have been in existence…and that sets a very high standard for my own writing."

Pamela draws on a wide range of inspirations for her more recent work. The torch song "Backseat," for example, is a radical departure from her previous efforts. It came about, she says, as a result of an observation at a party. "It Ain't Funny" is something else altogether—a bitter lament over the decline of Newfoundland's fishing industry, long a staple of the local economy. "Political posturing is now the ultimate insult / It's too little too late / What's left is up for sale / And the best small boatsmen in the world are on the dole." (Not exactly your usual pop subject matter.)

Pamela cites another reason for the move from traditional material. Many of the older people with large repertoires, including her main inspirations, are dying off. Benoit, for example, died September 2, 1992. "I just lost too many," she says. "The tradition is not as strong as it was when we were finding people. It was those older people that kept all those songs alive." Traditional culture, she adds, is simply "not as ingrained now as it was then."

Nevertheless, the tradition does live on and Pamela even finds her way to the occasional song session. "Anita (Best) makes sure that stays alive," Pamela says. "Parties often end up in songs and music because that's who we are. But I put a lot of energy into being a professional, and I don't have the luxury of socializing evenings as much as I'd like."

But even if Morgan won't be informally swapping traditional songs regularly, she's helping to keep Newfoundland's spirit alive in her own special way. An upcoming project will be a traditionally oriented one—a set of what she calls "lesser-known" Christmas carols. "I've never really made a distinction between the traditional and pop-oriented material in my own work," she says. "The original (songs) are influenced by my background in traditional music." From the choice of accompaniment to her direct, no-frills phrasing and singing style, it's clear that we'll be hearing the roots of Newfoundland in Pamela Morgan's music for a long time to come.

**newfoundland dance**: a lively, vigorous group step-dance.

1884 STEARNS 293 [At Bonne Espérance] Monday night, for our benefit, the natives performed a Labrador, or rather Newfoundland dance, at one of the native cabins near by. A crowd of about thirty assembled and danced till nearly morning. Their main object seemed to be to 'start the sweat, and see who could make the most noise.' It seemed as if the very house would come down over our heads as they hammered on the floor with their top-legged boots pounding with the full force of their powers.

# It Ain't Funny

Pamela Morgan

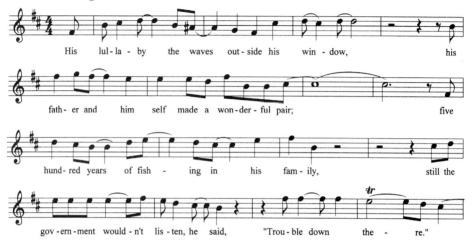

His lul-la-by the waves out-side his win-dow, his
fath-er and him self made a won-der-ful pair; five
hund-red years of fish - ing in his fam-ily, still the
gov-ern-ment would-n't lis-ten, he said, "Trou-ble down the - re."

It ain't funny—it ain't funny no more

Fat cat smirkin' in the land of plenty
Makin' jokes about a people and a culture from a gentler time
Sanctioned and applauded the gang rape of the place
But like any rape they blame the victim for the crime

It ain't funny—it ain't funny no more

Political posturing now is the ultimate insult
It's too little too late—what's left is up for sale
And the best small boatmen in the world are on the dole
Just stupid and lazy according to the *Globe and Mail*

It ain't funny—nobody's laughing now
It ain't funny—something has changed somehow
It ain't funny—it ain't funny no more

# More than a Monument: the Town of St. Lawrence Fights On

Luben Boykov

My name is Luben Boykov. I am an artist and a sculptor in St. John's, Newfoundland. Several hours by car southwest of St. John's there is a small town called St. Lawrence. In February of 1942, two US Navy ships were wrecked in a winter storm. Two hundred and three American sailors died, but one hundred and eighty-six men were saved. Now, fifty years later, the Heritage Society there wanted to commemorate the courageous rescue by the mine workers of St. Lawrence who pulled the drowning sailors from the freezing Atlantic and they commissioned me to create a sculpture for this purpose. But in talking to the people of St. Lawrence I came to realize that the sculpture was to be more than just a reminder of that event. I got a strong feeling that what I was about to create would become a symbol of the town itself.

This commission was special to me because the central idea behind the monument reflected a strong belief I have as an artist. I believe that works of art no matter how big or small or no matter where in the world they are made, I believe that they say to the world, "Look, I'm here, I'm not just a number, not just an industrial statistic, I'm worth something, I'm valuable in and of myself." The sculpture I would create was going to say just that. "Look, here is a town, a town that has value, a value which goes much deeper than the state of its industry or its economic conditions. Here is a community, with a past, and a present, and the life struggle which goes on. It is the life of its people which gives St. Lawrence its value. It's as simple as that."

After drawing and experimenting with ideas, I produced a small plaster model of the sculpture and took it to St. Lawrence. The model, or maquette as it is called, showed two figures representing a St. Lawrence miner hauling a drowning sailor from the water. The St. Lawrence Heritage Society had worked hard to get the sculpture project going and they would be the ones to oversee things through to the finish.

It was a Christian symbol that I adopted for the pose of the miner's figure: the crucifix, the suffering, the martyrdom. I realized that the sculpture could not be too general or abstract. It had to reflect certain particulars, but it also had to express a universal meaning. Of course, I was nervous. I hoped that the small scale figures conveyed the same sort of dramatic composition and the strength of feeling I intended for the final sculpture.

So much of what an artist does is plain hard work, so it really is important for the piece of work to have at its center strong emotions and powerful ideas otherwise the long hours in the studio would just turn into tedious labour. You have to have a conviction and an emotional engagement that makes the effort worth it. For me, there was no doubt—the people of St. Lawrence were my inspiration and the stories written on their faces and in their voices stayed with me….

There was sleet and snow and wind, and I said to my husband, "God help the poor Christians on the ocean tonight." Next morning when we got up, my husband looked out through the window and he said, "There's black people going up the road, where are they coming from?" And I said, "I don't know."

When the ship split, all the crude oil came out on the waves and it was so cold that it formed a hard surface just like tar on the water. And that's why it was almost impossible for the poor fellows to swim. They were getting the encouragement from the shore, people were yelling, "Come on, swim!" You know, that's how a lot of them were saved, just through encouragement, "You can make it!" And our men, you know, were right out to their hips in that cold water. Lots of them said afterwards, it was strange, they were just numb, they were working so hard trying to save these people, so many young faces crying out to be saved. They themselves didn't feel it, they didn't feel the cold.

Thirty men put a rope around me and held it and I went down 375 feet and come back with the man I went after. He was down on the beach. I walked over sixteen dead bodies before I got to 'em. And another man was holding out his hand like that and I never got to 'em.

They had sort of a hunch, would there be another ship? And they walked up a couple of miles further up the coast and, sure enough, there was another ship.

You couldn't believe it, I mean you couldn't believe it in your mind that there were any survivors, that there was anyone out in the wash. But now, they were there.

They were pulled from these terrible waves and these chilling waters and they were dragged up over the cliffs by the men. There was a whole group of men on the beach and in the water and another group of men on top of the cliffs. After that, then, they were taken by truck here into the town. Then they were taken into the homes all around if you could take one or you could take two, however many you could accommodate.

When my husband came, I suppose it was three or three thirty, and when the truck stopped in front of the house here, he got out, he had this man with him and he took him on his back and brought him up. He was just rolled up in a blanket with a suit of underwear on him. He sat on the daybed and he looked so cold and so miserable, he was just a kid really, about eighteen years old. I looked at him and I said, "Are you all right?" He looked at me, smiled and said, "Yeah, I'm fine."

As I worked on the details I kept hearing their voices and seeing their faces as they told me about that cold February night fifty years ago. The work on the sculpture progressed. It was time for the Heritage Committee to have a look at the first figure. I talked about the progress I had made so far and explained what would come next. Every next stage adds something more and more and it looks better and better. The method that is used in bronze sculpture is very old but there is new technology that makes it even more complicated. We use liquid plastic over the clay to create a negative mold, so the form can't change. Then the wax is poured into the negative mold and then you end up with a positive mold, like the clay.

Working so intensely to shape the human form for the sculpture, I couldn't help but be reminded of the bodies of the miners and of the sailors on that dreadful night, the images of bodies tossed about by the cruel sea. And before long I am thinking of that other cruelty: the miners' disease that took so many men of St. Lawrence from their families and from their community. It was discovered that radon had been escaping from the fluorspar in the mine for years, many became really sick, many died.

> For years and years I was working underground, and then we didn't know what was happening, a lot of fellows were after dropping out, eh? And this was this stuff, it would get them unseen.

> There's not so much widows anywhere else as there is in St. Lawrence. I think that if I had a son, I'd almost sooner see him starve than to go in under there.

> All those who worked in the mines, as far as I'm concerned, are just the same as those that went overseas and laid down his life overseas. They laid down their life for their country over there, well they laid down their life here in Newfoundland for their living.

Laying down your life for your living. That statement echoes through my mind. Is this the way it is supposed to be? I can't help thinking something has gone wrong. Should making a living be the supreme sacrifice? The words haunt me.

For St. Lawrence the ironies seemed to go on. Not only did they have to withstand the devastation of illness and death, but there was another twist. After the *Truxton* and *Pollux* tragedy, the Americans showed their appreciation to St. Lawrence by having a hospital built in the town. As fate would have it this hospital provided a lot of relief and care as more and more miners fell victim to radon sickness and silicosis from the mine. And sure enough, as fate would also have it, the hospital no longer seemed feasible or efficient and would have to go.

As my work drew closer to the finish, I heard over and over the determined voices of the St. Lawrence people. I had the distinct feeling that the whole monument project was about that determination to fight on that seemed to be the spirit of St. Lawrence.

At the foundry the men cover the wax pieces of the sculpture with a ceramic shell. Then they pour hot molten bronze into this space. The wax will be melted so it runs out of the shell and leaves the shape of the sculpture inside. Soon all the pieces will be together. I was getting excited to show the sculpture to the people of St. Lawrence.

At first I was very apprehensive. The major challenge for me was to combine two more or less incompatible threads in composition: on the one hand, the actual rescuing operation, and the miners' disaster on the other. The naval disaster occurred almost overnight, an event that was emotionally charged to the limit. The miners' disaster was a prolonged suffering stretched over decades full of personal tragedies and grief. The only way, I thought, to unify these two events with such a different duration in time was to use a powerful symbol, a symbol that would become the overriding theme of the monument. The entire tradition of St. Lawrence is based upon Christianity. It had played and still plays a very important role in shaping the customs, habits, morality and values of the people.

The miner's figure participates in the concrete action. He is interacting with the sailor's figure but at the same time he exists in a different reality, a reality with no time, eternity. The miner is hauling on the sailor's figure by means of a rope but there is no rope to be seen between the two figures and the space between them is empty. This is the space where self-denial, feat and valour reside.

So it was time for the artist's journey to end. I felt not only a sense of fulfillment and accomplishment but also a sense of honour to think that the symbol I have created will become a part of the voice of this courageous town.

*St. Lawrence Miners*, Luben Boykov

# Loss of a Friend: A Personal Memoir

**Irving Fogwill**

"The cradle rocks above an abyss, and common sense tells us that our existence is but a brief crack of light between two eternities of darkness." Thus, in fatidic accents, we are told by Nabokov that the whole of personal life is nothing but a mere moment of day between two endless nights: the first darkness being without personal existence, the second encompassing an eternal sleep; hence there are beginnings and endings for that brief crack of light. There are arrivals and departures. And darkness comes at noon sometimes. Darkness comes suddenly and leaves a stillness and an emptiness that no sound of sophistry can animate nor substance fill; and a grieving comes with that darkness that no balm of Gilead can assuage. Other voices will be heard in other mornings, and the lost, sweet voice may be heard in a dream, but the warm, living presence is gone forever. This is the mood of modern man; lonely and despairing, as in poet Arthur Symons's hauntingly beautiful lines—

> O water voice of my heart, crying in the sand,
>     All night long crying with a mournful cry,
> As I lie and listen, and cannot understand
> The voice of my heart in my side or the
>     Voice of the sea,
> O water crying for rest, is it I, is it I?
>     All night long the water is crying for me.
>
> Unresting water, there shall never be rest
>     Till the last moon droop and the last tide fall,
> And the fire of the end begin to burn in the west;
>     And the heart shall be weary and wonder
>             and cry like the sea,
> All life long crying without avail,
>     As the water all night long is crying to me.

But what of Love and Hope and Faith? Surely, these three words—the most beautiful and inspiring in the language—have more than an etymological meaning? For those of us who must try to continue to live out our brief span of light? Because we must go forward into the days that flow towards us. And shall we not go forward strengthened with the love we had for him, and shall always have for him? In the quiet hours, memory shall speak of him, of his limitless compassion for all God's creatures, of his profound concern for human kind, of his warmth and humour in greeting a friend—his smile so like the sunburst through a cloud. Memory speaks and tells us of his enormous sense of responsibility, of his sensitivity; and of a strange sadness that lay behind the brusque façade, pressing like a sudden cloud over the face of the sun. And in the quiet hours the thought comes through as to how great must be the weight of the burden and pressures on the brilliantly intellectual and perceptive spirits of this terrible age in which we live: on those rare and intense souls who seem to comprehend more clearly than the rest of us the nature and the catastrophic shape of things. But even the stoic bows his head to the terminal battle, as the trees to the hurricane.

What statement then can we make to the memory of our lost friend? Oh, how we should like to be able to place in an indestructible arrangement a few simple words of the language that will testify indelibly to his inviolable honesty and sincerity; to record simply the measure of his humility and compassion towards his fellow men to all creatures that struggle for breath, and of his anguish in the face of human pain and suffering for which he did what he could to alleviate. In his profession, and as a man, infinitely unselfish, what more could he have done? If the burden becomes too heavy; if the knowledge and comprehension of things overwhelm body and soul and the heart of a good man breaks, what then, my friends? Is it that a man lies down in darkness? And is that darkness an infinity of night? Perhaps it is. But what of Love and Hope and Faith? Perhaps all God's children got wings.

> Sing O Muse, Melpomene, of time in flight,
> And the few yesterdays our hearts enfold
> Of one now lost in the unanswering night:
> For brave men must go forward in the cold.

> For darkness comes at noon and good men die,
> And quietly are laid beneath the sod;
> Lie down in darkness under sombre sky
> To take their aching questions up to God.

**Excerpt from**

# The Rock Observed: Studies in the Literature of Newfoundland

Patrick O'Flaherty

In the grim spring of 1914, a Bonavista Bay man, George Tuff, thirty-two years of age, was second hand on the sealing vessel the *S. S. Newfoundland*. He was, though young, a veteran seal hunter, having first gone to the ice at the age of sixteen and having already lived through the *Greenland* disaster of 1898. Through hard work and caution, Tuff had done well. He was known as a careful man. Even Captain Abram Kean, the aristocrat of the sealing industry, knew and trusted him. As second hand, he did not have to go on the ice to kill a single seal. Success indeed! His job was to ensure the smooth operation of the ship itself. Nevertheless, on 31 March, at the prompting of his young captain, Wes Kean, Abram's son, Tuff volunteered to lead the *Newfoundland*'s crew a distance of about four or five miles over rough ice to Abram Kean's ship the *Stephano*, where the main patch of seals appeared to be. There he would be given orders by the great man himself. Tuff did his job. After four and a half weary hours, with the weather becoming dirtier and more ominous, he and his men— except for thirty-four, who wisely chose to leave the group and head back to their ship—reached the *Stephano*, where in view of the weather most of the men thought they would spend the coming night. But Old Man Kean, impatient to get on with his own hunt, and thinking no storm was in sight, had different plans. After bringing the *Newfoundland's* men near a small patch of seals two miles closer (as he thought) to their own ship, he told Tuff to get his crew underway and to head for the seals. Tuff would have to get his men back to the *Newfoundland* before nightfall, in weather that was looking worse and worse. By this time Tuff could not, in fact, see his own ship, but though worried by the increasing snowfall he said quietly: "I don't want to delay you, sir." In a few minutes he and his crew of one hundred and thirty-one men were on the ice, the *Stephano* disappeared into the surrounding snow, and, as his men started to question his leadership, the full horror of his situation struck home in Tuff's mind:

"There's a starm on, George."

"What we doin' here?"

Then an accusation, "George, ye're our leader, ye brought us here."

"What's goin' to happen to we, George?"

The situation, the magnitude of the responsibility, hit George Tuff perhaps for the first time. He was in charge now. He was no longer taking orders from Captain Kean, or from anyone else. There was nobody to take orders from. Slowly he was coming to realize the peril in which they had been placed. The anxious faces, the questioning eyes of the men clustering around him were too much. He was a man of limited capabilities, and to be responsible for them—many of them personal friends—was overwhelming. Tears rolled down his cheeks. "Cap'n Kean give me orders to kill seals an' go back to our own ship," he pleaded.

A murmur went through the crowd and reached Cecil Mouland and his buddies on the outskirts. "Tuff is cryin'," they said in wonderment.

The incident is related in Cassie Brown's fine book, *Death on the Ice* (1972). Like so many other episodes described in Newfoundland literature, episodes such as George Cartwright's slaughter of bears on the Eagle River, Norman Duncan's encounter with Uncle Zeb on the Great Northern Peninsula, Franklin Russell's visit to the Funks, and many more, Tuff's disastrous decision to take the crew of the *Newfoundland* onto the ice in perilous conditions seems a symbolic moment, rich with meaning. What are we to make of it? Is Tuff's obedience to Abram Kean a sign of social deference and the yoke of a dependent spirit inherited from the old outport way of life? An expression of the fatalistic mood we note in one of the melancholy Newfoundland ballads?

> The best thing to do is to work with a will;
> For when 'tis all finished you're hauled on the hill,
> You're hauled on the hill and put down in the cold,
> And when 'tis all finished you're still in the hole,
>   And it's hard, hard times.

Or are we rather seeing in the incident another spirit entirely, a manly but unspoken confidence of success and determination against great odds? Tuff, after all, was no callow youth, but an experienced seal hunter. He had confronted rough weather, knobby ice, cold, and risky situations time after time, and had not only survived but done wonderfully well. Was he thinking that he had survived the *Greenland* tragedy, and that surely he would never again have to experience such a horror? Was he acting in the spirit of another ballad, full of a sense of mastery and power?

> I'se the b'y that builds the boat,
> And I'se the b'y that sails her!
> I'se the b'y that catches the fish
>   And takes 'em home to Lizer.

Judgment balks. We are left with an episode of great dramatic power, make of it what we will. One thing we know. The long history of the Newfoundland people includes more than story-telling in the twine loft and cavorting on the landwash. It includes seventy-seven frozen bodies of the *Newfoundland's* dead sealers. And George Tuff's tears.

To explore the whole of Newfoundland's printed literature is to become aware of the richness of a body of writing long neglected, and to learn caution in interpreting it. It is also to be left with a sense of the utter inadequacy of familiar catch phrases often used by authors, phrases such as "the nature of Newfoundland life" or "the shape of Newfoundland history." So little is known about the true history of Newfoundland, and indeed about the character and motivation of many of those who tried to influence or describe it, that any writer who summarily reduces the complexity of Newfoundland's past or present to a ready formula must be regarded with great suspicion. The literature we have examined mirrors, rather than resolves, that complexity. If it lacks the symmetry and universality of great art, it is none the less important in what it reveals. Through it we see, at times only faintly, the epic story of a people's struggles against overwhelming natural forces and economic adversity. The fleeting illuminations we receive of men such as George Tuff fill us with admiration, awe, pride, and, on occasion, bitter regret and anger.

Now, thirty years into the Canadian confederation, the people of Newfoundland have at long last found a way out of economic uncertainty and hardship. What the future holds, who can tell? And who can say with confidence how much Newfoundland society has changed, in its essence, in the past three decades? One commentator has spoken with authority of the "overall influence" of the new mass media, pointing out that the effect "has been not only to put Newfoundlanders more closely in touch with North America but to make them part of it." This note has been sounded as well by other observers, who worry about the loss of the Newfoundlander's distinctiveness, and hold out a future of assimilation. Yet these may be perceptions based on imperfect observations. To look closely at Newfoundland life as it is lived, rather than fancied, is to be struck with the force of continuity rather than change. Writers come and go; but whatever has changed, the elements of wind, tide, and crag remain; and the people may be already too irresistibly altered, the stamp of an old land too firmly implanted in them, to respond as readily as some think to new influences. Their character, perhaps, has been formed, and

> ...will go onward the same
>
> Though Dynasties pass.

It is at least possible that, in opting as they did, in 1948, for a chance at a decent and secure mode of life, the people may have chosen, not assimilation, but a kind of freedom. If this is so, their old history may find a new beginning, and writers will discover in men like George Tuff the materials for a living literature.

# The Literature of Newfoundland: A Roundabout Return to Elemental Matters

## Adrian Fowler

> There was a new way of believing
> what ancestors had believed,
> and a roundabout return
> to elemental matters.

Tom Dawe's poem "Peggy," from which the epigraph comes, refers to a process of reassessment which is, I believe, fundamental to an understanding of twentieth-century Newfoundland literature. Peggy is a simple girl, "not like the others," who shocks people with her wild talk

> of trees shedding blood,
> and the devil's claws on haddock skin,
> and the claim of listening
> to what the animals said
> in the dark mangers
> on Christmas Eve,
> and visions of fairies
> by an old wooden bridge
> where a moon floated
> on the tops of water stalks.

The people in the small community where she lives make fun of her poetic imaginings, this girl who makes "scrawly pictures / of animals with wings" and cries "at the sounds / clicking in her aunt's knitting needles / evenings when the sea called." Years later, however, there is a change of attitude. When everyone has left the cove for good, and Peggy has died in a city somewhere, the people who once laughed at her now dream of going back

> to a cove of kind bliss
> and bobbing skiffs in blessed light,
> and quaint little houses
> with the good wives knitting.

There is, it seems,

> a new way of believing
> what ancestors had believed,
> and a roundabout return
> to elemental matters.

talk, even,

> of exiled poets
> scattered all over cities and towns,
> waiting out their lyric lives
> for a chance to go back there
> one more time.

This poem is one of the more recent, and one of the more profound treatments of attitudes towards the outport in Newfoundland writing. These attitudes constitute a central concern of twentieth-century Newfoundland literature—the place itself, and the meaning it has for those who live there. In the poem we are presented with three distinct ways of looking at the cove in which Peggy grows up. The first point of view depicts the outsider within the community. Peggy does not fit in because she lives too much in the world of sentiment and imagination, and the community has no time for these things. The second focuses upon the good old times. The unsentimental people who would not tolerate Peggy's musings now find themselves dreaming nostalgically of the "kind bliss" and "blessed light" that was, of "quaint little houses" and "the good wives knitting." The third considers the outport as an inspiration for writers. It is a variant of the second view but more complex because it's more self-conscious. The poet talks about his own kind, the writers exiled in cities and towns, but his ironic detachment remains intact as he presents them drawn to the lost world of their ancestors, obsessed with finding a way back through the transforming power of the imagination to a more elemental experience of life.

These three views of the outport correspond in a general way to the attitudes taken by three pairs of Newfoundland writers over the past fifty years; moreover, these attitudes represent a dialectical progression in relation to one another, just as they do in Dawe's poem. Margaret Duley and Harold Horwood deal with the plight of the gifted protagonist born into an intellectually stultifying environment. Ted Russell and Ray Guy, focusing rather upon the texture of ourport life, find it, on the contrary, to be a rich mosaic of wit, wisdom, and humane virtue. Al Pittman and Tom Dawe, more conscious of cultural dislocation, are concerned with building, or rebuilding, a bridge to the past.

Ted Russell was a bayman. Born in Coley's Point, Conception Bay in 1904, he spent most of the first half of his life in outports in all parts of Newfoundland as a teacher and a magistrate. After some years first as Director of Cooperatives with the Commission of Government and then as Minister of Natural Resources in the first post-Confederation government of Newfoundland, Russell started, in 1953, to write a series of monologues for the CBC *Fishermen's Broadcast* entitled *The Chronicles of Uncle Mose*. The monologues were designed to fit in with the particular concerns of the programme: current fish prices, new regulations, fishery policy, and local problems of fishermen. Russell's background and his early writing both indicate a flair for the didactic. The mandate to entertain and inform suited his talents and interests perfectly, and, being a learned man beneath the homespun persona of Uncle Mose, he would have been quite capable of pointing out that his objective was not far removed from Horace's advice to aspiring poets. The monologues, along with some eight plays, all written with shrewd wit and informed by humane values, have won for him an honoured place in post-Confederation Newfoundland literature.

The narrator of the *Chronicles* is Uncle Mose and he speaks a language that outport Newfoundlanders would immediately recognize as their own. With each succeeding tale, a picture emerges of Uncle Mose's world. We come to know the community of Pigeon Inlet, situated somewhere on the northeast coast of Newfoundland and the neighbouring communities of Hartley's Harbour and Muldoon's Cove. Gradually we get to know the characters: Uncle Mose himself, a bachelor about fifty years old who had moved to Pigeon Inlet some years before; Grandpa and Grandma Walcott, who treat Mose as though he was their son; Aunt Sophy, their widowed daughter, whom Uncle Mose tentatively courts; Grandpa's good friend, Skipper Joe Irwin; the hangashore, Jethro Noddy, and his ancient billy goat, King David; Paddy and Biddy Muldoon of the Irish Catholic community of Muldoon's Cove; the merchant, Levi Bartle; Josh Grimes of Hartley's Harbour, Uncle Mose's rival for Aunt Sophy's attention; and many others. We soon come to feel that we know these people intimately, their personal histories, their qualities and quirks of personality, and the relationships among them.

Russell was certainly aware of the wave of change that was sweeping the Newfoundland outports in the wake of Joey Smallwood's policy of industrialization in the 1950s. And although he voted for Confederation and acknowledged its benefits, he did not like what he saw happening to the fabric of outport life, and his writing became a one-man crusade against the idea of change for the sake of change. Thus the traditional values of the outport are exalted in the *Chronicles* and the folly of modern living is exposed. Uncle Mose always sounds balanced in his appraisal, however. He applauds many things about the new Newfoundland. The improvement in teachers' qualifications is one. The modernization of the fishery is another. As Uncle Mose puts it to a lady tourist: "'Tis nice bein' quaint and picturesque.... The trouble is there's not much money in it." And he is inclined to think that the youth of today are not half so bad as they used to be in his day. But when he considers such things as the commercialization of Christmas, the antisocial effects of television viewing, and the dubious economics of packaging food and other goods, he comes to the conclusion that the "only thing that saves us down here is that we're so far behind the times." This revolutionary notion, that by being behind, Newfoundlanders might in some ways be ahead, is an idea that was later taken up by Ray Guy and other writers.

One effect of modernization that Russell particularly deplores is the erosion of the value traditionally assigned to work in the Newfoundland outport and an increasing reliance upon welfare benefits. Typically, he expresses his views on the subject through the use of humour and homespun reasoning. When Uncle Mose asks Grandpa and

Grandma Walcott why they continue to work now that they have their pensions and don't have to work any more he gets this reply:

> "No," said Grandpa, "in one way we don't have to work any more. But there's other ways of lookin' at it. In the first place we like work. Perhaps we're old-fashioned. But we think that while people are workin' they're really livin'. But after they give up workin'—well, they're more or less just lyin' 'round waitin' to die."

> "And," chimed in Grandma, "in Pigeon Inlet there's no other work for Grandpa to do only catch fish, and there's no other work for me to do only look after him and help him make his fish."

> "But the Old Age Pension...." said I.

> "Yes, Mose," said Grandpa. "The Old Age Pension is a blessin' sure enough—and I'm thankful for it. But as far as I can see, somebody got to work and produce something or else there'd be no Old Age Pensions and no money to pay Old Age Pensions with. So, I feel that I ought to help these people who've got to work by doin' a bit of work myself. I sort of feel that it's a way for me to say 'Thank you' for my pension…and Grandma's, of course."

> "But suppose you got sick or crippled up with rheumatism," said I. "What then?" "Ah," said Grandpa, that'd be different. Then I'd have to give it up. But I'm not sick or crippled neither."

At a time when the outport way of life was being questioned and even attacked, Ted Russell confirmed the confidence of Newfoundlanders in themselves, their history, and the values which emerged from their struggle to live, against all odds, on the island. And while he talked a great deal of sense on such questions as why fishermen should be eligible for unemployment insurance benefits, and why some might regret the disappearance of small communities like Muldoon's Cove, he entertained the people. Grandpa Walcott is often the instrument here—"our oldest citizen . . a truthful man," says Uncle Mose. "If such a thing is possible, he's too fond of the truth. He's so fond of it that sometimes he stretches it a bit to make it go further." Grandpa Walcott's yarns are masterpieces of the genre, as anyone will agree after reading (or better still, hearing Russell himself read) "Geese" or "The Smokeroom on the Kyle."

Ted Russell was a man of deceptive simplicity. Though he was himself widely read in the great authors of English literature and the ancient world, he chose for himself the native genre of storytelling, and he mastered the art to such a degree that it is not inappropriate to compare him, at his best, with Mark Twain. He is not at his best in his play, *The Holdin' Ground*—*The Chronicles* are much stronger—but the extended metaphor of the holding ground demonstrates perhaps better than anything else his ability to say something profound in a simple way. The central concern of Russell's writing is social change. He not only accepted the inevitability of change, he welcomed it. But when does change in society become destructive? Looking at Skipper Joe Irwin's schooner riding at her mooring, swinging this way and that with the baffles of offshore wind from the hills, Grandpa Walcott is struck by the thought of how much the schooner is like the people of outport Newfoundland. A stranger might think he was adrift unless he knew about their moorings and their holding ground. Ted Russell was conscious of the forces creating cultural dislocation in Newfoundland in the 1950s and he lamented the results. His writing was an attempt to make Newfoundlanders aware of the dangers of losing their moorings and of the necessity of having a good holding ground below.

Ray Guy, born thirty-five years after Ted Russell, personally witnessed the cultural upheaval that Russell warned of. His home community of Arnold's Cove was designated a growth centre and became the recipient of resettled communities during the period of the Newfoundland government's centralization program. Later a $500 million oil refinery was built close by. It is hard to find a one-word description of Guy's career as a writer. Journalist, satirist, humorist, essayist—he is all of these, yet he is more than these. Politically he filled the role Harold Horwood had performed in his "Political Notebook" columns in the St. John's *Evening Telegram* during the 1950s, keeping the spark of democracy alive by his savage criticism of one-man rule within the government of Newfoundland. Culturally he took over from Russell as the keeper of Newfoundland's conscience. His influence upon Newfoundlanders' perception of themselves and their outport heritage has been enormous, and, as a writer, his talent cannot be disputed. While many of the columns he has written to deadline—as many as five a week—do not stand up to repeated reading, and while even the three collections of his writing by Eric Norman contain their share of these, there are a sufficient number of brilliant and historically significant pieces by Ray Guy to ensure him a prominent place in Newfoundland literature of the past twenty years.

Guy, unlike Russell, is not primarily a story-teller. Though many of his humorous feature articles on the effects of a prolonged winter, or upon ridding his apartment of rats, qualify as good yarns (and there is one truly beautiful story for Christmas), his real gift is not for telling stories. This may be because, unlike Russell, he does not have a good memory for stories. "I'm not so good at remembering the stuff I heard the old fellers talking about," he confesses. "Just bits and pieces is all I can remember." But he can remember, he says, "the Juvenile Outharbor Delights all right. Right down to the letter. Because I went through it." One of Ray Guy's strengths is indeed his astonishing memory for youthful experiences. He remembers all the sights, sounds, and smells of childhood, the vocabulary and the games. Catching tansys in the landwash. Heaving rocks at steerins. Copying clampers. Foundering cliffs. Jumping in the bog. What it was like to lie in bed listening to the pong of barrels popping in the cool evening air or the grind of the tide on faraway beaches on foggy nights. The church smells of dust and dilapidated cobwebs, sun-warmed varnish, mothballs off people's Sunday suits, musty prayer books, puffs of sharp coal smoke from the backfiring stoves. And the methods of getting sopping wet: "If the philosophical mood was on me I could stand twenty feet outside the door chewing the strap of my aviator cap by the hour, licking the raindrops off the end of my nose, heaving the scattered melancholy sigh and getting sopping wet right down to the knitted drawers." The memory of the child is a memory for concrete detail. Guy's recollections give us a very vivid picture of domestic and recreational life in the outport.

Guy has a passionate belief in the distinctiveness of Newfoundland as a country—a more traditional and less strident term than nation, which he rarely uses. He exhibits a pride in the language spoken by Newfoundlanders, a rhapsodic appreciation of the fierce beauty of the land, and a naked patriotism towards the historic struggles for the rights of settlement: "Praise God and all honour to our forefathers through generations who did never forsake this dear and fine Country." But if Russell depicts a kind of rural Eden, Guy's outport is unmistakably post-lapsarian. The abuse of the social welfare system, which he claims Smallwood encouraged, along with an industrialization policy that struck right at the heart of outport society through the centralization program, have demoralized the people, undermined their traditions of self-sufficiency, and destroyed their pride. He writes at times in barely concealed anger: "It was no small thing we had hold of and it is no small thing for it to be slaughtered out of hand at the whim of a single person." Sometimes his writing contains an undisguised call to join in the struggle to save the country: "Rage to change this island to what you think it should be. You have a right and you can. Because it's yours. Willed to you by your father's hand." And elsewhere: "we WILL have our soul back."

These quotes give a palpable sense of the intimate relationship Guy claims with his readers, and the fierce loyalty he has commanded makes it clear that he struck a basic, if almost forgotten, chord with his audience. Of course he has been attacked for romanticizing outport life, glossing over the hardships. In at least two places he answers these charges:

> There has been much exaggeration about outport life. There were all sorts of outports and in some the people were dispirited, mean and slovenly; in others, bright, content and lively.

> In one you would see an unmarried mother shut away with all the scorn and reproach of relatives and community turned against her until she could bear the weight no more and died. Just as surely as if she had been in the middle of Africa and cursed by a witch doctor.

> In another you would see the people say it was a shocking thing but it happens and they would call the little one no more than a "merrybegot" and it would be taken in with normal joy to get a fair share of whatever family and community gives.

> Hard times? In spots, it was. If we hadn't been so isolated and there had been a few more modern facilities handy perhaps my two brothers might have lived. But I certainly didn't think they were hard times then so why should I think so now.

Ray Guy was acquainted, then, with the harshness of outport life. So was Ted Russell. He had spent "the five hungriest years of the hungry thirties" in Green Bay and lived through the times that Horwood describes so luridly in *Tomorrow Will Be Sunday*. He could tell, as he said, "an equal number [of stories] far less amusing, but they are better left untold." For Russell, as for Guy, the hardship and the bigotry that undeniably existed in Newfoundland outports did not outweigh the extraordinary qualities of the people: their sense of humour, their warmth and hospitality, their self-reliance, their powers of endurance, and their ability to cooperate like a closely knit family in the frequent life-and-death crises they faced.

Along with Percy Janes, Al Pittman and Tom Dawe emerged as the most important Newfoundland writers during the 1970s. Both are poets, though Pittman's writing on the outport has been confined mainly to his plays, *A Rope Against the Sun* and *West Moon*. Pittman and Dawe represent a kind of synthesis in the dialectic outlined so far. In their attitude towards the outport they have gone beyond the conflict over its worth. Their work is characterized rather by a sense of irrevocable change, sometimes by loss. In this sense they are more modern than Russell or Guy. They are sympathetic to the values of outport life but they are not partisans in a debate. Their writing indicates an attempt to discover and recover what it was really like. They adopt, therefore, a more investigative posture and a more objective mode of presentation.

There is something almost archeological, for example, about Pittman's poem concerning the resettled community where he was born, "St. Leonard's Revisited." We find the poet and his companion, or companions, walking amid ruins:

> among the turnip cellars
> tripping over the cremated
> foundations
> of long-ago homes
> half buried
> in the long years' grass

The men hauling their traps offshore wonder about them, thinking almost that they are ghosts, because they have gone back

> over the thigh-high grass paths
> that led
> like trap doors
> to a past
> they could hardly recall

"Gram Glover's Dream" is similarly an attempt to reconstruct in the imagination an event remote from the poet's direct experience but symbolically of great importance to him. Once again the motif is of a community abandoned. As the line of men, women, and children winds its way over the snow away from a window through which the scene is viewed, an old woman at the very end has turned around for one last look. It is a poignant moment but it is presented without comment, just as it is in the David

Blackwood etching upon which the poem is based. Again, the superb "Lines For My Grandfather Long Gone" gives the impression of having been painstakingly recovered from memory, the poet digging carefully so as to bring to light as far as possible the original event as it was experienced.

Pittman's play, *A Rope Against The Sun*, represents a radical departure from the traditional treatment of the outport in Newfoundland literature in the extent to which it is so little concerned with community. Although the outport is authentically captured, the play's emphasis is rather upon individual lives. All of the characters in the play are frustrated in one way or another. All of them are animated by dreams and illusions, all tormented by the possibility, or likelihood, that the gap between dream and reality will never be closed. Father Power wrestles with his terrible loneliness, yearning for companionship but unable to imagine how it might be attained. Jake Connors despises his uselessness after a life of action on the water, and is anxious now just to lie down and die. Mrs. Ennis frets over the birth of the baby she is carrying, in terror that it will be born when the sunkers are breaking. And so on, for Nell Pittman, Joe Casey, Joe's wife Elizabeth, the schoolteacher Michael Kennedy, Billy Collins, and Jennifer Byrne. Only the young have much hope of resolving their problems. But we do not blame any of this on the community. Their problems are due to their humanity. They cannot be solved by social action. As an old man says in one of Pittman's "Notes to No One": "the only progress made is made privately."

In this respect they are no different from people anywhere, which gives them dignity in our eyes. We see them as no better and no worse than ourselves. They are our equals—we cannot imagine ourselves managing any better in their situation and we could not promise them that in changing their situation their problems would go away. Thus we do not ache to resettle these people in order to improve their lot. Their problems, like ours, are problems of the spirit or of the soul. When Nell Pittman sings "remember, lad, I lived for you / and lived quite all alone," she is in this sense singing for all the characters in the play, and all humans everywhere. Concerning the issues explored in *A Rope Against the Sun*, everyone lives quite all alone.

Pittman's most recent play, *West Moon*, has not yet been published, though it has been performed three or four times in various parts of Canada. In it he turns directly to the theme of cultural dislocation. Like *A Rope Against the Sun*, it is a "play for voices," only this time the voices are coming from a graveyard where, each All Souls Night, the dead are able to speak. Once again we come to know the characters as human beings first, and as outport Newfoundlanders second, as the various conflicts in their lives are revealed. But in the second part of the play, when they discover that their community has been resettled and that they have, therefore, been abandoned, we are almost persuaded to believe that the dead can weep. "In all the measure of time's turning, it may not matter that the dead are," says the narrator; "as long as the living live and remember." But what if ever, "in the measure of time's turning, friends were to forget friendship, lovers forget love. Then the dead would be dead indeed. And death would be their dominion." *West Moon* reveals Al Pittman's conviction that if we are to remain human, we must strive to maintain a connection with the past.

Tom Dawe is also concerned with building a bridge to the past. His poem, "The Bridge," which describes the destruction of an old wooden bridge, deals symbolically with the disconnection that has occurred. The bridge took the people of the community "across a salt pond / to the caplin scull," took children "to the swing of the tickle-ace" and "the wand-swish of fishing poles." Two brothers had been lost there, cats and dogs had been drowned there, and once the cove's best swimmer had broken his neck diving from the top rail. Then somebody decides these people don't need a bridge. Men arrive in shiny cars, promises are made, there is talk of money, and the bridge comes down.

The landscape of Tom Dawe's poetry is strewn with abandoned communities and the intrusion of modernity. In such poems as "At Western Arm," "Abandoned Outport," "House On The Coast," and "Stage," the mood is restrained but there is a definite sense of loss. "The Madonna," a short narrative poem, develops the idea of change more fully. Two modern youths visit an abandoned island where there had been a community years before. They are outfitted with powerful binoculars, an expensive camera, and a small rifle. Entering the old Catholic church they shoot holes in the windows, finally turning attention to the Madonna, a white marble statue which was one of the few things left behind when the people left:

> One bullet punched near the eye
> and fine particles trickled
> into the dark shadows near her feet
> of feathered stone.
> She still smiled gently
> below the now-marred eye…

So the old gives way to the new. And although the youthful vandals are not condemned—there is more idleness than pathology in their behaviour—there is a shiftlessness and destructiveness in the new that is disturbingly anarchic.

Dawe, like Ray Guy, has a good memory for childhood, as can be seen in such poems as "The Guitar Player," "Ghosts," "Outport Christmas," and "A Day in '45." In particular, he has a vivid recollection of the world of magic: fairies, ghost and the pagan sense of the interconnection of all things such as is represented by the belief of the old man in "The Old Man and the Moon." "God'll never let dem rech da moon," he says. For him the moon was a thing of power, intertwined with the sea, the tide, the fish he caught: "the moving herring-schools / mooned in the long night tides / and tangled in his waiting nets." He was part of these things, and they were a part of him.

The nostalgia for a simpler, richer past, the sense of loss and cultural breakdown is, however, counterbalanced in Tom Dawe's writing by a dark side. There is a perception of the workings of evil in such poems "Devil at the Dance," "Once by the Atlantic," and "Along That Coast." This last poem retells, without apparent interpretation, stories of a vessel having gone aground along a particular stretch of coast. There was "talk of wracking / and a false light / tied on a wandering goat / shifting somewhere in the cliffs." People remember hearing the cloven hooves go by. One man has fixed in his mind the image of a crucifix in lamplight which he saw looking back from the door on his way to salvage. And a woman, "in a chain / of grave-digging days," thought of all the widows in foreign places. Today men on that coast tell of "how their fathers slaved / dragging bodies from a winter sea," and they complain about "outsiders" coming in and giving the place a bad name, shooting at government signs marking where the wreck occurred. In this poem the dark side—"talk of wracking," "cloven hooves"—coexists with the heroic—"dragging bodies from a winter sea"—and the human sympathy of the woman for the foreign widows. None of this is disentangled. What actually happened we do not know—only stories about the event. The present is represented by the defensiveness of the people, recalling only the heroic and blaming the outsiders (are they outsiders?) for giving the place a bad name, and by "a long oil-tanker / [gliding) in the blue haze / of a far horizon."

Other poems, not exactly dark, are disturbing. Suspicion and menace emerge in "The Stranger," madness in "In Picasso's 'Madman'." The plight of the outsider is considered, sometimes sympathetically, from the outsider's viewpoint ("To a Poet"); sometimes less sympathetically, from the viewpoint of the insiders ("Noah"). Tom Dawe's poetry contains a depth and a complexity that are myth-breaking rather than myth-making. Al Pittman, on the other hand, avoids the outsider/insider stereotypes by creating characters whose aspirations and frustrations derive primarily from their humanity rather than from their identity as outport Newfoundlanders. In both cases this represents a progression beyond the perspective of Duley, Horwood, Russell, and Guy.

I am aware, of course, that comparing novels, humorous monologues, satirical essays, lyric poetry, and drama is a bit like comparing apples, oranges, tomatoes, bananas, and coconuts. The choice of genre certainly affects the treatment of theme. On the other hand, the writer's sensibility, and therefore his inclination to treat a theme in a particular way, no doubt affects his choice of genre. I have avoided this chicken-and-egg dilemma and concentrated more on effects than on causes. I am aware, as well, that except for Russell, the writers considered here are not exclusively concerned with the Newfoundland outport either as the main focus, or even as part of the background, of much of their writing. Nevertheless, the writing dealt with here is among the most important in the recent literature of Newfoundland, and the attitudes taken towards the outport represent shifting attitudes on the part of Newfoundlanders themselves. The fact that it plays such a major part in much recent Newfoundland writing is a measure of the extent to which national (now regional) identity has preoccupied writers in Newfoundland, and the extent to which views of the outport specifically have determined that sense of identity.

**Excerpt from**

# The Colony of Unrequited Dreams

## Wayne Johnston

On the third day, when we looked through the porthole at mid-morning, we saw something other than the single shade of white we had become accustomed to— the many subtle shades of white that comprised the ice-field.

It was several hours more before the master watch came down and told me to go to my sleeping quarters.

I did as he said. I heard the boiler being fired up and felt the ship begin to move through the ice pack, which had loosened because the wind had changed.

About three o'clock in the afternoon, they found what they were looking for. Far off on the ice, I saw a couple of dozen men trudging about in a circle. The shout no sooner went up that the men of the *Newfoundland* were found than the ship's whistle shrieked in celebration. I looked out through the porthole, but that side of the ship was at too oblique an angle to the rescue site. As the ship ploughed on through the ice, however, the stem slowly drifted starboard and I was able to see round the curvature of the hull. The men were not a hundred feet away, still tramping in a circle as if even the ship's whistle had not roused them, each man with his hand on the shoulder of the man in front. They were so coated in snow I could not tell what they were wearing or make out their faces, which were rimed with frost. Most of them were limping badly; outside the circle was a man walking an even slower circle of his own and at the same time holding beneath the armpits another man whose feet made a feeble step now and then but otherwise dragged behind him on the ice.

As we drew closer to them, some of them at last noticed the ship and stopped walking. Some dropped to their knees or toppled over onto their backs, others stared as if they doubted that what they saw was real. The crew poured over the side and led the sealers or carried them on stretchers to the ship.

We moved on. I had counted twenty-three men. That left eighty unaccounted for. I stayed at the porthole. The ship came hard about, and for half an hour we crashed on through the ice, then stopped again.

My heart rose when I saw what looked to be the balance of the crew standing on a mile-wide ice pan in the near distance. From on deck, there were shouts of "Hurray" and footsteps thumped on the ceiling overhead as once again the ship's whistle sounded.

Gradually we drew up close to the ice pan. Mooring lines with grapnels on the end were cast onto the ice, and the pan was slowly pulled towards the ship until it thumped against it.

For several minutes after the ship stopped, no one disembarked. I saw what I had not been able to through my binoculars: that these were not survivors but a strange statuary of the dead. I was not repulsed by what I saw. I could not take my eyes away.

Two men knelt side by side, one man with his arm around the other, whose head was resting on his shoulder in a pose of tenderness between two men that I had never seen in life.

Three men stood huddled in a circle, arms about each other's shoulders, heads together like schoolboys conferring on a football field.

A man stood hugging himself, his hands on his arms, shoulders hunched, in the manner of someone who has momentarily stepped out of his house into the cold in shirtsleeves to bid a guest goodbye.

One man knelt, sitting back on his heels, while another stood behind him, his hands on his shoulders, as if they were posing for a photograph.

Two sealers stood in a fierce embrace, the taller man with each wrapped round the other, holding him against his chest, while the arms of the shorter man hung rigid at his sides.

Four men lay on their stomachs side by side, all facing the same way as if they had lain down for some purpose or agreed together that they would.

Only a few men knelt or lay alone, perhaps those who had lasted longer than the others.

One man sat by himself, his elbows resting on his drawn up knees, his bare hands frozen to his face.

The storm had started out as freezing rain. A man who must have been among the first to fall lay encased within a mould of silver thaw.

I later learned that some who, in their delirium, thought they saw a light ran off in pursuit of it and were never found.

Joined in some manner of embrace were men who before this journey to the ice had never met, men who had outlasted those they knew best and for warmth or fellowship in death embraced some stranger.

They were all there, the boys too young and the men too old, who to get a berth had lied about their ages or agreed to half a share; boys younger than me and men older than my father.

Perhaps, too tired to walk but still standing, they had been buried in snow that had blown away when the storm let up, by which time they were rooted in the ice that lay like pedestals about their feet.

Some men lay in the lee of a low shelter they had managed to erect, a wall of ice and snow that was barely three feet high.

I recognized a few of them, but only because of some distinctive article of clothing, like the orange watch cap of the man who every morning made the tea. He lay on his side, his knees drawn up almost to his chest, his head resting on his hands, which were clasped in a prayer-like pillow, palm to palm.

They had been transformed by their passion on the ice. Each had assumed in death some posture emblematic of his life. Or else they were refined to men that no one knew, as if in each face and posture was inscrutably depicted the essence of the person they had been.

Everywhere lay evidence to futile acts of courage and self-sacrifice. A man stripped down to his undershirt and coveralls lay prone beside a boy bulked out in two sets of clothes.

In various places the snow was scorched where small fires had been lit. From each a smudge of soot trailed out, a stain left from the smoke that had been flattened by the wind.

I did not want to see them moved or see the scene disturbed. I closed the porthole and sat down on my bunk.

I heard above the wind and the droning of the ropes the sound of ice being hacked and chopped. I heard the coal crank of the hatch at the far end of the ship lurch into motion. The chopping and shouting and winching of the crank went on for hours. When it stopped, I considered opening the porthole but could not bring myself to do it.

I looked around the sleeping quarters at all the empty bunks. Not all the men had been lost. Not every bunk represented a man who would not be going home. It was impossible to tell which ones did. Three-quarters of them did, but I didn't know which ones. Except for the bunk of the man who made the tea.

Something deep within me, which I hadn't known was there, gave way. My body grieved but not my mind. I felt as though someone who was sitting right beside me was crying, and though I wanted to console him, I could not.

I felt the ship reach open water. The grinding of the ice against the hull ceased suddenly, the keel rocked from side to side until it balanced and we moved smoothly on. I got up and pounded on the door to be let out. As if, in all the commotion, I had been forgotten, I heard the sound of footsteps running. The hatch slid open and I saw the sky.

**sealing crew**: (a) organized group of men engaged in taking seals with nets near the shore; (b) group of men aboard a vessel, engaged to hunt seals on the ice-floes; CREW.

[1771] 1792 CARTWRIGHT i, 124 Two of the people belonging to the sealing crew came here this morning, to engage with me for the summer's fishing. 1861 DE BOILIEU 84 A sealing crew consists of not less than six men. [1891] 1978 *Haulin' Rope & Gaff* 35 Please pay attention for a while / And I will sing to you / A song about the *Greenland* / And her hardy sealing crew. [See 1906 quot at **sealing captain**.] 1924 ENGLAND 234 "Success to Every Man": De warriors o' de wooden fleet, / Dey soon will sail away, / in charge of 'ardy swilin' crews, / Wid colours flyin' gay! [1954] 1979 *Evening Telegram* 14 Mar, p. 8 He says the reason for this is that the sealing crews begin killing seals too early.

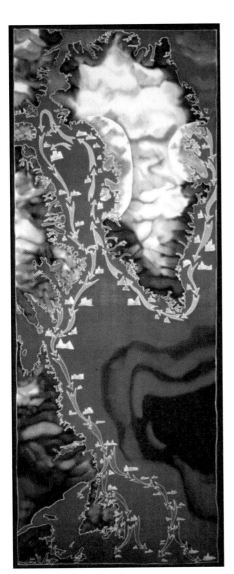

*Iceberg Alley*, Diana Dabinett

*Through vibrant colour and myriad forms of life, I attempt to present a unique view of the underwater world beyond the Newfoundland shoreline, the seabirds along its rocky cliffs and its bogs, forests and fields inland. The surface teams with details from the natural environment, but captures the duality of its fragility and durability under the harsh conditions of this edge of Canada. The subtlety of the sparkle of the sunlight, delicate petals, the sheen on a fish's side are captured in the freshness of watercolour or in the brilliance of procion dyes on silks. At times the fish swim off the surface and shimmer in schools in the three-dimensions of soft sculpture, or the viewer is enticed into a woodland walk through a silken forest with intriguing glimpses of ocean vistas.*

*In a continuous observation of the surrounding environment I build up a storehouse of experiences, memories that are supported by an expanding collection of reference photographs and scientific facts that, through contemplation and emotional response, provide the stimulus for my work. When the world's natural environment is threatened on so many fronts, it is time to look at what this province still has, to delight in its unspoilt variety and to preserve in our work some of the beauty and diversity that still remains.*

*My works on silk are hand-painted in the serti technique, using gutta as a resist and procion dyes applied in a wet watercolour style.*

— Diana Dabinett

# Doctor Olds of Twillingate: Portrait of an American Surgeon in Newfoundland

## Gary Saunders

"Belief in a doctor, any doctor, that's the thing."

— Captain Peter Troake

Doctor Olds and Twillingate Hospital were the last things on Captain Peter Troake's mind that chilly June morning in 1947 as he weighed anchor for Labrador and another summer's fishing. Standing in his greatcoat at the *Minnie B.*'s helm as she moved out into Durrell Arm, the short, energetic 38-year-old was thinking instead of his family, his crew, his vessel, of his provisions and what he'd forgotten, of whether the wind would breeze up, of how much ice they might meet above Cape John and if he would secure a good fishing berth this year.

Had all gone well with Captain Troake, Dr. Olds might have glanced out the east windows of his second-floor Operating Room later that morning and seen the *Minnie B.* clearing Burnt Island with two or three other schooners. He had known and liked Peter a long time. The Troakes of Durrell and Hart's Cove were rough and ready fishermen and sealers—among the best. Peter was only six when he jigged his first quintal of cod. When he was nine, his father took him down to the Labrador with the Summerville floaters, where, in the long subarctic days, the boy quickly learned to split fish on deck and salt it below. Pete liked to tell John how, beating up to St John's that stormy fall, hull down with green Labrador Number One, he had been seasick all the way. After Grade Five he quit school to help his father. At sixteen, eldest of ten children, he was a full shareman on the *Lone Star* and proud of it.

Now as then, Peter Troake relished this moment of leaving a safe harbour, the moment when his boat began ever so slightly to lift to the ground swell, when the rigging started its faint, rhythmic creaking like a fiddler tuning up. But he would feel better once Burnt and Gull Islands were astern, when he could sling overboard like old ballast all the petty vexations of gearing up for a long voyage and fix his mind on the days ahead. His eyes twinkled in a smile. In nine days he would be 39. He had his own new schooner. Jim Hunby the builderman had finished her in four months two winters past. Last summer she fetched home 850 quintals in one trip. This year they might even fare better.

He had other cause to smile. Last winter he had installed a new 10 HP *Atlantic* auxiliary engine in the *Minnie B.* All his life he'd worked under sail; there was nothing like it. But Labrador was a far piece and the competition was too keen to let the wind call the tunes. Peter Troake was in a hurry. As his sleek black schooner dove the grey wind-lop and sent the scattered ice pans wallowing turquoise in her wake, the *Atlantic*'s pulsing bass stole under the treble cries of gulls and terns to sweeten his joy.

Experience had taught him caution, however. Five minutes of neglect could cook a new motor. Better check it one more time, he thought.

"We had about a 15- or 20-knot wind and the schooner was lickin' along pretty good, seven or eight knots. I went below to screw the grease cups down to make sure there was plenty of hard grease for this new motor. 'Twas on the starboard side, and the grease cups were on the inside, so I had to reach over. I had on a pair of Army pants from when I was in the Home Guard overseas. And when I leaned over, the coupling set-screw on the shaft caught and hooked on those pants.

"And it turned round and broke my left leg in half. I went down between two timbers about two feet apart. If my leg had brought up on a timber he would have broken again. As it was, my pant leg went around and around the shaft until it stalled this new motor.

"When I got clear of the shaft, my foot was up there by my shin, bottom up. I took my foot up in my hand and had a look. Right on my instep there was something sticking up about the size o' the top of my thumb. This was the small bone o' my leg, but I didn't know it. So I took hold of that and pulled it out. It was broken off and ship-lapped—sticking out so far on one side, less on the other.

"I got savage mad then. It was spite kept me from fainting, perhaps. I don't know what fainting is. I've been in a lot of trouble in my time, but never felt like I was going to faint. A person can't brag about it though, because tomorrow I might see something to faint about.

"Well, when they saw I was in a mess—feller at the wheel looked down and got frightened to death—I bawled out and told him to tell Herbie Weir, my second hand with me, to run her in to the Arm. There was a nice swell on, a nor'east wind. 'And when you gets in,' I said, 'you sing out for someone to take me off.'

"Just at this time my brother Allan was going up in the trap skiff, and as he come abreast, the fellow who had the wheel sung out and told him the skipper was killed. Frightened Allan right to death! So when Allan passed us by, he jumps onto the schooner—didn't tie 'er on or nothin'! Away goes skiff! Another fellow had to shut the engine off. That's how excited Allan was.

"Anyway, they got the boat alongside for to bring me to shore. 'Boys,' I said, 'take me up.' But when they went to handle me they didn't know how. Because there I was, my leg all torn away, and the foot lodged so that when they went to pick me up it just about fell off. And there it was, swingin', right off on a thread, and they afraid to touch it.

"I said, 'Boys, take ahold! If 'twas a fifty-six-pound weight on there it wouldn't stop you, would it?' But they were afraid. I reached down then and picked it up and put it to one side. Because you couldet hurt me no more than I was already hurt, understand. I had all the hurt that I could have.

"Well, they put me on a handbar, with a mattress under and blankets over me, and they carried me over to Gillett's shop where there was a phone. There was not so many phones around then as now. Joe Elliott he come in, had a look at my leg and almost fainted off. 'Twas a Freeman man come and took me over to the Hospital. He belonged to the Hospital, was working there. He come and picked me up in a truck.

"Now, if you had a seen the blood! I never tried to stop it. I was going to, but said to myself, 'tis on the left side, and I might do damage. I've heard say that if you damp it and didn't wrap the bandage right you could have trouble. So I said, 'Let 'er bleed.'

"But if you saw the blood that run out of Peter Troake you would not have believed it…. You should see the mess you can make with blood! When I hoisted my leg up I'd put blood the length of myself every time my heart would beat.

"Going over to the Hospital, coming up the hill, I was starting to feel a bit comfortable….There was a light too, a dazzle, like when you rub your eyes too hard…. I started to feel right comfortable. Oh yes, that's how you die, you know. I haven't been dead yet, but I know how it is.

"They carried me in off the truck into the Hospital. And Dr. Olds comes in. 'Doc,' I says, 'I got me leg broke.' He pulls back the blanket and takes a look.

"'Yes,' he says, 'and a damned good job you did on it too.'

"'Doc, you're goin' to have to cut off my leg ain't you?'

"'Pete, I don't know. I want to try to save it, send you home on crutches with both your legs. But one thing I know for damn sure—if I try to save it, the ponds will be cracking before you get out of here. Are you game for that?'

"'If you are,' I says.

"'Good enough.' We shook hands.

"Then he says, 'One thing I'm afraid of—there's a piece of bone missing.'

"Right away I knew what he meant. It was the piece I took for a splinter of wood and hove down in the bottom of the boat. I told him and he sent an orderly who fetched it and cleaned it up. And with that we made for the Operating Room. On the way, one of the doctors said, 'We'll take off that foot before Christmas, Dr. John.' Dr. Olds only grunted.

"So they got me ready. My first cousin Rose Cooper was in the OR up there then and she said, 'Pete, b'y, when Dr. Olds comes in he might have to cut off your leg.'

"Now I don't know much about Heaven, but I know all about taking this ether. In my life I was put to sleep nine times. I know about going to sleep, know how to sleep good, go to sleep comfortable. And I know how to go to sleep for punishment too. Get so much of the ether in you, get crazy too, sometimes. The last time they put me to sleep with that, the nurses had a job to hold me on. There was none of this modem anesthetic then.

"Anyway, when Nurse Manuel put the cone over my nose she said, 'Take a deep breath, now, and do this, and do that.' Finally I started to get comfortable again. And all the pain leaves me…. I said to Nurse Manuel—I was just as sensible as could be—'If there's anything any better than this 'tis too good for Peter Troake.' Every pain was gone, see, every last twinge.

"Now Dr. Olds liked me; I don't know why. I don't know why, but he loved me. And I loved him. Nobody was ever better to me than him; my mother and father could be no better. He was my old bosom friend. And there was no man around the Newfoundland coast he'd sooner do a job on than me.

"I wasn't timid, see. One time up there I said, 'Doc, if you was to tell me, "Pete, I got to take your head off and slew it round and you can walk backwards," I'd say, 'Sir, you do it.' I believed that much in he. Belief in a doctor, any doctor, that's the thing. They can do all they can for you and if you don't believe, it won't do a peck of good.

"'Twas a woman named Betty who belonged down there to Change Islands, she took me out of ether. After a while I heard somebody calling 'Mr Troake, wake up.' Now, I didn't want to hear anybody call me that. Never liked this "Mister" stuff. Mother called me Peter and that's what I wanted. Anyway, it was 'Mr Troake, wake up!' Seemed like I was quite some time listening to this. By and by I opened my eyes.

"'Has Dr. Olds got my leg taken off?'

"'No.'

"'I don't believe it.' I was lying flat now, after taking that ether. 'Naw, I don't believe it.' I tried to sit up.

"'Oh, Mr Troake,' she said, 'you can't rise up, you got to 'bide flat.'

"I said, 'I got to see if that foot is taken off.' So she gives me a hand and lifts me up.

"The first thing I saw was my big toe sticking out of the bandage. Right there and then I knew what I was in for. I thought my leg would be taken off. I'd seen what a mess it was in, see. There was hard grease in this wound o' mine, there was pieces o' cloth, there was part of my sock—everything. I had picked out so much of it, but a lot still wasn't.

"Well, now, for Dr. Olds to put this together for me to have to rear this leg again…. I thought, 'This is it. I'm in this hospital for a good long time.'

"I was there 11 months and 24 days; nine months on my back, never moved one inch only when the nurses moved me. All this time my leg was hoisted about three feet, and there was a shot bag, a twenty-five pound bag of shot, on the bottom of my foot down there, and sandbags on me side. The lobster pot, I used to call it. And there was a light—it gave off heat—that was shining on it.

"At first I was tormented. Then I said to myself, 'You were stupid enough to get into the net, so now you've got to 'bide here.'

"Sometimes when the nurses come in, I'd say, My dear, 'tis no good for you to look in that lobster pot now 'cause the feller got that pot robbed for long ago.' That's how I'd be.

"Dr. Olds he'd come to see me three or four times a day. And at first he thought I was going to give up, that he'd have to take my leg off for to save my life.

"So the summer passed, and the fall. And the next spring Dr. Olds goes to the ice again to look for the cause of Seal Finger. And when he went, every guy in the Hospital from one ward to the other was saying, 'Well, Dr. Olds is gone, now we'm gonna *die* for sure….' I didn't think I was gonna *die*, but don't you think that we liked to see Dr. Olds go. It was a selfish thing.

"Now I don't know who the other doctor was that took his place. I know McGavin was there. It was another one, just before Dr. Olds come back, that X-rayed my leg. I didn't much care whether he did it or not; I wanted Dr. Olds. I shouldn't have been like that.

"He wasn't gone very long before he comes back. 'Skipper,' he says, your leg is gonna come out good. Yes, Dr. Olds will be pleased when he comes in.'

"By and by, Sir, in he comes. Don't know if he even went home when he come from the ice; up he comes.

"'Pete,' he says, 'you're gonna walk again!'

"I said, 'Doctor, I hear you. And I believe you.' I was sat up now; it was the only way I could think to keep going. And he says, 'Take the cast off and have a look. You're gonna cut that cast off.'

"'Can I?'

"'If you want to.'

"'I can do the job,' says I. 'But Doctor, don't you think it's going to be another operation to take that off?' I was half afraid of what I might see. They had it packed in tarry oakum for to keep down the stink. Before they did that, people couldn't hardly stand to walk by my room.

"'You've got to have it soaking wet first.'

"Well, he gave me something like a putty knife and they soaked the cast and there I was now, cutting it. I split it open all the way up. Probably I would have cut like blazes—I was so anxious to have it off—but Dr. Olds warned me my leg might be ulcerated. Anyway, I cut it open from my big toe right on up.

"Now somebody had to pull that cast around for to bend it abroad, because it wouldn't soak wet right on me; 'twas fastened. And when my leg come out of that cast—if you were haulin' out me heart it couldn't have been no worse.

"And oh, if you had seen what I saw then! The X-ray didn't show what the flesh was like underneath; 'twas only the bone that showed up. When they took that cast off, even Dr. Olds he got disgusted. It had been on so long, the cast ulcers were everywhere. And the linen that was wrapped around my leg under the cast—those ulcers had even grown out into that…arggh!

"He got down-hearted, the doctor did. I suppose he never thought it would be so bad.

"Well, we had to wait so long for those ulcers to heal up. For a while it was all one sore, then finally it was two. Three or four times he operated. The last time, the sore was down to the size of a fifty-cent piece. When he put the bones together that last time, he had to cut and ship-lap them.

"One day, after he got it to his satisfaction, he asked me to try my leg. But I was afraid to put my weight onto it. He said, 'For Christ's sake, Pete, put it to the floor. Put it whichever way you feel comfortable.'

"I did; it seemed okay. And after dodging 'round the bed once or twice I said, 'Doctor, why did you turn my foot in a little bit like that?'

"'Pete,' he said, I thought it would be better to have it turn in than turn out.'

"'Well,' I said, 'that sounds sensible too. Because if I'm goin' to the woods I won't need so big a path!' We had a good laugh.

"'Pete,' he said, 'that's better than an artificial leg.'

"'Yes, guaranteed, brother.' Your own leg is always better, even with a limp.

"After I was all better he said one day, 'Pete, who do you thank for your leg?'

"'Doctor,' I said, 'I thanks you and the Lord, Sir.'

"'Pete,' he said, 'guts and contentment.'

"'Well, no; I wouldn't say that,' I said. 'Because I could have all the guts I like and if you hadn't done the job you did do, I'd have lost my leg from gangrene.'

"So I got out of there with only a limp and a cane and a bill for $360.38. 'Twould have cost me $946.38 but I was on the Blanket Contract and that took up the slack. A patient don't want to get better and then get a bill that will kill him."

"Now if there was a meter put on that leg to measure the miles that I've a-covered on he since then, a person would be amazed. I had over fifteen vessels in my time. I was forty-nine years on the Labrador, up and down the Labrador all my life. And in 1950, when I lost the *Lady MacDonald* in the ice up in the Straits of Belle Isle with a heavy load of seals, we had to walk down the Straits nearly five miles to the *Linda May*. And after that I was on the *Christmas Seal* for twenty years.

"I'm not saying no other doctor could have done what Dr. Olds did; I couldn't say that. I'm not saying he was the best. Nobody is the best; there is no best. I'll say one of the best, because he would try what another doctor wouldn't. There were people come from Montreal to get cured by him. There were people on the mainland that were told they couldn't be cured and they come to him. A lot of people he took chances on. They had to die anyway, but a lot are living today thanks to him. And I'm one of them.

"Because I guarantee you no doctor in Newfoundland would ever try to do what he did for me. Because I only had one inch—one inch—of good flesh left on my leg when I went in.

"That's why I say he and me and the Lord done it.

"But all Doctor Olds said was, 'Pete, guts and contentment.'"

**myrrh** n also **murr(e)**, Possibly from the biblical association of myrrh and frankincense. Cp *OED* ~ [1] 1 (esp 1672 medical quot); see also FRANKINCENSE, FRANKINTINE*, FRANKUM GUM, TURPENTINE. The resin of a fir or spruce tree, freq in home remedies; also attrib (P 133-58).

P 65-64 Turpentine on trees is called 'mur.' Mur is put on cuts to cause a cure.
T 396/7-67 There was a myrrh you could use, what you get out o' the woods—a good medicine for inside use and outside use...I've drink molasses an' myrrh. C 67-16 Go to the wood-pile and get some myrrh; then we won't need any stitches to keep the cut together. C 68-10 He hurried into the near by woods and in a few moments came back with a handful of mur bladders. These he squeezed out and mixed with molasses. The cut (about 1/2 inch deep) was covered with this mixture and wrapped with white cloth. In just one week my leg was completely healed.
C 70-15 [He] went out into the garden where there was an abundance of balsam fir, and he brought back a strip of rind on which there were a number of 'myrhh bladders.' He cut open the bladders and squeezed the 'myrrh' on the cut. Of course the bleeding stopped, and within a few days the cut had healed nicely. 1972 MURRAY 240 They often made use of 'murre' or the turpentine 'bladders' found on the bark of fir tress to dress the cut. 1976 *Decks Awash* v (5), p. 16 I know of a man who believed that turpentine (murr) from the fir tree was a cure for TB. He went about with a teaspoon bursting the bladders on the trees and swallowing the stuff. He died at the beginning of an elderly age, but not from TB. The murr was supposed to be good for cuts and to stop bleeding. Whether it had any healing qualities is a matter of conjecture, but one thing is certain, if a wound was clean and bandaged and plastered with murr, it was not possible for any outside bacteria to infect the wound.

# We Will Remain

## Shane Mahoney

ive hundred years we have stood our ground, living like small birds in the talons of a hawk. We forever expected hardship, and in finding the strength to endure gathered a quiet dignity that sustained our lives and our people in this wild and predatory home. Selected by the cold reason of English merchants and the sorrowed passion of Irish famine and rebellion, we were amongst the strongest, most stubborn and most desperate of these unrelenting nations. Hunters of the sea, we fed ourselves, raised our children and buried our dead. Like so many packs of wolves we sought the protective coastal margins and staked territories that kinder generations called communities. And there we killed to survive and bred to succeed.

From the harshness of this existence there emerged a society which inherently recognized the value of cooperation. Evolved out of necessity, this capacity flourished in gentler moments to become something greater, a truly human identity that could reflect a sincere and selfless concern for others. This Christian-ness was not set amongst us by God's tinkers, but rather by our closeness to extinction. Indeed, our elaborate humanness was liberated by our essentially animal natures, set loping in full stride within our literally animal lives. At times, this great ideal, long sought by the religions of humankind, rose incarnate and walked amongst us. Lives were given so that others might live, and sorrow and joy became communal rites. In the welcoming of strangers, in the true generosity unhindered by material wealth, and in the honest acceptance of ourselves as mere mortals, we, this nation, arose above the world of idolatry and showed to others who came here a better way.

So many times we defied the odds. We sought the farthest coves and hid from the great greed of Britain, ignoring her edicts that proclaimed we could not stay. In small boats we ventured seaward and sifted from the cold salt plain hordes of living things that so often demanded their share of human misery. We were educated by Nature herself, the highest clergy, and learned to trust our instincts to master tide and weather. Without compass we sailed over fogged shoals and alongside escarpments of black rock that mirthlessly welcomed the errant crew. From stony, acid soils we coaxed reluctant food, itself a gift from the sea, nourished as it was by the scattered silver dead or by the wind-ravished kelp that perished upon our rocky shores. We grew lean in our expectations of life, unalterable in our fierce determination to persist, and greedy for our chance to live.

And so, do they think we are finished now? Destined to become pickled specimens on some laboratory shelf? Will the little gods of elsewhere ordain it so? Are they about to teach us what we do not wish to know or worse what we ought never to have needed? Will they parade their fool's wisdom once more, and prance naked in the King's new clothes, all the while wielding their traitorous lightning, designed to dazzle and kill? So be it. We are Newfoundlanders. And some old child amongst us will point to the naked arse rambling up the road.

We are indebted only to Newfoundland for our identity. No man or god may take the credit or the blame. No man or god will recreate us. It was in this crucible of fog enshrouded rock that we literally created ourselves. We emerged coincident with our uniqueness, crawling upwards from the centuries of struggle. Like all natural formations, we bear the unmistakable signs of struggle, or advances and retreats, of blind alleys chosen and then abandoned. We have not always courted the truest hearts, nor have we always acted with honour. Be we were never afraid to fight. The seeds of weakness are recent monsters that have flourished in a brief interlude of unnatural ease.

Already the ice is returning, however, beckoning our old talents. So to those who decry the emergent indifference and opportunism, the puss-choked sores on the face of our culture, and to those who sadly believe that this latest crisis is truly our last, I would gently ask them to listen. Listen. Listen quietly to the more ancient rhythm, the faint drumming echoing backwards from the temporary present to the more concrete past, of something powerful, sure, and proud. Forever rising, forever falling, like the sea that runs through our salted existence, it is always there. Along the dark road home we will meet ourselves, and in the instant of recognition the doomsayers and false priests will be slain.

Newfoundland…and her people…will remain.

**nipper**[1]: n

1 A large biting mosquito; GARNIPPER: gally nipper.

[(1663) 1963 YOUNGE 60  In July, the muscetos (a little biting fly) and garnippers (a larger one) will much vex us.] [1819] 1978 *Beothuk Vocabularies* 46 Nipper—bebadrook. 1854 [FEILD] 70 The title or name [Nipper's Harbour] is rather an alarming one, particularly to thin skinned Southerners, as the Nipper is the largest and most formidable of the mosquitoes. 1861 *Harper's* xxii, 744 Mercy! who ever saw the flies and nippers so bad as they! 1893 *Trade Review Christmas No 14* The operator in charge waged a daily and [nightly} war against insect life, viz.:—black files,[mosquitoes], nippers, horse and sand flies. 1913 THOMAS 191 All day long the black flies made our lives miserable, and as night approached the 'nippers' took their place. [1926] 1933 GREENLEAF (ed) 251 "Change Islands Song": The weather still got hotter, plenty nippers, flies and stout. T 45/6-64 [tall tale] Nippers was that thick that they come and used to drive their thorns down through the bark-pot. According as they drove them down, he used to clench them, and by and by they got that thick on it that they rose the bark-pot and went away with it. C 68-23 We didn't want [the frog] to die because we were told that frogs used to eat nippers (mosquitoes) and we didn't want to hurt anything that helped to destroy the nippers. 1973 PINSENT 56 All Ruth could seem to do was point to the door, which made about as much impression as a nipper's bite on an elephant's arse.

2 In various ball games, the catcher.

M 69-2 The millyer and the nipper were similar to what is today the pitcher and the catcher.

# Newfoundland

**E. J. Pratt**

Here the tides flow,
And here they ebb;
Not with that dull, unsinewed tread of waters
Held under bonds to move
Around unpeopled shores—
Moon-driven through a timeless circuit
Of invasion and retreat;
But with a lusty stroke of life
Pounding at stubborn gates,
That they might run
Within the sluices of men's hearts,
Leap under throb of pulse and nerve,
And teach the sea's strong voice
To learn the harmonies of new floods,
The peal of cataract,
And the soft wash of currents
Against resilient banks,
Or the broken rhythms from old chords
Along dark passages
That once were pathways of authentic fires.

*Red is the sea-kelp on the beach,*
*Red as the heart's blood,*
*Nor is there power in tide or sun*
*To bleach its stain.*
*It lies there piled thick*
*Above the gulch-line.*
*It is rooted in the joints of rocks,*
*It is tangled around a spar,*
*It covers a broken rudder,*
*It is red as the heart's blood,*
*And salt as tears.*

Here the winds blow,
And here they die,
Not with that wild, exotic rage
That vainly sweeps untrodden shores,
But with familiar breath
Holding a partnership with life,
Resonant with the hopes of spring,
Pungent with the airs of harvest.

They call with the silver fifes of the sea,
They breathe with the lungs of men,
They are one with the tides of the sea,
They are one with the tides of the heart,
They blow with the rising octaves of dawn,
They die with the largo of dusk,
Their hands are full to the overflow,
In their right is the bread of life,
In their left are the waters of death.

*Scattered on boom*
*And rudder and weed*
*Are tangles of shells;*
*Some with backs of crusted bronze,*
*And faces of porcelain blue,*
*Some crushed by the beach stones*
*To chips of jade;*
*And some are spiral-cleft*
*Spreading their tracery on the sand*
*In the rich veining of an agate's heart,*
*And others remain unscarred,*
*To babble of the passing of the winds.*

Here the crags
Meet with winds and tides—
Not with that blind interchange
Of blow for blow
That spills the thunder of insentient seas;
But with the mind that reads assault
In crouch and leap and the quick stealth,
Stiffening the muscles of the waves.
Here they flank the harbours,
Keeping watch
On thresholds, altars and the fires of home,
Or, like mastiffs,
Over-zealous,
Guard too well.

*Tide and wind and crag,*
*Seaweed and sea-shell*
*And broken rudder*
*And the story is told*
*Of human veins and pulses,*
*Of eternal pathways of fire,*
*Of dreams that survive the night,*
*Of doors held ajar in storms.*

# Author Index

Author Unknown, 268

Anonymous 49, 265

Artiss, Phyllis 173

Avis, Nick 248, 249

Beckel, Annamarie 25

Bouzane, Lillian 133

Bown, Addison 75

Boykov, Luben 44, 283, 286

Broomfield, Samuel 267

Buchanan, Roberta 105

Bursey, Wallace 17

Burt, Robert 19

Butt, Grace 122

Cahill, Tom 113

Candow, James 60

Carroll, Daniel J. 264

Cartwright, John 59

Cook, Michael 10, 45, 51

Cormack, W. E. 50

Crummey, Michael 190

Dabinett, Diana 305

Dalton, Mary 60, 135

Dawe, Tom 54, 245

Editors 72

Fennelly, Ray 214

Fitzhugh, Lynne 168

Fogwill, Irving 166, 287

Fowler, Adrian 247, 292

Fraser, Janet 149

George, Cliff 56

Glover, David 85

Goudie, Elizabeth 180

Greene, Richard 216

Hall, Pam 212

Hansen, Ben 221

Hart, Anne 200, 270

Hamilton, Lady 23

Hillier, Raymond 197

Holmes, John 29

Horwood, Harold 91

Inglis, Bishop John 34

Johnston, Wayne 36, 302

Kelland, Otto 148

Knowling, Kathleen 179

Krachun, Peggy Smith 150

Leonard, Peter 143

Leyton, Bonnie 134

Long, Gene 107

Maggs, Randall 153

Mahoney, Shane 312

Manak, Mabel 269

Marshall, Ingeborg 10, 13, 22, 55, 57, 61

Martin, Harry 266

McGrath, Carmelita 155, 233

McGregor, John 32

McNeill, Leonard 184

Minty, Dennis 65, 71, 215

Morgan, Bernice 124

Morgan, Pamela 282

Moore, Lisa 253

Murray, Neil 103

Norman, Robert O. 12, 52

Obed, Ellen Bryan 207, 210

O'Flaherty, Patrick 289

O'Neill, Paul 18

Paddock, Harold 275

Parsons, Paul 246

Pastore, Ralph 11

Paul, Randolph 66, 67

Payne, Jim 243

Pittman, Al 38, 138, 212, 213

Pittman, Ken 27

Porter, Helen Fogwill 274

Power, Gregory 111

Pratt, E. J. 314

Pratt, Mary 189

Provincial Archives 73

Puddester, Sharon 136

Ralph, Wayne 219

RCA Theatre Company 223

Rendell, Susan 157

Roberts, Gildas 250

Rogerson, Isabella Whiteford 74

Rosato, Eamonn 198, 199

Rose, Clyde 272

Roseman, Ken 277

Rubia, Geraldine 86

Ryan, Beth 30

Saunders, Gary 88, 306

Shanawdithit 32, 33, 34, 35, 47, 48

Shepherd, Helen Parsons 156

Shepherd, Reginald 167

Slade, E. 19

Small, Larry 102

Smallwood, Joseph R. 127

Smith, Sherry 183

Squires, Gerald 16, 41, 44, 137, 206

Stockley, Eleanor Cameron- 68

Story, Kirwin & Widdowson 84

Strowbridge, Nellie 252

Tomova, Veselina 213

Udell, Janice 262, 263

Vine, Andy 182

Wade, Michael 242

Walsh, Des 17

Wangersky, Barbara Pratt- 251

Wellman, Jim 145

Williams, W. P. 110

Winter, Kathleen 141, 164

Winter, Michael 93

Wornell, A. C. 261

# Title Index

Adam and Eve on a Winter Afternoon, 155

All Gone Widdun (Excerpts), 25

The Announcement of the Rooster Tax, 111

Arctic Fox, 208

As Loved our Fathers (Excerpts), 113

At Red Indian Lake, 18

Ballad of Captain Bob Bartlett, Arctic Explorer, 261

Be Sure to Bring the Kids to See Finding Mary March, 29

bedoret ahune, 66

Beothuk IV, 17

Beothuk Bark Canoes (Excerpts), 57

The Beothuk of Newfoundland (Excerpt), 55

The Black Tie, 122

Borrowed Black (Excerpts), 210

The Bowl, 133

The Broadcast (Excerpt), 145

The Brule Men, 143

A Chant for One Voice, 91

The Colony of Unrequited Dreams (Excerpts), 36, 302

dead Indians, 60

Dictionary of Newfoundland English (Definitions), 87, 104, 132, 140, 154, 188, 232, 276, 281, 304, 311, 313

Dictionary of Newfoundland English (Excerpt), 84

Dictionary Sam, 86

The Dig, 12

Down by Jim Long's Stage (Excerpt), 212

Dr. Agnes C. O'Dea, 270

Doctor Olds of Twillingate (Excerpt), 306

Eighteen, 149

Elemental Poem, 105

Empty Nets, 243

Excerpts from a Diary, 34

Excerpts from a Journal, 41

Film Injects Beothuck Legend with Life, 30

Finding Mary March, Film Script (Excerpt), 27

Goin Hout, 85

Greenhair Goes for a Smoke, 153

heart of the rock, 67

Help Me, Hepplewhite, 200

A History and Ethnography of the Beothuk (Excerpts), 10, 13, 22

The Home, 197

The Hunt, 102

If Sonnets Were In Fashion, 245

In Memoriam: Captain Arthur Jackman, 264

In Memoriam: Cassie Brown—A Tribute, 274

In the Chambers of the Sea, 157

In There Somewhere, 54

The Incubus, 233

It Ain't Funny, 282

Jeans, 150

The Labradorians (Preface), 168

Let Me Fish Off Cape St. Mary's, 148

Let There Be Peace Among Us All, 69

The Literature of Newfoundland, 292

Liverpool Mercury (Excerpt), 19

London Times (Extract), 50

Loss of a Friend: A Personal Memoir, 287

Mary March, 19

Message, 247

Miracles, 190

More than a Monument, 283

Newfoundland, 314

The Newfoundlander (Extract), 49

Newfoundland's Dream, 110

Noel Dinn, 275

now that there are no cobblestones, 17

Obligatory Beothuk Poem, 60

Old Flame, 250

On a Wing and a Wish (Excerpts), 213

On the Rim of the Curve (Excerpt), 10, 45, 51

Pamela Morgan: A Voice for Newfoundland's Roots, 277

A Picture of the Past, 75

A Piece of Toast, 164

Portrait of the Artist as a Young Mortician, 138

The Prisoner, 166

A Profile of Georgina Ann Stirling, 72

The Public Ledger (Extract), 49

Purgatory's Wild Kingdom, 253

The Rain Hammers, 242

Raku: Sod, 135

Reports and Letters by George C. Pulling (Excerpt), 61

The Rock Observed (Excerpt), 289

A Seaman of the White Fleet, 219

Seasons, 103

Second Heart, 93

Shaa-naan-dithit, or the Last of the Boêothics, 32

Shanadithit, 38

Shanadithit: The Musical (Excerpts), 68

Shanawdithit's Dream, 52

Shanawdithit's People (Excerpts), 11

Some Labrador Narratives by Nat Igloliorte, 173

springsmistory, 249

A Statement, 267

Suspended State (Excerpt), 107

Terras de Bacalhau (Excerpts), 223

Text of an Address, 127

This is My Home, 266

To Be a Bee, 252

To Mark The Occasion, 124

To Miss Twillingate Stirling, 74

To Whittle an Alder Whistle, 88

Tragedy of CF-BND, 184

Tribute to James (Jimmy) Butler, Blacksmith, 265

A Tribute to Michael Cook, 272

A Tribute to Samuel Broomfield, 268

A Tribute to Samuel Broomfield, 269

waking from a dream, 248

We Will Remain, 312

The White Fleet, 216

Wind in My Pocket, 209

Wind Song, 207

With Love from the Andes, 141

Woman of Labrador, 182

Woman of Labrador (Excerpts), 180

Woman of Labrador (Play Excerpts), 183

# Text Credits

Every reasonable effort has been made to trace the ownership of material reprinted in this book and to make full acknowledgement for its use. The publisher would be grateful to know of any errors and omissions so they may be rectified in subsequent editions.

The publisher thanks the following for their permission to include these texts in this book:

ADAM AND EVE ON A WINTER AFTERNOON, from To The New World by Carmelita McGrath

ALL GONE WIDDUN (Excerpts), Annamarie Beckel (Breakwater Books Ltd.)

THE ANNOUNCEMENT OF THE ROOSTER TAX, Gregory Power

AS LOVED OUR FATHERS (Excerpts), Tom Cahill

AT RED INDIAN LAKE, Paul O'Neill

BALLAD OF CAPTAIN BOB BARTLETT, ARCTIC EXPLORER, A. C. Wornell

BE SURE TO BRING THE KIDS TO SEE FINDING MARY MARCH, John Holmes

BEDORET AHUNE/HEART OF THE ROCK, Randolph Paul

BEOTHUK IV, Wallace Bursey

BEOTHUK BARK CANOES (Excerpts), © Canadian Museum of Civilization, text by Ingeborg Marshall, Mercury series, Canadian Ethnology Service, paper no. 102

THE BEOTHUK OF NEWFOUNDLAND (Excerpt), Ingeborg Marshall (Breakwater Books Ltd.)

THE BLACK TIE, Grace Butt

BORROWED BLACK (Excerpts), Ellen B. Obed

THE BOWL, Lillian Bouzane

THE BROADCAST (Excerpt) from the Ghetto Program by Jim Wellman

A CHANT FOR ONE VOICE, Harold Horwood

THE COLONY OF UNREQUITED DREAMS (Excerpts) by Wayne Johnston. Copyright ©1998. Reprinted by permission of Alfred A. Knopf Canada, a division of Random House of Canada Limited.

DEAD INDIANS, Mary Dalton

DICTIONARY OF NEWFOUNDLAND ENGLISH (Definitions), Story, Kirwin & Widdowson (University of Toronto Press & Breakwater Books Ltd.)

DICTIONARY OF NEWFOUNDLAND ENGLISH (Excerpt), Story, Kirwin & Widdowson (Reprinted with permission of University of Toronto Press)

DICTIONARY SAM, Geraldine Rubia

THE DIG, Robert O. Norman

DOCTOR OLDS OF TWILLINGATE (Excerpt), Gary Saunders (Breakwater Books Ltd.)

DOWN BY JIM LONG'S STAGE (Excerpt), Al Pittman (Breakwater Books Ltd.)

DR. AGNES C. O'DEA, 1911-1993, Anne Hart

EIGHTEEN, Janet Fraser

ELEMENTAL POEM, Roberta Buchanan

EMPTY NETS, Jim Payne

EXCERPTS FROM A JOURNAL, Gerald Squires

FILM INJECTS BEOTHUK LEGEND WITH LIFE, Beth Ryan

FINDING MARY MARCH, FILM SCRIPT (Excerpt), Ken Pittman

GOIN HOUT, David Glover

GREENHAIR GOES FOR A SMOKE, Randall Maggs

HELP ME HEPPLEWHITE, Anne Hart

A HISTORY AND ETHNOGRAPHY OF THE BEOTHUK (Excerpts), Ingeborg Marshall (McGill-Queen's University Press)

THE HOME, Raymond Hillier (Flanker Press)

THE HUNT, Larry Small

IF SONNETS WERE IN FASHION, Tom Dawe

IN MEMORIAM: CASSIE BROWN—A TRIBUTE, Helen Fogwill Porter

IN THE CHAMBERS OF THE SEA, Susan Rendell

IN THERE SOMEWHERE, Tom Dawe

THE INCUBUS from Stranger Things Have Happened by Carmelita McGrath

IT AIN'T FUNNY, Pamela Morgan

JEANS, Peggy Smith Krachun

THE LABRADORIANS (Preface), Lynne Fitzhugh (Breakwater Books Ltd.)

LET ME FISH OFF CAPE ST. MARY'S, Otto Kelland

THE LITERATURE OF NEWFOUNDLAND, Adrian Fowler

LOSS OF A FRIEND: A PERSONAL MEMOIR, Irving Fogwill

MARY MARCH, Robert Burt

MESSAGE, Adrian Fowler

MIRACLES, Michael Crummey

MORE THAN A MONUMENT, Luben Boykov

NEWFOUNDLAND, E. J. Pratt (University of Toronto Press)

NOEL DINN, Harold Paddock

NOW THAT THERE ARE NO COBBLESTONES, Des Walsh

OBLIGATORY BEOTHUK POEM, James Candow

PAMELA MORGAN: A VOICE FOR NEWFOUNDLAND'S ROOTS, Ken Roseman ©1996 The Sing Out Corp. Used by permission, all rights reserved.

A PICTURE OF THE PAST by Addison Bown from Tempered Days, G. J. Casey & Elizabeth Miller, eds.

A PIECE OF TOAST, Kathleen Winter

PORTRAIT OF THE ARTIST AS A YOUNG MORTICIAN, Al Pittman (Breakwater Books Ltd.)

THE PRISONER, Irving Fogwill

A PROFILE OF GEORGINA ANN STIRLING, Editors

PURGATORY'S WILD KINGDOM, Lisa Moore

THE RAIN HAMMERS, Michael Wade

RAKU: SOD, Mary Dalton

REPORTS AND LETTERS BY GEORGE C. PULLING (Excerpt), Ingeborg Marshall (Breakwater Books Ltd.)

THE ROCK OBSERVED (Excerpt), Patrick O'Flaherty (University of Toronto Press)

A SEAMAN OF THE WHITE FLEET, Wayne Ralph

SEASONS, Neil Murray

SECOND HEART, Michael Winter (Porcupine's Quill)

SHANADITHIT, Al Pittman (Breakwater Books Ltd.)

SHANADITHIT THE MUSICAL (Excerpts), Eleanor Cameron-Stockley

SHANAWDITHIT'S DREAM, Robert O. Norman

SHANAWDITHIT'S PEOPLE, (Excerpts), Ralph Pastore

SOME LABRADOR NARRATIVES BY NAT IGLOLIORTE, Phyllis Artiss

SPRINGSMISTORY, Nick Avis (Breakwater Books Ltd.)

SUSPENDED STATE (Excerpt), Gene Long (Breakwater Books Ltd.)

TERRAS DE BACALHAU (Excerpts), RCA Theatre Company

TEXT OF AN ADDRESS, Joseph R. Smallwood

THIS IS MY HOME, Harry Martin

TO BE A BEE, Nellie Strowbridge

TO MARK THE OCCASION, Bernice Morgan

TO WHITTLE AN ALDER WHISTLE, Gary Saunders (Breakwater Books Ltd.)

TRAGEDY OF CF-BND, Leonard McNeill (courtesy Them Days Magazine)

A TRIBUTE TO MICHAEL COOK, Clyde Rose

A TRIBUTE TO SAMUEL BROOMFIELD, Author Unknown (courtesy Them Days Magazine)

A TRIBUTE TO SAMUEL BROOMFIELD, Mabel Manak (courtesy Them Days Magazine)

WAKING FROM A DREAM, Nick Avis (Breakwater Books Ltd.)

WE WILL REMAIN, Shane Mahoney

THE WHITE FLEET, Richard Greene

WIND IN MY POCKET (Excerpt), Ellen B. Obed (Breakwater Books Ltd.)

WITH LOVE FROM THE ANDES, Kathleen Winter

WOMAN OF LABRADOR, Andy Vine

WOMAN OF LABRADOR (Excerpts), Elizabeth Goudie

WOMAN OF LABRADOR (Play excerpts), Sherry Smith

319

# Visual Credits

Music prepared by Fergus O'Byrne

All page bars and photos that appear on the introductory pages are courtesy of Breakwater Books Archives.

Illustrations on the following pages custom created by Boyd Warren Chubbs: 9, 75, 91, 93, 101, 157, 163, 190, 196, 200, 233, 241, 253, 260, 312

11: BBL Archives; 16: Gerald Squires; 18: BBL Archives; 23: National Archives of Canada; 26: BBL Archives; 28: BBL Archives; 32: Newfoundland Museum; 33: Newfoundland Museum; 34: Newfoundland Museum; 35: Newfoundland Museum; 42: BBL Archives; 43 (top & bottom): BBL Archives; 44: Gerald Squires & Luben Boykov; 46: BBL Archives; 47: Newfoundland Museum; 48: Newfoundland Museum; 50: BBL Archives; 51: BBL Archives; 53: BBL Archives; 56: © Canadian Museum of Civilization, End profile of Beothuk canoe replica made by Shanawdithit, drawing by Clifford George, Mercury series, Canadian Ethnology Service, paper no. 102; 57 BBL Archives; 58: BBL Archives; 59: PANL; 64: BBL Archives; 65: Dennis Minty; 66: BBL Archives; 67: BBL Archives; 70: BBL Archives; 71: Dennis Minty; 73: PANL; 134: Ray Fennelly; 136: Sharon Puddester; 137: Gerald Squires; 156: Emma Butler Gallery; 167: Emma Butler Gallery; 179: Kathleen Knowling; 189: Mary Pratt; 198: Eamonn Rosato; 199: Eamonn Rosato; 206: BBL Archives; 207: Shawn O'Hagan; 208: Shawn O'Hagan; 209: Shawn O'Hagan; 211: BBL Archives; 212: Pam Hall; 213: Veselina Tomova; 214: Ray Fennelly; 215 (top & bottom): Dennis Minty; 221: Ben Hansen; 222: BBL Archives; 246: Emma Butler Gallery; 251: Emma Butler Gallery; 262/263: Janice Udell; 286: Luben Boykov; 305: Diana Dabinett.